SEEING THROUGH GOD

SEEING THROUGH GOD

A Geophenomenology

John Llewelyn

INDIANA UNIVERSITY PRESS
Bloomington and Indianapolis

PUBLICATION OF THIS BOOK IS MADE POSSIBLE IN PART WITH THE ASSISTANCE OF A
CHALLENGE GRANT FROM THE NATIONAL ENDOWMENT FOR THE HUMANITIES,
A FEDERAL AGENCY THAT SUPPORTS RESEARCH, EDUCATION, AND PUBLIC PROGRAMMING
IN THE HUMANITIES.

THIS BOOK IS A PUBLICATION OF

INDIANA UNIVERSITY PRESS
601 NORTH MORTON STREET
BLOOMINGTON, IN 47404-3797 USA

HTTP://IUPRESS.INDIANA.EDU

Telephone orders 800-842-6796
Fax orders 812-855-7931
Orders by e-mail IUPORDER@INDIANA.EDU

THE PAPER USED IN THIS PUBLICATION MEETS THE MINIMUM REQUIREMENTS OF AMERICAN
NATIONAL STANDARD FOR INFORMATION SCIENCES — PERMANENCE OF PAPER FOR PRINTED
LIBRARY MATERIALS, ANSI Z39.48-1984.

MANUFACTURED IN THE UNITED STATES OF AMERICA

LIBRARY OF CONGRESS CATALOGING-IN-PUBLICATION DATA

LLEWELYN, JOHN.
SEEING THROUGH GOD : A GEOPHENOMENOLOGY / JOHN LLEWELYN.
P. CM. — (STUDIES IN CONTINENTAL THOUGHT)
INCLUDES BIBLIOGRAPHICAL REFERENCES AND INDEX.
ISBN 0-253-34346-1 (ALK. PAPER) — ISBN 0-253-21639-7 (PBK. : ALK. PAPER)
1. ENVIRONMENTAL SCIENCES — PHILOSOPHY. 2. ENVIRONMENTALISM — RELIGIOUS ASPECTS.
3. PHENOMENOLOGY. I. TITLE. II. SERIES.
GE40.L54 2004
304.2 — DC21   2003011795

1   2   3   4   5   09   08   07   06   05   04

IN MEMORIAM
PÁLL ARDAL
LARRY BRISKMAN
MICHAEL HAAR
JOHN JENKINS
REDVERS MARTIN
ABEL AFAON MORGAN
GEORGE MORICE
JOHN O'NEILL
ALUN JOHN MORRIS VIRGIN

AND OF THE EARTH
IN WHICH THEIR EARTH
HAS COME TO DWELL

...BOB PETH A WELODD LLYGAD
AR HYD WYNEB DAEAR LAWN

...EVERY THING THAT EYE HATH SEEN
UPON THE WHOLE WORLD'S FACE

—WILLIAM WILLIAMS PANTYCELYN

CONTENTS

PREFACE

According to which of the several possible senses is given to the title of this book, a different answer has to be given to the question posed in the title of the book's closing section. In the space between these titles these senses are exploited. The object of the experiment conducted there is to explore the technology of looking in response to the look of things. I do not attempt to define the word "thing," although — especially in my final chapter — I do give attention to matters relevant to how things are distinguished, in more than one meaning of this term. By things I mean primarily earthly things other than human beings but including non-human animals, and by earthly things I mean not only things belonging to our planet but things belonging to the universe as a whole, whether they be things of the natural universe or artifacts, things created or otherwise made out of natural elements. By elements I sometimes mean the traditional four — earth, air, fire, and water — as these figure in the reflections of Greek thinkers. But at other times the elements I refer to are the entities or events seen as fundamental in modern sciences. For it is a subordinate aim of the book to bring out that one way to achieve its principal aim is to look again closely at methodologies adopted by at least some modern sciences. In doing this I discover in the so-called tough-minded resources of Western science what is usually taken to be most at home in the so-called tender-minded practices of Eastern religion. Not only in this respect are we too ready to oppose the East to the West; we are also too ready to oppose science to poetry and, more generally, to art and, still more generally, to aesthetic experience. I give a phenomenological description of a moment in which the imagination is seen to be exercised in very much the same way in all of these spheres. From that description it appears that in all of these spheres that moment has an ethical or religious or ethico-religious dimension. By religious I do not mean theistic. This does not prevent my touching from time to time on the topic of salvation as theisms variously understand this term. Where that topic is raised here, what is most at stake is the salvation and perishing of the earth and the temptation to dishonor it into which we are led by our honoring of a Platonic or God-promised heaven. So this book may be regarded as a work of mourning for the victims of martyrs indecently preoccupied with their own salvation, whose victims include not only human beings but also things, whether things of the earth or things like the effaced statues of the Buddha in the Bamiyan valley, whose feet once touched the earth but whose eyes were averted from it toward some world other than this one. An equivocal mourning therefore, on the threshold of this world, a mourning whose equivocality equals that of this book's title and is marked by the ellipsis that suspends from its epigraph the words

> Y mae gwedd dy wyneb grasol
> yn rhagori llawer iawn
> ar . . .

> The beauty of thy face,
> plenteous in grace,
> excels by far . . .

ACKNOWLEDGMENTS

I thank the editors and publishers of *Eco-Phenomenology: Back to Earth Itself,* Charles S. Brown and Ted Toadvine, eds. (Albany: State University of New York Press, 2003), *Post-Structuralist Classics,* Andrew Benjamin, ed. (London: Routledge, 1988), *Research in Phenomenology* 17 (Leiden: Brill Academic Publishers, 1987), and *Research in Phenomenology* 31 (Leiden: Brill Academic Publishers, 2001), for permission to adapt here contributions to those volumes in, respectively, chapters 1, 4, 5, and 6.

I thank Janet Rabinowitch, Dee Mortensen, Jane Lyle, Tony Brewer, and Carol Kennedy at Indiana University Press, the staff of the libraries and of the computer service at the University of Edinburgh, my brothers Howard and David for their technical and philosophical assistance, my ever-forbearing wife Margaret and our sister, Monica, for enabling me almost always to keep at least one foot on the ground that is the topic of this book.

SEEING THROUGH GOD

1

PROLEGOMENA TO ANY FUTURE PHENOMENOLOGICAL ECOLOGY

WHAT IS PHENOMENOLOGY?

Is phenomenology a help or a hindrance to a philosophical ecology or a philosophy of the environment? It might seem to go without saying that before this question can be answered definitively, the terms in which it is posed would have to be definitively defined. But not even provisional definitions are easy to give at the outset for some of the terms. Recall, to begin with, Merleau-Ponty's acknowledgment in the preface to *The Phenomenology of Perception* that no definitive answer has been given to the question, What is phenomenology? It may well be that phenomenology is essentially resistant to being defined, if to define is to deliver an account of an essence understood as a statement of necessary and sufficient conditions. So if phenomenology is, as is sometimes said, the science of the essence of what appears, there would apparently be no essence of phenomenology and no phenomenology of phenomenology. But if, as is commonly said, phenomenology is a descriptive science, then its findings need not be essences understood as necessary and sufficient conditions for something. If we still want to say that what it seeks to describe are essences, essences will have to be more flexible,

1

for example clusters of features of which a more or less large number will belong to what instantiates the concept in question, no particular one of the cluster being bound to belong to each instance. It is not surprising that the concept of phenomenology has to be understood as a family resemblance if it includes phenomenology of conception, phenomenology of perception, and phenomenology that comes to exceed both conception and perception in the course of the history of the word's use by, to go no further back in the history of philosophy, Hegel, Husserl, Heidegger, Merleau-Ponty, Levinas, and so on. As the bearer of the first of these proper names would insist, given that there is a historical dimension to the logic of the Concept as such, there is a historical dimension to the logic of the concept of phenomenology.

According to the construal of essence as family resemblance, historical circumstances play a part in determining which features belong to the cluster of those from which different selections are made in different exemplifications of a concept. This historical dimension of conceptuality is acknowledged in the appeals to etymology that are made sparingly in the style of phenomenology practiced by Heidegger in *Being and Time* and less sparingly in the style of thinking, no longer called by him phenomenology, to which he later turned. Making an appeal both to the etymology of a concept and to the concept of etymology, it is illuminating to note that the Welsh word usually translated as "essence" or "quintessence" is *hanfod*. The second syllable of this verbal noun is a mutation of *bod*, which is equivalent to the verbal noun "being." The first syllable, deriving perhaps from the obsolete preposition *han*, meaning "out of" or "from," has the sense of descent, as in *hanes*, history or story, and the further sense that what the story would tell is clandestine, something concealed. This last notion is conveyed in Latin and Greek by the prepositional components of *substantia* and *hypostasis*. It is the notion of property, propriety, or properness conveyed by *ousia*. This ontological notion corresponds to the phenomenological notion that to get to the truth of something is to unconceal, as suggested by the Greek *a-lētheia*. According to Heidegger there is more than correspondence here. "Ontology is possible only as phenomenology."[1] "Phenomenological ontology" is a pleonasm. That this is so is spelled out in the words *Sein* and *Da-sein*. "Sein braucht Da-sein." Being needs and uses Da-sein. The *Da* is the where and opening of the appearing and concealing of being.

Of course, one immediately wishes to interpolate, what is hidden may be a ground or it may be a causal or historical antecedent; of course, it goes without saying that we must distinguish chronological or temporal genesis from logical origin or ground. But the two words "of course" themselves sometimes hide what is not a matter of course and does not go without saying. If the principle of all principles of phenomenology according to Husserl is self-evidence,[2] the self-evident must be scrupulously distinguished from what only appears to be self-evident. Here we strike again upon one of the features that belong to that selection of features highlighted in Heidegger's conception of phenomenology. Linguistic appearances to the contrary, phenomenology is the study not only of what appears (*phainomai*), but also of what disappears. Were we not already aware that Heidegger takes seriously the thought he sees expressed in the word *a-lētheia,* the thought that there must be an original darkness for something to come to light, we might wonder whether Heideggerian phenomenology is in contradiction with phenomenology more naively understood. We might wonder whether his phenomenology of the concept of phenomenology exemplifies the paradoxical capacity of a concept to include mutually incompatible features in the cluster of those upon which users of the term denoting it draw in different contexts. Writers who have speculated on the genetic analysis of concepts include Dugald Stewart, Payne-Knight, Karl Abel, Freud, Wittgenstein, and Robert Musil. The last three of these have noted that a semantic cluster may embrace opposite elements. Of a concept such as premeditated murder, justice, or scorn, Musil writes, "a multiply branching and variously supported chain of comparisons is possible among various examples of it, the more distant of which can be quite dissimilar to each other, indeed distinct from each other to the point of being opposite (*Gegensatz*), and yet be connected through an association that echoes from one link to the next."[3] This does not render the term that denotes such a concept unusable, since the concept is not defined in the Aristotelian manner by necessary and sufficient conditions or genus and differentiating property (the way President Clinton defined "sexual relations"?), but is one based on family resemblance (the way "sexual relations" was defined by the President's critics?). Does the admission of this degree of openness of texture put an end to logic, reducing logical or conceptual necessity to anthropological, psychological, historiological, or sociological contingency? Not if the concept of logical necessity is itself based on family resemblance so that logical necessity is not simply opposed, as the necessity of systems of formal logic and mathematics is traditionally opposed, to the empirical contingency usually associated with the sciences of anthropology, psychology, and the like. It is precisely this opposition between formally rational necessity and empirical contingency, hence the opposition referred to earlier between logical origin or ground and chronological or temporal genesis, that Husserl and those inspired by him portray as derived by abstraction from and dependent for its meaning upon motivation by involvement in a concretely inhabited world. Meaning is not originally either meaning defined by the principle of non-contradiction or meaning defined by empirical ostension. This dualism of meaning, one of the "dogmas of empiricism," presupposes what Husserl calls a lifeworld and Wittgenstein a form of life. It is this that gives point both to the formally analytic a priori and to the synthetic a posteriori.

Kant had already argued that this dualism presupposes the synthetic a priori. But he had argued this by transcendental deduction from what he claimed to be the fact, one agreed upon by rationalists and empiricists alike, that human experience is chronologically successive. Husserl and Heidegger (and Bergson), in their different ways, set out to show that this alleged fact is one that holds at best only for the temporality of the world of Newtonian science. They maintain that this chronology of clocks, and the synthetic a priori concepts and principles deduced as the condition of its possibility, presupposes a temporality of pre-conceptual experience. This pre-conceptual experience is not that of an inner psychological continuum of impressions or ideas or contents, an internal projection or reflection of the external world of physical objects. As Heidegger in particular tries to show, this pre-conceptual experience is not initially a perceptual one in which a subject represents an object either in the space of an external world or in the space of what is taken as that world's internal duplicate. Rather is it in the first place one in which the opposition of a subject and an objective external world is shown to be an outgrowth from a complex bedrock of one's behavitive being-in-the-world.

ECOLOGIES AND ENVIRONMENTS

The hyphens in this complex *in-der-Welt-sein* are Heidegger's reinterpretation of the hyphens in the complex of *noesis-noema* and *cogito-cogitatum* that are fundamental in Husserl's essentialist phenomenology. It is the sense given to these hyphens on which hinges the answer to the question whether Husserlian or Heideggerian phenomenology is a help or a hindrance in articulating a philosophical ecology or philosophy of the environment. If the Husserlian *noema* and *cogitatum* are intentional accusatives, we shall have reached a field of research more fundamental than that of the empirical or theoretical objects of the natural sciences. But will we not have stayed with the same structure of objects or objectives over against subjects? And if transcendental subjectivity constitutes objectivity, is not objectivity a way of being subjected to the subject? If so, will not the objects (*Gegenstände*) of the natural world of which the phenomenological objects (*Objekte*) present the form also be subjected to the subject, perhaps subjugated by it? It may be said that the inference that it will be is invalid, because for something to be subjected to or subjugated by something else it must first be there, already constituted, as Husserl would say, and it is in the manifold intentional acts of *noesis* or *cogitare* that this constitution consists. A chef who puts together the ingredients of a Christmas pudding is neither exercising mastery over the pudding nor releasing it from bondage. Until the pudding is made, it is only to the ingredients that the chef can be doing either of these things.

Does not this clarification leave standing the fact that all *noesis* is understood by Husserl as an act of meaning or intending? Here another clarification is called for. Does one perform two acts of will whenever one does something and means to do it? If one does, must one not perform an

4

infinite series of acts, therefore none? However, without supposing special acts of will, and without supposing that intentionality as a phenomenological feature either of all mental acts or of all consciousness implies that something is performed willingly (for what is done unwillingly may also display intentionality in the sense described by Husserl and Brentano), is not this mental intending still haunted by a ghost of will even when this is no longer conceived dualistically as a ghost in a machine or on analogy with a pilot in a ship? Otherwise, how are we to explain the translation in some contexts of Husserl's word *meinen,* "to mean," by "to want to say," *vouloir dire,* a French expression that, anyway, echoes the expression *sagen wollen,* which is already used in German as one alternative to *meinen,* as illustrated in Hegel's discussion of sensible certainty in *The Phenomenology of Spirit*?[4] Both are ways of marking that someone wants, wishes, or desires what she or he does or says to be taken as such and such, for instance, considering here only acts of speech, as predicating a property of a thing or as a denial, as a question or, indeed, as the expression of a want, wish, or desire. So they are expressions of the subject's subjectivity, whether or not through their noematic objectivity they necessarily subject the things of the subject's environment to that subjectivity. Even if those things, human or non-human beings, are not enslaved to the human ego, the human ego seems to be accorded a certain priority. The ego is at least their master in a metaphorical sense. And that bodes ill at least for a deeper philosophical ecology.

A sense of what a deeper philosophical ecology might be can be conveyed by contrasting it with a philosophical ecology that is compatible with the at least figurative dominion of the ego that appears to be implied by the account of the noetic-noematic structure given so far. The advocate of this shallower version could begin to dispel the impression of egological dominance by saying that other egos have the same access to power over me as I have to power over them. As Hegel in his phenomenology of recognition and Sartre in his phenomenology of the look maintain — the first optimistically, the latter pessimistically in *Being and Nothingness,* though less pessimistically in *The Critique of Dialectical Reason* — arrangements can be instituted by which conflicts between the interests of human beings can be at least temporarily resolved, and through them one ego will be making concessions to another. These arrangements will have to include ones that safeguard the sustainability of the natural resources necessary for the survival of human society. They may go so far as to include ones that foster concern for the welfare of non-human beings. Nevertheless, at the shallowest end of philosophical ecology, that concern for the welfare of non-human beings will be dictated ultimately by concern for the welfare of human beings. Shallow ecologism thus described would be an environmentalism that sees the non-human as the environment of the human.

It is to a shallow ecologism of this sort that the hyphen of the noetic-noematic structure of Husserlian phenomenology seems to point — at least as we have analyzed it so far. Very much the same has to be said of the first stage of the analysis of Da-sein's being-in-the-world carried out in *Being and Time*. That first and, Heidegger insists, provisional stage describes how everyday Da-sein inhabits its world for the most part. That *Welt* is an *Umwelt*, where the *Um* not only marks Da-sein's being *surrounded by* its world, but also marks the world's being *for* Da-sein, *um-zu*.[5] First and foremost, the world occupied by everyday Da-sein is not a totality of objects or things present to consciousness. Nor is it a totality of facts — which in any case are liable to be regarded as abstract and complex objects or things. It is rather a totality of utilities and disutilities, a totality of routes or barriers to the discovery or production of goods that are expected to answer human needs or desires.

A theological turn will be given to the discussion at this point by some. They will maintain that the world's answering to human needs and desires has to be subsumed under the human being's answering to God and that the adjustment of the world to humanity is not a humanocentrism, but a ground for seeing human life in relation to a non-human center. Taking this turn would entail discussing whether the theological philosophy of ecology that might emerge from doing so would still be a shallow ecology. One recalls Heidegger's warning, considered disingenuous by many of his readers, that when he writes of Da-sein's propensity to fall prey to the world (*verfallen*), this term is not to be taken to express any negative value judgment.[6] If, as Heidegger implies, "inauthentic" (*uneigentlich*) in his use of the term does not express a value judgment either, it follows that a conception of ecology that sees the world as subservient to man and an ecology that sees the world and man as subservient to God are both inauthentic. Any conception of Da-sein and Da-sein's *oikos* is inauthentic if Da-sein's being-in-the-world is not ultimately for the sake of being. Both the humanocentric and the theocentric ecologies, whether we call them shallow or deep, see the human being as "fallen among objects in the world," rather as an apple might find itself fallen among other apples on the ground in Eden or elsewhere. This is how these ecologies see not just human or non-human beings of the world. If the humanocentric ecology makes room at all for an otherworldly being called God, both it and the theocentric ecology see all beings as "fallen among objects in the world." For God's or a god's being a being in a world other than ours is in Heidegger's sense a mode of worldliness, a mode of his or her or its being "with us," albeit, so to speak, in a room for whose door we may not possess the key: present in the mode of absence. Heidegger is not the first to observe that even to place the Deity beyond our world in a superworld of its own is to bring it down to the level of apples, sticks and stones, cabbages and kings. God is thereby de-divinized. Being is more holy than a God so conceived — and Heidegger says this too of such a reifying conception of the Good and of value quite generally.

This is why no negative value judgment is being made when he writes that Da-sein has a propensity to fall prey to the world and to occupy its world in an inauthentic way. This statement is a phenomeno-ontological one. Such statements are value-neutral. My value judgments, whether expressing a positive or a negative evaluation or indifference, evince my having fallen prey to the world. But what this means is simply that they are ontic judgments I make of beings in the world, including human beings, regarded inauthentically as simply entities alongside me. In authentic regard beings are regarded in their being. What does this statement mean? Can it be understood in a way that does not subordinate beings to being? If being is more divine than God understood as a being, is it not *a fortiori* more divine than any other beings too, especially if these are understood as having been created by God? Is this to say that being is higher or deeper than beings? If so, would a deep ecology whose depth is the depth of being be an ecology that sacrifices beings at the altar of being? The thought that it would might arise from the tendency manifested throughout the history of metaphysics to construe being as a being of one sort or another. And this thought is encouraged by the assertion that being is higher or deeper than beings. However, what is higher or lower than a being is another being. Being as such, being as expressed by a verbal noun, is not a being, any more than a verbal noun is a noun, however difficult it may be to avoid construing it as one. That is why the history of the many different metaphysical constructions of being as a being has to be deconstrued and why it is so difficult to do this even with hindsight — perhaps precisely because of hindsight, because deconstrual seems to require us to jump over our own shadow.

A section of a chapter of the book in which this difficult deconstrual is written up would deal with the history of the topic with which this present chapter began, phenomenology. That chapter would show in detail how Heidegger's phenomenology of time as the meaning of being relates to Husserl's preoccupation with the temporality of consciousness. That chapter would stress, as it must be stressed here and now, that although intentionality may, as noted earlier, retain a trace of will (the "faculty" given prominence in the German Idealism, Kantianism, and Neo-Kantianism from which Husserl and Heidegger strive to become disentangled), the will of any individual Da-sein is minimal in what Husserl calls passive intentionality, passive genesis, and passive synthesis. It would be all too easy to reify passive intentionality and to see it as an impersonal force in conflict with the intentionality of individual Da-sein. But we can think that Husserl admits this reification only if we forget his insistence that the point-source of temporality cannot be named. For an analogous reason no such "dialectical" conflict between Da-sein and *Sein* can have a place in the interpretation of *Being and Time* if what Heidegger does in that book is extend and bend Husserl's teaching of the unnamability of the genesis of time into a teaching of the meaning of being. As already noted, Da-sein and *Sein* use and need each other, but in the way that in the *Sein* of Da-sein the genitive is double, both objective and subjective, as grammarians say, if misleadingly in this

7

context of all contexts; for Da-sein is not a subject and *Sein* is not an object, since neither *Sein* nor Da-sein is primarily an entity, although they may be inauthentically thus ontically conceived. This does not mean that there cannot be a Da-sein. Heidegger regularly uses "Da-sein" as a placeholder for what other philosophers call and sometimes he himself calls a human being, *Mensch*. What he aims to convey in using this word is that Da-sein is indeed a placeholder. Ontologically and existentially, Da-sein is the "where," the *Da*, that makes being possible, makes being its possibility, its *Seinkönnen*. As Heidegger says of language, traditionally proposed as that which differentiates man from non-human animals, Da-sein is the house of being, being's *oikos*, the ecologicality of being.

A philosophical ecology deeper than one concerned only with the human being's environment would be one that follows up the consequences of the thought that as well as having an environment the human being is part of the environment of non-human beings. Would it follow that the kind of theological ecology referred to above is deeper than one-sided humano-centric environmentalism? Not necessarily, if to say that one account is deeper than another is to say that it is more comprehensive, wider. For it is not clear that an account according to which whatever is non-human is for the sake of the human is any less comprehensive than one according to which whatever is non-divine is for the sake of the divine. "Deep ecology" is not a notion for which we can realistically expect to find generally agreed necessary and sufficient conditions. At the present moment in the history of reflection upon it there is no agreement on the list of features upon which applications of the expression would draw. Definition is bound to be somewhat stipulative. This does not mean that it is bound to be arbitrary. Reasons are required and a case has to be made out. Paradoxical though it may seem, cases may have to be cited without our being able to define the concept under which it is claimed that they fall. Here there is as much learning to be done as there is teaching. Here the distinction between definition and description breaks down. Merleau-Ponty says of Husserlian phenomenology that "It is a matter of describing, not of explaining or analysing."[7] Nor of defining, one might want to add, since what Husserlian phenomenology purportedly describes is essences. And Heidegger says that the expression "descriptive phenomenology" is tautological.[8] But what is it to describe an essence? What is it to describe? Wittgenstein bids us consider how many different kinds of thing are called "description."[9] Might not one of these things be definition according to necessary and sufficient conditions or by genus and differentia as in classificatory botany? If so, such definition could not be simply opposed to the description of essence. On the other hand, the essences that phenomenology is said to describe could still be more open-textured. Whether they are or not will depend on what we learn when we patiently allow our descriptions and definitions to be guided by "the things themselves," by the *Sachheit* of the things under investigation, where, let it be noted in anticipation, the German word *Sache* corresponds with the English word "sake."

So Heidegger writes of phenomenological description that it "has the sense of a prohibition, insisting that we avoid all nondemonstrative determinations." Here demonstration is showing, in the sense of the Greek word *phainesthai,* which, let it too be noted in anticipation again, is middle-voiced. Hence, in applying Heidegger's phenomenology to phenomenology itself and to ecology, how tightly or loosely these are to be defined or described remains to be seen. And if, with regard to the *logos* of phenomenology or ecology, a modern Socrates objects, as the ancient Socrates so often does to his interlocutors, that he is asking not for stories but for an *eidos,* a sharply delimited specification of essence, he must be told that stories and histories may be what the situation asks for here, the *hanes* of *hanfod* referred to above. He must be reminded of Aristotle's advice not to expect in fields of discourse such as ethics what might be sought in mathematics.[10] Giving reasons for defining deep ecology in this way or that, and giving reasons for advocating deep ecology rather than shallower varieties, will be in large part the telling or retelling of stories, describing concrete experiences, perhaps performing them in one way or another.

PERFORMANCE

One way of moving beyond phenomenological description or of rethinking description as performance is illustrated by the history of Heidegger's move "through phenomenology to thought."[11] If phenomenology entails a move from philosophy that sets up the definition of essences or concepts as its ideal to philosophy that describes best by giving examples or exemplars, Heidegger's later thinking entails a move that supplements such description with performance, the singing of song, in both a wide and a narrower sense of the word. Indeed, with the help of, although not always in unison with, Hölderlin, Goethe, George, Mörike, Rilke, and the thinker-scientist-poets by whom Plato and Socrates were moved, not always successfully, to try to write sober prose, Heidegger sings the word "word" and thereby each thing that calls to be called by a name or a proname, a noun or pronoun or some other part of speech. Perhaps the philosopher and the poet and the scientist working together may alter by complicating what one may risk calling a *Weltanschauung,* notwithstanding Heidegger's qualms about what goes by that name. This word may be risked because it can mean both how human beings regard the world and how the world regards human beings, how it concerns us. To think regard in this latter ethical or "ethical" sense, which may be "deeper" because presupposed and therefore prone to be hidden by the former sense, is to rethink the sense and directionality (*Sinn*) of the hyphens of noesis-noema and of being-in-the-world. This is what

Heidegger's thinking of the ecology of what he calls the Fourfold (*Geviert*) or Fouring (*Vieren*) would do, with its emphasis upon the interdependence of the components, which he calls earth, sky, mortals, and gods, and his emphasis upon their being each of them according to its own way of being or essencing, *fügsam seinem Wesen*.[12]

Is Heidegger's emphasis equal? Or does it reflect the priority given to the human being in the chorus from *Antigone* that Heidegger quotes?

> Wonders are many on earth, and the greatest of these
> Is man.

As earlier with "deeper," so now with "greatest," priority must be heard in Heidegger's terms as priority of the ontological over the ontic. He is invoking Sophocles in the service of giving the philosophical reminder that Dasein, "man," is the *locus* and *logos* of being. No slur is being cast upon beings that are un-*Da*. Heidegger is simply spelling out preconditions of both casting slurs and praising to high heaven. These include the notions of fairness and unfairness, justice and injustice, truth and untruth presupposed in judgments we make about things natural, non-natural, or super-natural. But the truths of such judgments presuppose in turn primordial truth as the disclosure, *a-lētheia*, and opening that is Da-sein's *Da*. Similarly for the justice or injustice of such judgments. They too presuppose primordial justice, the order that the particle *fug* echoed in Heidegger's *fügsam* is intended to denote, itself an echo of the Greek *dikē*, meaning an original justice or organization of the world, on which Heidegger bases his fourfold ecology.

No particular order of evaluative priority can be inferred from this basis as to the worth of, say, the organic in comparison with the inorganic or the earth in comparison with the sky. The constituents of Heidegger's fourfold are incomparable, for they are not separable from one another. Each is implicated in and implicates the others.[13] So if any of these regions is for the sake of another, it is also for the sake of itself. This does not mean that a thing belonging to one region cannot be for the sake of another thing of that region or for the sake of a thing of another region. It does however suggest that when such supposed intra-regional or inter-regional subservience is placed in the wider co-regional perspective, invidious comparisons cease to be attractive. In the words of the poet, scientist, and phenomenological ecologist John Muir, who is remembered by an inscription on a granite slab in Wisconsin as "the most rugged, fervent naturalist America has produced, and the Father of the National Parks of our country":

> Poison oak or poison ivy (*Rhus diversiloba*), both as a bush and a scrambler up trees and rocks, is common throughout the foothill region up to a height of at least three thousand feet above the sea. It is somewhat troublesome to most travellers, inflaming the skin and eyes, but blends harmoniously with its companion plants, and many a charming flower leans confidingly upon it for protection and shade. I have oftentimes found the

curious twining lily (*Stropholirion Californicum*) climbing its branches, showing no fear but rather congenial companionship. Sheep eat it without
apparent ill effects; so do horses to some extent, though not fond of it,
and to many persons it is harmless. Like most other things not apparently
useful to man, it has few friends, and the blind question, "Why was it
made?" goes on and on with never a guess that first of all it might have been
made for itself.[14]

If it might have been made by God, it is made to His Greater Glory only if
God makes it for itself and us for ourselves. So a sustainable human economy would be sustained justly, *fügsam*, only if it cooperates with a sustainable
economy for non-human beings, with an environmentalism that is not uni-
directional, but a synergic ecology. An opening is made for this thought
when Heidegger reminds us and himself that being needs beings, and when
in saying this it is not only human or Da-sein-ish beings that he means.

No more can be claimed here than that an opening is made for this
thought. Heidegger's phenomenology and the "other thinking" he de-
clined to call phenomenology does not entail this other thinking of the non-
human other. It only enables it. It enables it precisely by softening the
hardness of the logical must, by passing from phenomenological methodology to hodology, to a being underway — *tao*, he is ready to say[15] — on a path
that this other thinking suggests we could follow if we could learn again to
think deponently, depositionally, to speak in something like the middle
voice, poised between the putting of a question and being put into question,
in the pause of the open question, on the way to language, in the moment of
the *question-savoir* for which *savoir* is no longer an *avoir* and least of all a
s'avoir, a self-possession.[16]

At the end of the *Cartesian Meditations* Husserl writes:

> The Delphic motto, "Know thyself!" has gained a new signification. Positive
> science is a science lost in the world. I must lose the world by *epochē*, in order
> to regain it by universal self-examination. *Noli foras ire*, says Augustine, *in te
> redi, in interiore homine habitat veritas*.[17]

Heidegger's phenomenology of inauthentic everyday being-in-the-world
and of falling into entanglement in it echoes Husserl's words. Following a
way toward which Husserl's words point, therefore, in the pause of phenomenological suspension, which is a losing of the world of objects and of the
self as having fallen among them, he finds the world given back. It is given
back not just to oneself, but to itself. Acceptance of the invitation to enter
into yourself, *in te redi*, leads to an *in te redditus*, a gift of the world that is a
foras ire, an exiting from interiority through the world's being accepted as a
gift, and therefore as a ground for gratitude.

Gratitude to whom or Whom, to what or What? What Heidegger calls
seinlassen, letting-be, lets us leave this question open, at least for a moment,
now and then. It allows us to not close off the thought that gratitude may be

due simply to the things themselves, and that this dueness may be the ligament, alliance, reliance, and truth of the *religio* treated in the work, *De vera
religione,* from which Husserl's citation from Augustine comes. If, following
Augustine, Descartes found God already at home in the *cogito,* following
Heidegger following Husserl one may find that the interiority of that home
is an exteriority in which one is not altogether at home, but *un-heimlich.* This
is in part because one cannot be grateful to oneself. It cannot be to oneself
that the debt of gratitude is due. But gratitude and its owing are not enough.
It is not enough because its owing is still owed to a self-owning. It is a return
for services rendered to me. Even if I think I am not worthy of the benefit I
have received, even if what is conferred is a sheerly gratuitous grace, I am
still at the center of my world—or at one of its centers if the geometry of
that world is the geometry of an ellipse. To be elliptical is to fall short, to
be incomplete. But the ellipsis described by gratitude does not fall short
enough. Its incompleteness is insufficient, so to speak, because it is described in terms of sufficiency and its lack. Here we have to speak so-to-
speakingly not because we have to speak metaphorically in the semantically
semiological sense of metaphor. Nor is the having-to of our having to speak
so-to-speakingly the having-to of the hard logical must. Both harder and
softer than the must of logical entailment is the must of a necessity that
is not based on my need or on a logico-conceptual requirement of my
language, but on the absolute need in which other things stand. Here *Notwendigkeit* undergoes a *Wende der Not,* a turn of need (to which we shall
return in Chapter 2). Another thing's absolute need is not and is not based
on a particular lack. In that sense it has no basis. My response to it is both the
most and the least gratuitous response in the world. In the phenomenology
of Husserl the motivation of the intentionality of consciousness, even when
it is complicated by his references to passive genesis, is (on the assumption
that one's own self is the center) centrifugal. The response that is due to
another's absolute need, absolute responsibility, is motivated otherwise.
The intentionality of its motivation is (still on the assumption that one's own
self is the center) centripetal, an affection from outside that bypasses my
consciousness—and my subconsciousness and unconsciousness too, if these
are conceived as subliminal analogues of consciousness.

JUSTICE ADJUSTED

In my trans-humanistic response to the humanism of the other human
being toward which Levinas works in response to the essentialist phenomenology of Husserl and the eksistentialist phenomenology of Heidegger, the
moment when, now, then, always, and always already, I am addressed by the
other human being is also the moment, the momentum, the movement,
and the motivation, when any existent whatsoever addresses me, whether or

not it, he, or she speaks the same language as I do — or any language at all where language is taken in the traditional Aristotelian way as a property that distinguishes the human from other living beings. My response to the address of another human being is not a response to the other's being an instance of the concept humankind. It is, as Levinas puts it, a response to the other's face. The other's face is the other's non-phenomenal singularity. Singularity is not particularity. The singularity beyond the sign, the uniqueness that in *Otherwise Than Being or Beyond Essence* Levinas calls a face and a trace, is beyond essence in this Aristotelian sense and beyond essence or *essance* in the verbal sense of *Wesen*. But is it beyond being? How can it be beyond being (and non-being), beyond *Sein* and Da-sein (and *Nicht-sein*) if, when we try to extend the application of Levinas's word "face" to all things, we extend it to every thing's to-be?

The being beyond which Levinas's title says his doctrine goes is not just the *existentia* of Scholasticism. It is also being as taken beyond *existentia* by Heidegger: being as thought not through the Latin third person *est* or the German *ist*, "is," but through the first person *bin*, with its sense of to dwell and to shelter, as in German *bei*, the *bu* of Sanskrit, the Scandinavian *by*, and the Scots *burgh*.[18] When this sense is read back into the Latin *existentia*, being regains the sense in which to-be-there, Da-sein, is to inhabit a world, not just to be in the space of a world in the manner of un-Da-sein-ish objects.

As Heidegger's later thinking of things in the ecology of the fourfold can help us understand, once we come to think of things as other than only objects, their being too is seen as more than Aristotelian *hoti estin* or Scholastic *existentia*. This does not mean that all things are now seen to exist in the manner of Da-sein. It means rather that they exist in ways of their own that may be Da-sein-ish or not, but are never the way only of objects over against subjects or indeed of objects over against Da-sein. A thing is no longer a mere what. But its existence does have a way, a mode, perhaps a mood. There is an adverbial how to it, which makes it possible for us, if not for it, to ask what it would be like to exist in that way. This makes a lot of sense at least for animals, even if to ask this question of plants and the non-living will be judged by many to be an indulgence in pathetic fallacy. If pathetic fallacy is the projection of human or Da-sein-ish capacities upon the non-human and non-Da-sein-ish, then pathetic fallacy does not respect the differences among the many ways of being. Ecological *Fügsamkeit* is flouted. The challenge is to maintain respect for an ecological justice that allows for difference without dominance. The challenge is to rethink justice in the way it is thought in Plato's *Republic,* but in a way in which the republic extends beyond the human and beyond the vertical hierarchy of the great chain of being, in a way that would mean refiguring justice in the soul so that the purely rational and the purely sensory would be abstractions from and aspects of an irreducibly ambiguous imagination. One platform from which to launch this idea would be the imagining of an original position like that imagined by John Rawls, except that we are to imagine a state in which it is not only undecided what role in society we are to fill, but undecided also whether we are to be human or non-human and in what way non-human.[19] The idea of metempsychosis could have a similar effect. If you are to come back into the world as a chicken or a fox, you may be strongly inclined in your lifetime now to take out membership of the Society for Compassion in World Farming and the League Against Cruel Sports. Ecological ethics built on such a foundation would, however, be an ethics based ultimately on self-interest. This ethics would still be a trans-humanly ramified prudence.

If we look to Kant or Levinas for the basis of a trans-human ethics that transcends prudence, we come up against the fact that both of them restrict underivative ethical responsibility to beings that speak. Levinas argues persuasively that ethics grounded solely in respect for a universal moral law is a violent masquerade of ethics because it fails to respect the other human being in its singularity. An ethics in which respect is limited to my being face to face with another would also be violent, because it is blind to the injustice it is bound to do to the third party. So respect of both kinds, for the case and for the face, have somehow to be hybridized if an ethics that is not glorified prudence is to be possible. In other words, Levinas retains a certain sort of systematicity, but it is not one in which terms are defined by their internal relations, as in the structuralism that was all the rage when he was writing his major works. Levinas has more than one way of maintaining the difference between terms. My difference from another human being is established first by my restrictedly egological enjoyment within the walls of my home. This corresponds with but is not equivalent to Heidegger's saying that for Da-sein to exist is to dwell. One reason why this is not equivalent is that according to Levinas the eksistentiality of Da-sein as described by Heidegger is so preoccupied with what it is *for* that it cannot admit Da-sein's enjoyment of what it lives *from.* My egological separateness and independence get "accomplished" and "produced," according to Levinas's genealogy of ethics, when the other human being picks me out, makes me stand out as a uniquely singular one from the impersonal one of *das Man,* by charging me with a responsibility unshared by anyone else. It is only through this asymmetrical relation of relations that human sociality can be ethical.

Whatever one may think of the bearing that Levinas's phenomenology or post-phenomenology has on the phenomenological ontology of *Being and Time* (the work of Heidegger to which he says he is attending above all), is it unthinkable, horrified though Levinas would be at the thought, that his doctrine and Heidegger's doctrine of the fourfold might be adapted to each other to produce at least a prolegomenon for a future ethical ecology? Recall that the regions of things that make up the Heideggerian fourfold (though we are not committed to a fold of only four) and the things of those different regions belong to each other. This does not mean that we possess them or that they possess us, any more than that we possess ourselves (*s'avoir*). Possession and the belonging, *zugehören,* of which Heidegger writes in "Das Ding" is for him more like a *zuhören,* one thing's so-to-speak hearing the voice of another. The openhanded non-possessiveness of this so-to-speak hearing and speaking is not altogether unlike that of the caress of erotic love with its accompanying sweet nothings expressed in not yet fully formed sentences, which according to Levinas anticipate the fully articulated ethical saying in which I am possessed by the other. For Levinas too possession is the hearing of voices, a kind of persecution mania, ethical psychosis, madness that is the "accomplishment" of rational responsibility because never accomplished, always beyond limit, infinite, unfinished: never enough, because absolutely beyond sufficiency.

But while what obsesses in what Levinas calls possession and psychosis is the other human being, it has to be asked why the other that obsesses me cannot also be the non-human. Levinas's reluctance to take this question seriously is connected with his fear of "hasidic" (Buberian), inebriated participation and confusion of every being with every or any other. As noted earlier, he sees a provisional salutary solution in the hypostasis of an ego enjoying itself, enjoying itself by enjoying the fruits of the earth from which it lives, a state which, whether or not it is prior to or presupposed by the being-thrown-ahead of itself of everyday Da-sein, still, like this latter, lives its life without questioning that the world is for the human ego. Another salutary solution is intimated in the following words of John Muir:

> The one deer that he started took a different direction from any which this particular old buck had ever been known to take in times past, and in so doing was cordially cursed as being the "d—dest deer that ever ran unshot." To me it appeared as "d—dest" work to slaughter God's cattle for sport. "They were made for us," say these self-approving preachers; "for our food, our recreation, or other uses not yet discovered." As truthfully we might say on behalf of a bear, when he deals successfully with an unfortunate hunter, "Men and other bipeds were made for bears, and thanks be to God for claws and teeth so long."[20]

It has to be conceded that any ethics or "ethics" based on this reminder might be only a glorified prudence and utilitarianism for non-humans, or for humans and non-humans, which latter, as Muir here implies, may include God. How much less exclusive can one get? Levinas is more exclusive than Muir. He does not think that a non-human and non-divine being might have a sake whose center of gravity is itself. This is a difficulty for him because a sake or, as he would say, a face is that which speaks. To face is to say, *dire.* But he himself underlines that this saying is not the speech-act that is distinguished from and opposed to what is said, the *dit.* It is the saying, the *Dire,* that allows this opposition to be made. So, rather as Levinas equates the face's saying with the looking at me of its eyes, can we not say of non-human beings that we regard them not simply as objects, but, as Levinas himself occasionally says of human beings, that they *me regardent,* that is, they are my concern? (We return to this matter in Chapter 9.)

Heidegger writes in "Das Ding": "Remembering them in this way, we let ourselves be concerned by the thing's worlding being (Dergestalt andenkend lassen wir uns vom weltenden Wesen des Dinges angehen)."[21] He goes on: "Thinking in this way, we are called by the thing as the thing. In the strict sense of the German word *bedingt,* we are be-thinged, the conditioned ones. We have left behind us the presumption of all unconditionedness." On the one hand, the conditionedness here is not just one of alimentary and other suchlike causal dependence. Nor, on the other hand, does it mean only that the worlding of other things is dependent upon the thinking and speaking that mortal things do. Nor, thirdly, is the different way of thinking that is envisaged simply a different *Weltanschauung,* if this is understood as a different attitude (*Einstellung*) taken up toward things, and if this in turn is understood as seeing things in a new framework (*Gestell*). That would still be representation, seeing things as objects, even if in a more complicatedly objectivating way. If the new thinking called for is ecological, it must be so in a non-objectivating way, and it must also be in some sense phenomenological, notwithstanding Heidegger's avoidance of this word because he and we have used it so much that it has become a concept we believe we have grasped. For Husserl phenomenology is motivated by the imagination.[22] So it can survive as a living science only if the imagination continues to be open to risks, including the risk to which Levinas fears it is exposed, the risk of defacing the human being. One of the risks to which phenomenology is exposed is that of seeing the non-human being as only for the sake of the human being or Da-sein. From poets and scientists phenomenological ecology may learn not only to be concerned with arriving by variation in imagination at invariants; it may learn also a capacity for the incapacity that leaves room at the edge of the *oikos* for the wild, the undomesticated.

ANCILLAE PHAENOMENOLOGIAE

Himself a man of science, but of science otherwise imagined, John Muir writes of men of science:

> The men of science and natural history often lose sight of the essential oneness of all living beings in their seeking to classify them in kingdoms, orders, families, genera, species, etc. . . . while the Poet and Seer never closes on the kinship of God's creatures and his heart ever beats in sympathy with the great and small as earth-born companions and fellow mortals dependent on Heaven's eternal laws.[23]

The same must be said of the science of ecology. The aesthetic, the ethical, and the scientific belong to each other. Together they make up an ecology, like the so-called faculties of the mind that in Kant's three Critiques read together are mapped on to the imagination writ large, larger than Plato's republic.[24]

Philosophy has traditionally been ready to listen to the sciences. It has sometimes been ready to think of itself either as the highest of them or as the handmaiden of the highest of them, the science of God. Whether or not phenomenology considers itself to be a science, any future phenomenological ecology will continue to listen to the natural and human sciences if its imagination is to be stretched not only toward the planet ("planetary thinking"), but toward the universe and the universal via the generic, the specific, and the particular. But if phenomenological ecology is to be fully attentive, its imagination will keep the particular in touch with the singular. That is to say, it will remain ready to listen also to the poet; and if its phenomenology is a science, it will also be an art. Heidegger writes that thinking, instead of taking up a different point of view, is called to make a step back, a *Schritt zurück*. Among other things Heidegger invites his reader to do is reread the so-called Pre-Socratics, who were scientists and poets and theologians and thinkers before the faculties of the mind and of the universities were separated, and before the faculty of philosophy was sectioned off into logic, philosophy of science, epistemology, metaphysics, ethics, aesthetics, political theory, philosophy of history, and so on. But this step back is to be made in order that we may make a step forward. It calls to be made in the pause, the halt (*Aufenthalt*) of *Ent-sprechen* between stepping back and stepping forward. (Chapter 6 pauses to think again of this pause.) *Entsprechen* is to correspond, co-respond. But spelled as Heidegger spells it, with a hyphen, it can be heard simultaneously as dis-speaking, sygetics, the ringing of silence, *das Geläut der Stille*. An antecedent of this has already been heard, Levinas says, in the Saying that is not the correlative of a said, but the ethical and anarchic passivity without which language is no more than a *flatus vocis*, hot air.[25] Notwithstanding all the burdens and aporias it brings already when confined to relations among beings that "have the word," is not responsibility shirked unless it is directed, and as directly, to beings that do not have the word? Do not "dumb creatures," those passed over in silence who cannot speak for themselves, call to be spoken for in the most serious sense of the word "call," a sense that crosses Heidegger's *Heissen* with Levinas's *Dire*? A limiting case of such advocacy would be saying that we should respect and acknowledge the meaningfulness of the silence of the beings on behalf of whom we speak. But, if only in order for there to survive beings toward whom this respect and acknowledgment is to be shown, our speaking on their behalf may have to take the form, despite the risk of appearing paternalistic, of protesting against certain practices, for example, the poaching of tigers in Thailand ("the East") to turn their bones, claws, and penises into allegedly tonic tablets or aphrodisiac soup for men rich enough to afford them, and the clubbing and, sometimes while they are still alive, the skinning of cubs of the rapidly dwindling population of seals in Canada ("the West") in order to provide fashionable garments for women.

The risk of sinking into the neutrality of the impersonal being of the "there-is" remains. So too, however, does the opposite risk of a parochiality in the scope of our conception of justice. Both risks can be met if the Good, the *epikeina tēs ousias*, is the beyond *of* being, being's beyond, commanding beings not hierarchically from above, but at the heart of a chiasmus. Levinas's fear of suffocation in being is a figment of a neglect of imagination, a neglect of that without which reason is empty and sensibility is blind. If phenomenological ecology is ontological it will also be ethical, the ontological and the ethical exceeding each other chiasmically. The ethical will in turn be chiasmically crossed with the aesthetic, and poietic representation as the production of something standing for something or somebody will be crossed with practical and political representation as somebody standing up for something or somebody. Only in this way will philosophy, not least the philosophy of Heidegger or the philosophy of Levinas, make belated acknowledgment that it has let preoccupation with one's own death or lethal indifference to other human beings turn its regard from the perishing or destruction of non-human beings.

So far these prolegomena for a non-exclusive phenomenological ecology have included God or gods among the non-human beings that compose that ecology, while allowing that this inclusion might be of a non-human being or of non-human beings entering into the *oikos* from an absolute exteriority. However, in responding to the questions just touched on of the death of the personal subject or of the personal as such, and of the death or destruction of the other, a thoroughly non-exclusive phenomenological ecology cannot exclude a priori what is proclaimed as the death or destruction of God. On one interpretation of this, what is proclaimed is that God is killed by being represented as a being. Bearing in mind that two of the three passages cited above from John Muir have invoked God as Creator, and taking as points of departure our citation of Heidegger's statement that being is more divine than any being and our more recent remarks about creative *poiēsis*, phenomenological ecology might find a future in going back to Husserl's thought that the engine of phenomenology is imagination. Your imagination and mine, but also imagination as it speaks to us through language, which Heidegger calls the house of being, being's *oikos*. One word that is spoken through this *ecologos* is the word "divine." The — or a — so-called root meaning of this word is to shine. It communicates therefore with *mico*, to flash, as of the imagination.

It is no surprise then that, as observed in our opening section, the concept of phenomenology is always liable to surprise us, that it is always on the move, always beginning again, always ahead of itself, if its motor is imagination, *Phantasie*, understood not as a power to conjure images, but as something like middle-voiced *phantazesthai*, where creative power is inseparable from patient *attente,* responsive attention, feel, touch, tact, attempt, temptation. Understood in this way, imagination exceeds itself only because it lets itself be exceeded, allows itself to be overcome by surprise. As *ecologos,* the language of imagination has the "divine tendency," *die göttliche Neigung,*[26] to open itself to what is not yet at home in the *oikos.* It is therefore open to the surprises thrown up in its own verbal play, for example the surprise that the so-called root meaning of shining attributed to "divinity" branches out also into "divining," prophesying, guessing. So if it is no longer thinkable that God is a being, it may still be thinkable that God is the human being's being kept guessing: shining, but also being kept in the dark, the provocation of imagination understood not as the power to produce images, but as patience before the unimageable. Therefore if imagination is the handmaiden of phenomenology, so also would be theology — or what we will find a reason for preferring to call theography.

2

GAIA SCIENZA

THE GAIA HYPOTHESIS

How sinister is it to say, as Heidegger said to the interviewer of *Der Spiegel,* that only a God/god can save us—where the German convention for writing nouns leaves it ambiguous whether in translating Heidegger's remark into English the initial should be in the lower or upper case?[1] In either case, he can be taken to have meant that there is nothing we can do except listen more closely. And his remark, in however apocalyptic a tone it may have been pronounced, can sound infuriatingly irresponsible to anyone for whom it seems extremely urgent that we should do something to save not just, as he says, "us," but them, those other than us, whether human or not, whether by the non-human be meant the sky and earth in his and Hölderlin's senses of these words, or whether with James Lovelock we refer to it more comprehensively as Gaia.[2] Or are we being too pessimistic, indulging a Pascalian fascination with the thought of being on the edge of an abyss?[3]

Heidegger would say that his apparent complacency is neither pessimistic nor optimistic. His remark to the interviewer from *Der Spiegel* simply acknowledges that to suppose one can devise a technique or strategy for over-coming an ultimate danger is to reinforce the ultimate danger itself. The danger lies precisely in that supposition. The ultimate danger is that of mistaking a symptom for the constitution of a malaise. Unlike at least some sorts of disease, if a sickness of worldhood is to be remedied, it can only be by letting it take its course, prescribing no regime, only preparing the way for one.

Whether or not Heidegger's response is pessimistic or optimistic or nei-ther, Lovelock's is the one or the other or neither depending on how one answers the questions, For what or for whom? According to his hypothesis, Gaia will look after herself. Geological evidence suggests that life will be preserved through the evolution of conditions that will protect it from ex-tremes of heat or cold.

> This [hypothesis] postulates that the physical and chemical condition of the surface of the earth, of the atmosphere, and of the oceans has been and is actively made fit and comfortable by the presence of life itself. This is in contrast to the conventional wisdom which held that life adapted to the planetary conditions as it and they evolved their separate ways.[4]

So the hypothesis bodes well for life in general. But the influence of the biosphere on the atmosphere is not necessarily good news for life in its human manifestation. That thought has at least the salutary effect of lead-ing human beings to adopt a less anthropocentric perspective. It would still be a somewhat geocentric one, however, insofar as while remembering mother earth one forgets for instance Mars, as Lovelock says he was able to do when the idea of the hypothesis came to him while doing research into the problem of the pollution of interplanetary space and "Working in a new intellectual environment, I was able to forget Mars and to concentrate on the Earth and the nature of its atmosphere."[5] That concentration still has an enormously wide focus. But we should also pan back, Pan back, so that Mars and the other planets re-emerge into view in order that we may ask of the starry sky above whether it is outlawed by the standard of the moral law within. Should we not work toward working in another new intellectual environment, one in which the moral significance and moral depth re-ferred to in the title of a book by Lawrence Johnson extends to everything and every thing that exists, or at least to every existent other than oneself, as was argued in *The Middle Voice of Ecological Conscience,* published in the same year as Johnson's *A Morally Deep World: An Essay on Moral Significance and Environmental Ethics?*[6]

That argument will be taken a few steps further here in fulfillment of the promise made through the epigraph of the postface of that earlier book, which borrows Heidegger's statement in the afterword to "What Is Meta-physics?" "Das folgende Nachwort ist . . . ein anfänglicheres Vorwort," to which I lend the meaning that a postface is a preface to a deeper beginning.

The deeper beginning looked for is the beginning of deeper and wider ecology, though one that leaves a niche for shallow ecology understood as an ecology motivated by enlightened human self-interest. Johnson's environmental ethics too does this, and I shall build on some of the things he says.

Before considering his morally deep eudaemonism I comment on a version of morally shallow contractualism, indicating why that falls short. In the course of these two discussions it will become plain why, notwithstanding the very high regard in which I hold the work of Jeremy Bentham, John Stuart Mill, and Peter Singer, I believe that utilitarian accounts fall short and that we must look beyond them and beyond morally shallow contractualism. I advocate a morally deep contractualism that is social but at the same time natural in that non-human beings are parties to it through human advocates.

MORALLY SHALLOW CONTRACTUALISM

Peter Carruthers's *The Animals Issue* is a book that would have beasts issue two by two from the protection of the ark of morality. Apparently too from his home. On the back of the book's jacket we are told that the author "has, at various times, been the owner of numerous cats and a dog, to all of whom he was devoted. He now has young children instead." The force of this "instead" will emerge as we consider some of the arguments leading to what the author describes as his book's "most important practical conclusion."[7]

Carruthers equates the possession of moral standing with the possession of rights. He limits the possession of moral rights to those who in principle can claim them or those — for example human babies, human mental defectives, and senile human beings — who resemble sufficiently those who can claim rights to be granted them in order to ensure social stability and to escape the dangers of finding oneself on a slippery slope when one asks how intelligent right-holders must be. No such risk is incurred, he maintains, as between humans and animals. We are able to distinguish between them well enough to forestall the Kantian argument according to which we have an indirect duty to be concerned for the welfare of animals since lack of concern for their welfare is likely to lead to lack of concern for the welfare of fellow human beings. Carruthers nevertheless agrees with Kant that we do have indirect duties to be kind to animals, but for two different reasons. First, in being cruel to animals we offend the sensibilities of animal lovers. Second, the indifference a person shows toward animals is a state of character that that person might manifest toward other rational agents. This point is perhaps not entirely consistent with what I have taken to be his dismissal of Kant's argument from contamination, an argument to which we shall return when we come to expound Johnson's eudaemonism. Carruthers dismisses the Kantian argument from contamination because, he says, human beings are more discriminating than Kant's argument suggests, and "That someone can become desensitised to the suffering of an animal need not mean they have become similarly desensitised to the sufferings of human beings — the two things are, surely, psychologically separable."[8] It also merits mention in passing that this capacity to discriminate is likely to be affected by human-animal organ or gene transplantation, to the point at which the concept of cannibalism, already blurred by a non-symbolist interpretation of the Christian Mass, becomes further complicated when one asks whether after the organs of a pig injected with human genes have been removed in the neighboring organ farm its remains may be served up in the hospital's wards for breakfast. Similar complications are introduced by the results of research into the linguistic ability of some animals, for example chimpanzees. After considering some of these results *The Animals Issue* concludes that even if it be granted that certain animals may be credited with linguistic capacity, that capacity does not stretch to the rationality required for the long-term planning and long-term desires necessary to the ability to be partner to a contract. This calls for not merely technical intelligence but social intelligence, more specifically for possession of the concept of what it is to act under a rule and possession of the idea of what it would be like for all others to act under the same rule.[9]

Although I have already conceded that it is pedagogically persuasive for the defender of the moral standing of non-human beings to at least begin with resemblances between humans and animals — and the point of resemblance consisting in the fact that they both suffer seems to me to be one to which no one should deny moral relevance — making moral standing dependent upon the possession of properties similar to those possessed by humans is ultimately too exclusive. I am aware that the perspective I advocate is one that might well be considered dangerous and daft. That it would be considered dangerous by the author of *The Animals Issue* will shortly become clear. That it would be considered daft is evident from his argument for rejecting the idea that human beings might be contractual advocates for animals. Referring, as our opening chapter did, to John Rawls's idea of an original position in which human beings are as yet ignorant of what their place in society will be,[10] he argues:

> Once it is allowed that animals may have representatives to speak on their behalf behind the veil of ignorance, there seems to be no good theoretical reason why other sorts of thing should not have representatives also. Why should there not be people detailed to defend plants and micro-organisms, or indeed mountains and ancient buildings? Moral rights would then become rampant, in a way that would, I think, be acceptable to no one.[11]

If this proliferation of moral rights should seem to be acceptable to anyone on the basis of the historical fact that not so long ago women and slaves would have been thought not to be entitled to have a voice or advocate in the imaginary (Rawlsian) or real (Scanlonian) contract,[12] Carruthers will point to the historical fact that such exclusions were based on mistaken beliefs, for example the belief that slaves were of lower intelligence. But could it not be said that some have denied moral standing to animals on the basis of the mistaken belief that humans but not animals have immortal souls, that animals but not humans are machines, or that animals are not conscious of pain?

Carruthers agrees that the principle of reflective equilibrium demands that an acceptable moral theory must not conflict either with too many empirical beliefs or with too many widely held commonsense moral intuitions. Among beliefs of the latter kind with which he holds a moral theory should be consistent he includes what he claims to be "the almost universal human belief . . . that the interests of an animal count for precisely nothing when set against the suffering of a human being."[13] It is "hugely counter-intuitive," he says in criticism of the utilitarian perspective, that there would be nothing to choose between saving an animal or a human being if it is open to us to save one but not both from sadistic torture and if the balance of pleasure-pain is the same in each case, or that we would be morally bound to save not the human, but the dog or even a creature of greater life expectancy than a human being or a dog. But this is a criticism of the utilitarian perspective in general, one that leads me to reject it too. It does not settle "that the interests of an animal count for precisely nothing when set against the suffering of a human being." An argument against this contention is forthcoming from further reflection upon another of Carruthers's scenarios, that of the fire at the kennels where we have to sacrifice either the life of the kennel-master or the lives of the dogs. Would those who believe robustly that the interests of an animal count for precisely nothing when set against the suffering of a human being not begin to waver at some point if the sacrifice necessary to save the kennel-master is that of a hundred dogs, a thousand, a million, six million? If it be replied that our morality is not fitted to cope when circumstances exceed a certain degree of extraordinariness, that is a reflection of the conservatism implied by "our morality." But circumstances are sometimes extraordinary, and if when they are we decide to leave judgment in suspense, it is still a decision that is made. Instead of saying that this would be a suspension of morality as such, should we not say that it is only a suspension of our morality, and a sign that it might be time to widen its horizons?

After its earlier chapters have produced an argument to show that morality is a social contract that denies moral standing to beasts, the last chapter of *The Animals Issue* presents, albeit tentatively, an argument that would, if it is valid, finally sweep away the last chance of getting animals rescued by an ethical ark built according to utilitarian specifications. It would destroy this last chance by demonstrating the moral irrelevance of animal pain. That the neo-Cartesian argument of the final chapter will not be invulnerable to objection can with hindsight be seen to emerge quite early in the book. There the author says of a caterpillar pierced by a pin that although a human being observing the caterpillar's wriggling might think that the caterpillar is in pain, this behavior is probably due to a tropism, so that "the nerves sensitive to the presence of the pin feed directly into the muscles responsible for the subsequent movement, without any intervening cognition" — as if, although there is sensitivity, there is no conscious pain, because there is no cognition.[14] It becomes clearer in the last chapter of the book that Carruthers takes consciousness to imply cognition, and holds that for cognition there must be self-consciousness, meaning that the subject of the experience must be able to identify the experience as its own and as an instance of a certain kind. There must be something that the subject's experience is like.[15] There must be consciousness. He goes on to suggest that if it is only human beings that are capable of conscious experiences so defined, the pains of animals will make no moral claims upon us, for if there is nothing that the animal's experience is like for that animal, hence nothing that it is like for that animal to be the subject of non-conscious pain, then it can make no claim on our sympathy.

Now although in the circumstances so described empathy may not be possible, sympathy seems to be possible and appropriate. It can only seem otherwise if it is assumed that consciousness cannot be pre-reflective.

Carruthers suggests that his contractualist conception is probably innately selected for by human evolution. If that is so, it is not surprising that his contractualist conception of morals gives priority to the survival of humans. Nor would it be surprising if within the parameters of the contractualist conception animal welfare is always overridden by human welfare, as illustrated by the fact that whereas that thou shalt not murder is a conceptual truth available for the defense of human beings, no such conceptual truth seems available for settling a debate about bringing about the death of the animal, for it remains an open question whether or not one should kill. That one should not kill does not begin to look like a conceptual truth. On the other hand, that other things being equal one should not be cruel does appear to follow from the concept of cruelty with equal necessity whether that concept be used of human conduct toward other human beings or toward animals. And this is an argument for allowing that there is at least one segment of the sphere of direct moral significance that humans and animals share.

The perspective of rule- or practice-utilitarianism keeps open the possibility, foreclosed by contractualism as defined by Carruthers, of extending a moral social contract to a natural contract in which not only do contractors get delegated to speak on behalf of animals, but in which every contractor, every human being, is an advocate not only for herself or himself, but also for non-human beings. The apparently very Western, indeed, as Nietzsche describes it, very English, perspective of utilitarianism in that respect overlaps the so-called Eastern perspective of *wu-wei*, which, as will be argued further at the end of this chapter and in the next, is a perspective implicit in the very methodology of Western science. It is implicit even in the methodology that in Carruthers's moral science is referred to as the principle of reflective equilibrium. For that principle requires a balance between theory and the data of ground-floor moral intuition. It therefore depends on the dialectic of determinant and reflective judgment in which reflective judgment dares to think that even the most fundamental theoretical categories are not immune to revision and that the values they incorporate are exposed to revaluation. The recklessness and caution of this reflection represents the tender-mindedness that must accompany the tough-mindedness of science if science is not to be stopped in its tracks by the weight of its own dogma. The categories that frame our questions or demands demand categorically to be called into question. This metacategorical imperative "Let" is announced in something like the middle voice, the voice that lets be heard the voice of the other, not only the human other, but every single singular other, including the animal other, be it the elephant who might be named Ganesh, the ape who might be named Hannuman, or the dog who might be named Anubis or Bobby or Bobbie.[16]

Having expressed reservations over the requirement of social contractualism that all moral subjects be capable of language and over the utilitarian tendency to require of moral subjects that they be capable of suffering, do I contradict my desire to preserve moral relevance for difference if I associate every difference with need? Does this not simply replace one resemblance between humans and non-humans with another? The contradiction is only apparent. The attempt to find a commonness of need is an attempt to find a non-exclusive condition for any existent to qualify as a focus of prima facie responsibility. The concept of need ranges at least as widely as the concept of harm or deprivation. But this point of resemblance through need, thanks to which every thing is granted a face, allowed to be the singular subject of ethical regard in the dimension of, let us say, justesse, is consistent with a pluralism of morally relevant features in the dimension of justice. So in this latter realm of claims and counterclaims it may be important to seek not only resemblances but differences. And it will therefore be important to remember that humans may be legitimately regarded either as animals or as Da-sein — nothing Heidegger says is inconsistent with this — and that, as well as speaking of the animals issue generically, one should look closely at the differences among species and individual living creatures and at the resemblances and differences between these and the inorganic world. It will be important, for example, when considering the relevance of contract to the moral standing of animals not to overlook such observations as those Frans de Waal reports in his *Chimpanzee Politics*, where with reference to his study of chimpanzees at Arnhem zoo he writes:

chimpanzee group life is like a market in power, sex, affection, support, intolerance and hostility. The two basic rules are one good turn deserves another and "an eye for an eye, a tooth for a tooth."

The rules are not always obeyed and flagrant disobedience may be punished. This happened once after Puist [a senior female] had supported Luit in chasing Nikkie. When Nikkie later displayed at Puist she turned to Luit and held out her hand to him in search of support. Luit, however, did nothing to protect her against Nikkie's attack. Immediately Puist turned on Luit, barking furiously, chased him across the enclosure and even hit him. If her fury was in fact the result of Luit's failure to help her after she had helped him, this would suggest that reciprocity among chimpanzees is governed by the same sense of moral rightness and justice as it is among humans.[17]

This chimpanzee morality would be a morality of politics, marketing, and trade-off in which it is in body language that claims are expressed. If it is conceivable that the chimpanzees might extend their morality to include their human keepers, it is also conceivable that human morality might extend to the chimpanzees. In that case it is conceivable that Carruthers might at least allow one exception when, in what he describes as the most important practical conclusion of his book, he declares of animals in general that there is no basis for extending moral protection to them beyond that which is already provided, and that "those who are committed to any aspect of the animal rights movement are thoroughly misguided."[18] Anyone anywhere? And was the bill to prohibit hunting with hounds passed in the British and Scottish parliaments since the publication of *The Animals Issue* thoroughly misguided? The book's "most important practical conclusion" is largely motivated by the belief that feelings of sympathy for animals "serve only to divert attention from the claims of those who do have moral standing, namely human beings." When on the last page it is asserted that these feelings are "partly dependent upon the false belief in the equal moral standing of animals," one is confirmed in the suspicion raised earlier in the book that it runs together the question whether animals have moral standing with the question whether they have "*equal* rights with human beings, consistent with their different needs and capacities."[19] Now although every holder of rights has an equal right with every other to have its rights considered (otherwise it is not a holder of rights), in concrete circumstances even a right possessed by a particular human being may not carry equal weight with that possessed by another human being. And it is only in actual or imagined concrete circumstances that a right possessed by a human being can be weighed against that which an animal might hold. I say this on the assumption that the social contractual model, the model centered on bargaining and the claiming of rights, is the only right model for ethics. But I hope we can go at least one step beyond that, one step further for nonhumankind. I hope we can make sense of the extension of that model to one centered on a socio-natural contract in which advocates speak for those who cannot speak for themselves. This extension is an extension of the imagination. In arguing for an ethics centered on others' needs I am arguing that ethics has many mansions, so that perhaps the animal rights movement is indeed misguided if in emphasizing rights it assumes that where there is no right there is no responsibility. The reciprocating engine of rights is introduced, as it is by rule-utilitarianism, in order to serve as a governor for excesses of act-utilitarianism, such as the principle of the general substitutability of sentient beings provided the balance of pleasure-pain is not altered. But does not an ethics of exchange call for an excess and substitution of a different kind: my substitution for the other, my readiness to die — or to live and donate my savings in order to save him or her or it? If a responsibility or a duty is always correlated with a right, perhaps it is with your right that my responsibility is correlated, not with any right of mine. Whether or not I have a right is irrelevant to whether or not I have a responsibility. And I have a responsibility the moment you have a need, whatever your standing in the so-called great chain of existence. Moreover, you have a need as soon as you exist, the need that at the very least, other things being equal, your existence not be put at stake. Thus Proposition 6 of Part 3 of the *Ethics* of Spinoza, "Every thing, so far as it is in itself, endeavours to persevere in its being," is found to play a crucial and positive role within the context or non-context of the asymmetry of face-to-face address in the proto-ethics of Levinas. This being so, perhaps an abbreviation may be made in the chain of ideas making up what I shall call a deontological argument. That implicative chain stretches from the idea of the existence of an entity other than myself to the idea of its need to the idea of its good to the idea of my responsibility. If the first idea in this concatenation implies the last immediately, and if existence is not a predicate, we may have found that the readmission of non-human beings into the ark of direct ethical significance does not turn even on the resemblance they share with human beings of being in need. One thing does not resemble another in point of existence. Their existence is what their resemblance — or lack of resemblance — presupposes. Large questions remain as to the daftness or otherwise of positing the existence of, for example, numbers, as to the *ti estin* of the *hoti estin,* and as to whether existence has no kind, only one kind, or many kinds. However, starting from the *hoti estin,* from the that it is of what is other than me, we may be able, as I have hinted, even through scientific method, to take one small step or two for non-humankind toward the inclusion of Gaia and the starry sky above within the field (*nomōs, iworu*) of direct ethical regard.

MORALLY DEEP EUDAEMONISM

I shall now summarize rapidly the points made by Lawrence Johnson that I am almost entirely willing to endorse, in order to bring out why I suspect that the environment of his wide and deep ecology is yet not wide and deep enough.

To express my suspicion in a word, it is that, like Lovelock in the paragraphs from which I have quoted, Johnson zooms in so close with his ethical lens that the zoological, in the broadest possible sense of what has life, is all that is left with moral standing in its own sake — not to say without qualification in its own right. He argues that what has underivative moral standing must have an interest and what has an interest is what can have well-being. This leads him, if I read him correctly, to limit the scope of moral standing to living beings, with the exception of one sort of being, whose moral status, however, is derivative from that of human beings in a manner I shall explain when I have sketched the stages on his way to this corollary. To say that the balance of pleasure and pain can provide a necessary condition or criterion of morality is objectionable, Johnson maintains, because, as conceded in Peter Singer's version of Benthamite utilitarianism, sentient beings could be eliminated and replaced by other sentient beings without offense provided the balance of pleasure over pain were unreduced.[20] Johnson's objection is well made. A parallel objection holds against Kantianism if Kant is taken seriously when he says that the moral dignity of persons stems from the moral law they represent. Although that law is infringed, according to him, if one person wills her or his own or another's death, it is the universal law as such from which the goodness of a good will derives. That it is the will of *this* person is morally neither here nor there. True, the moral law operates upon teleological maxims that may distinguish this from that person's psychological personality. This has led at least one philosopher, J. J. C. Smart, to assert that Kant is a closet utilitarian.[21] Although there is more to be said for this interpretation of Kant than one might at first suppose, it is seen to be untenable once one accepts that there is in Kant an element of the idolatry of law from which Jack Smart would like to have utilitarianism saved.

However, with Bentham and against R. G. Frey, Johnson argues that although the capacity to feel pain is not a necessary condition, it may be a sufficient condition for moral significance. Frey denies this, and denies that animals can have morally significant interests, because he holds that to have an interest is to have a desire and to have a desire is to have language; but animals lack language.[22] This denial has been widely questioned, for instance by Stephen Clark and others in a publication on the capacities of chimpanzees.[23] But one should also question whether the case for the moral standing of non-humans should be grounded simply on resemblances they are claimed to have with humans. On its own, that approach leaves too many non-human beings out in the cold. However, I share what I think is Stephen Clark's view, that an argument based on resemblance is one pedagogically efficient place at which to start.[24]

Johnson too questions the thesis that no non-human animals have language. That thesis is questionable because it takes too propositional a view of the capacity to be conscious of having a desire, which, according to Frey, having a desire presupposes. Frey identifies this consciousness with having a belief and, following Davidson, identifies belief with belief in the truth of a sentence. This semantic theory of belief, as we might call it, is incredible. Fido can desire a bone without being able to formulate his desire linguistically, unless Fido's tugging at his lead as he nears the butcher's shop amounts to linguistic formulation, which Frey denies. He maintains that if Fido is to have an interest that will serve as the basis for his having moral significance, he must have linguistic capacity of the sort that will enable him to formulate a claim. Admittedly, a comatose human being cannot make such a claim, but Frey allows that such a being can have a morally significant interest on the basis of the desires it would have if it were not comatose and were therefore able to exercise the thinking and linguistic capacity we associate with being a normal human being. Nevertheless, although Frey denies that non-humans have moral significance, he allows that they may be wronged. Kant's reasons for saying this are available to Frey; that is, although it is open to him to say with Kant that one can have indirect obligations in respect of animals, one cannot have direct obligations that respect animals: one's obligations or duties in respect of animals are derivative from one's direct obligations or duties toward beings who can have obligations to oneself.[25] However, Johnson confesses to being puzzled as to how Frey can consistently allow that animals can be wronged. He expresses this puzzlement in a manner that may seem slightly slipshod, but is in fact perceptively and revealingly careful. "I find Frey rather mysterious here," he remarks.

> He seems to be tying interests to rights, then saying that animals have a moral status of some sort even without rights and interests. For my part, I am content to leave the problematic concept of rights out of account altogether, as being more rhetorical than illuminating. I tie interests directly to injuries and benefits, and argue that anything that can be injured in its own right has an interest in not being injured, and that anything that can be benefited in its own right has an interest in being benefited.[26]

Has Johnson left the problematic concept of rights, in the plural, out of account if he centers his account on the notion of what a being can suffer or enjoy in its own singular right? Does this phrase "in its own right" reintroduce a notion of natural right and maybe even natural contract, in the sense of the title of the book by Michel Serres?[27] And is the apparent shift of ground in fact a marching on the spot because the terms to which it purports to move depend for their sense on the concept of legal right and social contract, whether or not these are avowedly or unavowedly conceived in terms of a mythological or theological covenant? An alternative is to interpret the phrase "in its own right" ecologically, in a way to which I shall later return. However, let me first finish my résumé of Johnson's theory of moral significance.

So far I have mentioned nothing in that theory with which I wish to disagree. Nor do I have cause for complaint when Johnson goes on to say that although having desires may be a sufficient condition for having moral standing, it is not a necessary condition, so it is not a sufficient and necessary condition as the capacity to feel pain seems to be in the utilitarian theory presented by Singer. "In general," Johnson writes, managing to sound like Heidegger and Aristotle at one and the same time, "it is by no means the case that our primary values spring from our desires, as from some axiological Unmoved Mover. Our most central desires spring from our most central being, and are a matter of what contributes to our wellbeing."[28] And wellbeing extends beyond desires, certainly beyond desire for pleasure and the absence of pain. Human well-being extends beyond that, and human being, whose being Heidegger calls world-forming, *weltbildend*, in his lectures of 1929–1930, has that much in common with the being of the plant, whose being, though discussed by Heidegger in those lectures, is left in an even more ambiguous state than that of the stone, whose being is first said by him to be poor in world, *weltarm*, and then said to be *weltlos*, without world and without environment.[29]

Johnson is rather clearer than Heidegger is about the difference between the plant and the stone. He is very much in favor of the idea that a plant can have a well-being, but stops short of granting this favor to the stone. His argument in effect blocks a riposte that some philosophers have made to Kant's admission that we have a derived duty to animals on the grounds that in permitting humans to act cruelly to them we would be cultivating an attitude that might lead to violence toward human beings. The riposte is the observation that on this argument, other things being equal, it would be at least derivatively immoral to strike stones. Johnston forestalls this reply by affirming that one can do moral wrong only to what can have well-being and by denying that stones do. Or at least — and this explains the slight reservation in my preliminary remarks about the point at which my agreement with him comes to an end — rocks, to wit such rocks as Ayer's Rock and geological formations such as the Grand Canyon, may be valued in their own right, but the basis for the appropriateness of that valuing is not that they have wellbeing, but that valuing something for its own sake is conducive to the wellbeing of human beings.

Of course, if the names Ayer's Rock and Grand Canyon are taken to stand for ecosystems, then they do have moral significance in themselves, for they have interests and so well-being consisting in what Lovelock calls their homeostasis or what Johnson, following Sagan and Margulis, suggests it would be preferable to call homeorhesis in order to escape the implication that ecosystematicity is static.[30] And when the names Ayer's Rock and Grand Canyon are so regarded, included in the ecosystems they name would be human beings, in particular, respectively, the Australian Aborigines and Native Americans. However, regarded as individuals on their own, such geological entities do not in themselves have moral significance, whatever may be their aesthetic value or value as symbols and archetypes helping human beings to achieve a wider and deeper order in their psychological or spiritual lives.

Johnson is willing to go a little further than this, but he does not go quite far enough. His view seems to be that things he considers in themselves incapable of interest, hence incapable of well-being, are capable of *moral* relevance only on account of the effect they have on human and other beings that have interests and well-being. Johnson speaks of the Nazi officer who on his morning journey to check the operation of the ovens at Buchenwald paused to admire the grandeur of the mountains and in the evening returned to enjoy listening to Mozart in rooms on whose walls hung paintings appropriated from foreign museums. Such a person, he writes, would have lived a life that was better for himself if he had been more compassionate to fellow human beings, and in any case "if someone does not find something to value in Mozart or the Grand Canyon, there is something missing in that person"; "if we, individually and as societies, learned to develop values genuinely conducive to our wellbeing, we would then treat the environment, and one another, and ourselves quite a lot better." However, he adds, this better treatment of the environment is not a *morally* better treatment of what is not itself a biospheric ecosystem, living species, or individual. Only such beings have well-being, that is to say, health. His concluding words are these:

> Morally we ought, as best we can, to allow the living world, and the entities thereof, in their diversity, to thrive in richness, harmony, and balance. In all things we must ask whether our actions are conducive to, or at least compatible with, the fullness and wellbeing of life. Thereby we may better live deep and worthwhile lives in a deep and valuable world.[31]

On the previous page he has been slightly more guarded. What he says there is that "The depth of moral significance extends at least to the depths of the living world." It is not entirely clear why he says "at least." Perhaps this phrase is no more than an indication of the tentativeness with which he admits he proposes the account I have just summarized of the way he sees the non-moral value of certain non-living entities contributing to the well-being of living human beings and hence having moral significance. No less tentatively, I want to give other reasons, as I have begun to do here and elsewhere, why we should retain that guarded "at least." We should retain it in order to retain underivative moral significance for beings that are not or not believed to be living, whether or not we consider that this underivative moral significance presupposes that such entities are capable of well-being as Johnson defines this. So if the biosphere is defined in such a way as to exclude, for example, Mars, this will not entail that Mars is not an object of underivative moral significance.

PROTOGAIA

Of course, no entity we can think of is excluded from the biosphere if inclusion in the biosphere is achieved by inclusion in the thoughts of living beings. This inclusion by way of what used to be called Cambridge predicates is not what I take Lovelock to understand by inclusion within the biosphere. The biosphere in his sense is Gaia, understood as our earth. But is not the biosphere in that sense only part of the ethosphere (recalling that the Lexicon records that the plural *ēthea* named places haunted by beasts, before it came to name the abodes of human beings)? Do not the galaxies belong to the moral kingdom of ends? Is not taking a less telescopic view of the moral realm a morality of the parish pump? Not because it may be discovered that there is life on Mars. Nor because it may be that there is life *in* Mars, as there is according to Leibnizian, Whiteheadian, and other pan-psychic accounts of matter. Let the matter that makes up Mars, Ayer's Rock, and the Grand Canyon be as inert as one can imagine, these entities are morally significant as beings in their own right. Simply as beings, as entities in their *hoti estin,* in their existential *that,* whatever their *ti estin,* whatever their *what.* Simply in their very extantness or standing they have moral standing. Although whatever exists has a what, whether that what be described as an essence or not, its existing, its *Wirklichkeit,* independently of how it exists, in abstraction from its real predicates, from its *Realität,* confers upon it a need, namely the minimal need that, other things being equal, its existence not be curtailed. This is how to interpret the above-cited Proposition 6 of Part 3 of the *Ethics* of Spinoza: "Every thing, so far as it is in itself, endeavours to persevere in its being," *Unaquaeque, quantum in se est, in suo esse perseverare conatur.* Another being's to-be-or-not-to-be is for me already a moral question. I say "another being's" and "for me" because each I endeavors to persist in its own being anyway as a matter of fact, but in doing so it is liable to put the existence of other beings at risk. Morality is not magnified prudence, and the distinction between prudence and morality is the distinction between myself and others. Morality is not enlightened self-interest. It is enlightened other-interest. That "interest," however, is either too weak if it means no more than being among (*inter-esse*) or too strong and question-begging if it is used in the sense given first in the *Concise Oxford Dictionary* (though sixth in the *Collins Concise English Dictionary*), namely that of legal concern, title, claim, or right in property. It is hardly surprising, as I have already said in discussing the arguments of Carruthers, that if interest is understood in this sense, the kind of moral theory based on the concept of interest turns out to be one of contractual rights.

Further, instead of making moral significance pivot on either desire or well-being, should we not cast need in that role? The word "want" might perform the same function in the sense it has in "for want of a nail the shoe was lost." And an attraction of using the word "want" is that its sense ranges over the privations of inanimate as well as animate beings, and overlaps with the sense of desire. It may be objected that defining morality in terms of another's need or want in the sense of lack makes morality undemocratically patronizing, thereby defeating the original aim of defining morality in these terms, the aim of retaining the greatest possible width for the constituency of legitimate claimants to moral standing. This objection is met if, without need or want in the sense of lack being equated with desire, the desire to desire is one kind of want or need. An attraction that the term "need" offers over the term "want" is its connection with the idea of necessity, that is to say, *Not* and *Notwendigkeit* in Nietzsche's and Heidegger's sense of *Wende der Not,* a turn of adversity or emergency.

If the word "well-being" is intended as a translation of *eudaimonia,* we are projected immediately into the sphere of *daimonia,* psyche or life, and perhaps into the sphere, if it is one, fully rounded or broken, of what David Krell's remarkable *Daimon Life* teaches its readers to understand by its title.[32] Making moral significance dependent upon well-being understood as *eudaimonia* immediately puts at risk the chance of securing moral significance for the unliving. And it is this chance that my book aims to save, even if the saving of it remains haunted by a certain insecurity.

GEOETHICS EAST AND WEST

One way by which one might attempt to keep open this chance is by turning to the East. This is why it is necessary to underline the differences between enlightened self-interest, associated with the phase in the history of the West called the Enlightenment, and enlightenment as associated typically with practical or mystical traditions of the East. In making this distinction one should not forget the mystical traditions of the West. Nor should one forget that long before Japan learned to outstrip the West in the Baconian will to compete with nature to the point of making nature its slave, the turns in Taoism and Buddhism to such tender arts of cooperation with nature as *wu-wei,* letting-be or going with the flow, were sometimes reactions to preceding epochs of bellicose triumphalism. *Wu-wei* is indeed a way, like *tao.* It is not a method as conceived by Western philosophers of science. It is not an inquisition or extorsion, twisting nature's arm. No one should be surprised that *tao* is mentioned in the course of Heidegger's placing of *Gelassenheit* and *Seinlassen. Tao* and *wu-wei* are mentioned also in *A Morally Deep World* and in *The Middle Voice of Ecological Conscience.* Mention of *wu-wei* is made in this last in the course of an attempt to sketch a proto-ethics for an ecology following the contours of Hölderlin's and Heidegger's Fourfold. The book's postface attempts to show how, if ecology is to have an ethical dimension, it must reconstrue the world of measurable and countable objects or processes as this is regarded by classical science. However, the phrase "as this is regarded" must be handled with care. An adaptation of the Heideggerian thinking would still suffer from parochialism if it could not find a way of extending moral regard to the objects of science quantitatively described. A *protogaia scienza* would be inconsistent with its own pretensions to largesse if it assumed a priori that entities as regarded by natural science could not be objects of moral regard. A reconstrual of the manifold of science as a Fourfold would seem to imply a willingness to forfeit the hope of quick cognitive and technological profits that might be made by modern scientific methodology. It would seem to imply at least the patient waiting of *wu-wei*, the qualified resignation of Heidegger's seemingly fatalistic "Only a *Gott* can Save us." For even the ways of Western mysticism have been unlearned by the West, and relearning them or coming to be at home in their Eastern near-equivalents might well take more time than either Westerners or Easterners have left to enjoy those quick returns.

It is therefore timely to entertain a hypothesis that may appear to run the risk of falling into the trap brought to our attention by Heidegger, the risk of pointing to a method when what is called for is the preparation of a way. In fact, the proto-gaia hypothesis points through method to a proto-methodological way. In so doing it may appear to incur another risk, that of falling into the trap set by Lovelock of presumptuously and anthropocentrically supposing that Gaia cannot look after itself. What the proto-gaia hypothesis supposes is rather that human endeavor, as one fold of manifold Gaia, may be not only one way by which nature may be denatured but also one way through which Gaia may be enabled to look after herself. Perhaps the best hope of learning to mend our ways before time runs out for us and for those other entities, processes, or states that we have not yet destroyed is for the West and the Westernized East to look into so-called Western scientific methodology itself for a place in which something like the so-called Eastern way of thinking and being may be not transplanted, but found already growing, though in need of being brought on and brought to light. The expression "so-called" is repeated in the preceding sentence lest we forget either that the West also has a mystical tradition or that the East too has its analytic logic and epistemological methodologies, for instance those of the systems of Nyāya and Vaiśesika. But what is being proposed in this chapter is that we should look for a route to a pan-ecological ethics not only in the direction of Eastern holistic meditation, where such routes are today commonly sought, but in what is widely considered to belong to the essence of the West, the very citadel of scientific method as propounded, for example, by Descartes and Bacon.

3

OCCIDENTAL ORIENTATION

Perhaps at the very heart of what are generally considered to be paradigm cases of a methodology that dominates nature and puts her inquisitionally to the test, perhaps in the methodology of Bacon, Descartes, and Kant — whose first *Critique* cites in its epigraph Bacon's declaration "I am labouring to lay the foundations . . . of human utility and power" — may be discerned a pointer to a way of saving a chance for a geoethics that is not only consistent with but implied by that methodology and is therefore a necessary, albeit commonly forgotten, condition of the consistency of Cartesian and Baconian scientific methodology. This necessary condition is that rule of Bacon's method implied in the aphorisms advising man to become once again a child, submitting himself to and following nature.[1]

But what does following nature mean? It may not mean following a rule. It may mean not following a rule. And a child may be unruly. It may be irregular and unregular. It may resist regulation. And if it is an infant, *infans*, not yet in possession or not yet in the possession of much or any language, it will not have any *regulae* to which to appeal, least of all a regulation that prescribes or permits the relaxation of regulation. It is beyond an adult's capacity to become a child again in that sense without a loss of competence with language, such as happens in senile decay. Bacon's scientist keeps his wits about him, so the childhood of the child he is advised by Bacon to become must be a second childhood, related to the first in a way analogous to the way intuition or *scientia intuitiva* in the doctrine of Spinoza is related to feeling, with discursive ratiocination coming between. Intuition is a second nature that supervenes when reasoning skills requiring step-by-step mediation give way to a capacity to see that returns to an immediacy comparable with the immediacy of the first nature of sensory experience and feeling.

DESCARTES DEFENDED

This second nature is the destination which in Rule 10 Descartes calls sagacity.[2] Rule 11 shows that sagacity is not simply a destination external to a method considered as a route to it. The relation between them resembles that between method and result in the Hegelian dialectic. It is a dialectical relation in being an internal one in which the travail and the travel of inference leads to a wisdom that is not purely speculative, but increasingly informs the practice in which the rule of method is applied. Rule 11 states:

> If, after we have recognized intuitively a number of simple truths, we wish to draw any inference from them, it is useful to run them over in a continuous and uninterrupted act of thought, to reflect upon their relations to one another, and to grasp together distinctly a number of these propositions so far as is possible at the same time. For this is a way of making our knowledge much more certain, and of greatly increasing the power of the mind.[3]

The method and the result are apparently conceived as separate when Rule 1 states: "The end of study should be to direct the mind towards the enunciation of sound and correct judgements on all matters that come before it." But to make sound and correct judgments in the plural, judgment in the singular is required. And Descartes's word for this is "sagacity." Part of the story being told here is being told when it is said that the meaning of a proposition is the body of propositions that support it, and this idea is commemorated in the fact that the German word *schliessen* means either to infer or to conclude. Indeed, this idea is encapsulated in the fact that the English word "conclusion" refers not only to a proposition but also to the inferring of it from other propositions. And although the Latinate word "proposition," on account of the component "position," lends itself to being construed statically, this component is translated by *Satz*, which can mean a movement, as in music, and a jump, as in Heidegger's title *Der Satz vom Grund*. Cartesian sagacity is the ability to move in the right direction and to reduce the distance one must jump. Without it, without judgment, judgments may be true, but they will not be sound, and they will not be even correct if correctness means that they have been reached by moving in the right direction. This is why, although Descartes distinguishes sagacity from sharpness or perspicacity (*ingenii acies*), he defines the latter as the capacity — *ingenium* means capacity as well as mind — to see the simple. But the simple can be identified only in contrast with the complex, and vice versa. The simplicity of the tree can be perceived only in connection with its context, say the wood. Simplicity is a relation, so simplicity is complex. This holds for the simplicity of what Rule 9 calls "the smallest and most easily mastered things" (*ad res minimas et maxime faciles*). It may seem that this superlative "most" turns out to be a comparative in the light of Descartes's admission that

> some things are from one point of view more absolute than others, but from a different point of view more relative. Thus though the universal is more absolute than the particular because its essence is simpler, yet it can be held to be more relative than the latter, because it depends upon individuals for its existence, and so on.[4]

Notwithstanding this and the statement that "Certain things are likewise truly more absolute than others, but are yet not the most absolute of all," Descartes does not conclude that the class of what is most absolute is null.[5] He goes as far as to say that he is speaking of hierarchical series like that of individual, species, and genus, where the intermediate item is absolute in relation to one of the extremes but relative in relation to the other. This does not mean that there is nothing that is most absolute. The most absolute in such ordered series are the most simple, and these are what he calls simple natures.[6]

However, the items he calls simple natures are so described because they are reached by a process of simplification. The absoluteness of their simplicity is methodological and epistemic, not ontological or physical. Their simplicity is not that of physical atoms or of ultimate metaphysical kinds or Platonic forms. Nor, on the other hand, is their simplicity arbitrary or conventional, for although the simplicity of simple natures can be said to depend upon a choice, this choice depends upon evidence; the simple is that which is most easily understood. Thus "*intuition* is the undoubting conception of an unclouded (*purae*) and attentive mind, and springs from the light of reason alone; it is more certain than deduction itself, in that it is simpler" (Rule 3). The words "more certain" may be taken to refer to a psychological characteristic, but only if this is understood as a criterion of knowledge, the benchmark of which is the indubitability of *cogito ergo sum*, where the *ergo* marks the limit of the distinction between intuition and deduction. This *ergo* also marks the zone where psychology, epistemology, and theology run into each other. In one of his replies to one of the sets of objections to the *Meditations* collected by Mersenne, Descartes defines scientific knowledge as knowledge involving deduction. Since he argues that the reliability of deductions is dependent upon God, he denies that the atheist can have scientific knowledge. This, he says, does not prevent the atheist having intuitive knowledge. But the acceptability of this statement is questionable if the standard of evidence for intuitive knowledge is that of *cogito ergo sum,* and *ergo* is the sign of deduction. The *ergo* is retained in the *Discourse,* gets dropped in the *Meditations,* and returns in the *Principles.* This may be evidence that Descartes is embarrassed by the question whether the atheist can know anything — an embarrassment that would not be removed by replacing the *ergo* with a comma, a hyphen, a dash, or a sheer gap. But it may be evidence of a casualness arising from the fact that Descartes is not embarrassed by this question. If the atheist is someone who says "I believe that there exists no God," once he can be brought to entertain the hyperbolic doubt that he himself exists he will be implicated in the inconsistency of denying the existence of the infinite being without which, according to the arguments of the Third and Fifth of the *Meditations,* he cannot have the idea of himself as a doubting and therefore finite being. It can only be because his ideas have not reached a sufficient degree of clarity and distinctness that he can believe that there is no God.

Descartes argues that, given the distinctness and clarity of the idea of God, an idea which will include that of His undeceivingness, it will be unreasonable to maintain that knowledge of the world is unobtainable in principle. Now it may be about such knowledge — physical and mathematical knowledge, not any knowledge whatsoever involving deduction — that Descartes is talking when he says that the atheist can have no scientific knowledge. But his rejection of general skepticism regarding the possibility of knowledge of the world leaves room for him to say that such knowledge, despite its being based on foundations that are absolute in the sense already described, is not absolute in another sense. As explained in the Sixth Meditation, the refutation of general skepticism about the possibility of knowledge of the physical world does not exclude the possibility of error about particular matters of fact, but even the logical and mathematical truths of which we can be certain owe their truth to the will of God. We cannot comprehend how God might have made it false that the radii of a circle are all equal. Although this mathematical truth is a necessary one, its necessity is no more independent of the will of God than the creation of the world is independent of his will.

These mathematical truths, to which Descartes, following Mersenne, applies the adjective "eternal," are the foundations of natural science.[7] Yet their foundationality is not intrinsic to them. So the universality of the natural science that Descartes claims to be within the reach of man is a qualified universality. And the mood in which Descartes advances his claim is colored by a degree of humility. The least one can say is that the Cartesian scientist is not playing God. In this respect Descartes's pretensions are more modest than those of Father Mersenne, for the latter believes that in our belief in eternal truths we are in possession of something that flows from the essence of the Divine mind.

But we have already seen that more than this can be said in defense of the view that the Cartesian scientist does not lord it over nature to the extent that he is reckoned to do in most recent representations. We saw that the Cartesian methodology calls for scientific deduction to be reduced as far as possible to intuition. For Descartes *intuitus* is a form of receptivity. We also saw that his method calls for a certain sagacity. This is a keenness of insight acquired indeed by exercising a power, but a power over oneself, a power that increases one's perspicacity and judgment through the practice of eschewing precipitate judgments and exposing one's prejudices, one's inherited and habitual prejudgments, to the test of clarity and distinctness. When in the *Discourse* Descartes reduces his twenty-one rules of method to four — an economy that compares well with God's condensation of his ten Commandments into two (Mark 12:31) — the first rule of his new short list is

> to accept nothing as true which I did not clearly recognize to be so: that is to say, carefully to avoid precipitation and prejudice in judgements, and to accept in them nothing more than what was presented to the mind so clearly and distinctly that I could have no occasion to doubt it.[8]

Although what God knows is what God wills, human knowledge is obtained, according to Descartes's account, through the will's refusal to assent to what is not clear and distinct. We must distinguish "that faculty of our understanding by which it has intuitive awareness of things and knows them, from that by which it judges, making use of affirmation and denial" (Rule 12) and so making use of the will; "no direct experience can ever deceive the understanding if it restrict its attention accurately to the object presented to it" (ibid.). This allots an important part to the will, but it is not one in which the will imposes itself upon nature. It is one in which the will is directed toward itself, in order that the mind may be allowed to open and be free to receive the light. The rules of method are rules for a practice by which one learns to control not nature, but the natural scientist's will. It is a practice analogous to the spiritual exercises of Ignatius Loyola and the disciplines of Buddhism: *Buddhi* means *intuitus*.

According to his statement under Rule 3, in his "new use" of the term *intuitus* Descartes follows only "the meaning of the Latin." Rational intuition means tuition by what enters in. Therefore even if it is an innate idea that enters into the attention of the mind, it is as passive an affection as is sensory intuition. Activity belongs to the attention and to assent. So an initially noematic status belongs even to the simple natures that Descartes deems to be innate, whether they be the simple natures of the purely material sort, such as figure, extension, and motion; of the purely intellectual sort, such as knowing, doubting, ignorance, willing; ones that are common to both of these kinds, such as existence, unity, and duration; or principles of logic that permit these ideas to be linked, such as the principle that things that are the same as a third thing are the same as each other (Rule 12). But if even the purely intellectual natures or essences can have this noematic status, it is difficult to see how that can be its ultimate status. This is why there has to be a rationalist equivalent of the dictum "Nothing is in the intellect that was not first in the senses," and this is what Leibniz supplied when he tagged on to this dictum "except for the intellect itself." It was precisely this tag and hints from Locke that put Kant on the way to overcoming the opposition between metaphysical rationalism and empiricism by suggesting to him that the grammatically accusative and objective status of at least some of the so-called simple natures would have to be denied in favor of a subjective and subjecting role without which there could be no objectivity.

Subjecting. Subjugation? When in a philosophy of science it is argued that ideas traditionally supposed to be objects of the understanding are formal concepts that the understanding itself imposes upon its content, holding it in its firm grip, as the words "concept" and *Begriff* suggest, cognition would seem to have become inquisition. And this appearance is strengthened when these formal concepts are called categories. For to categorize is to arraign and accuse. This is what the term means when Aristotle uses it, even if that force is not obvious when *katēgoria* is translated as "predicate." Aristotle's categories are the most fundamental predicates, the highest kinds. Although — following this translation — a primary substance like Aristotle himself is said by him not to be a predicate, to describe him as a substance is to ascribe a basic logical predicate. It is to answer in the most general way possible the question "What?" Similarly with the other categories in his list, quantity, quality, relation, place, date, and so on, which in Kant get subdivided on the one hand into categories properly so called, the structures of the intellect, and on the other hand into the forms of sensibility, namely space and time. When Kant says that what he calls categories are active and what he calls forms of sensibility are passive, he is making a logical distinction in terms of two of the other categories that are included in Aristotle's list. Aristotle's list is drawn up on the basis of observation of modes of speech. Kant, followed by a succession of German Idealists, chides Aristotle for not producing a decent deduction of these allegedly ultimate frames of reference. Because his grammatical classification extends no further than those of the noun, the verb, and perhaps the conjunction and the article,[9] this grammatical classification, even when supplemented by his distinctions between kinds of judgment and inference, would be too threadbare to employ even as a mere guiding thread for a classification of categories of the understanding. Kant does not content himself with following the hints his list of logical forms of judgment is deemed to offer for the discovery of a list of epistemological categories. He purports to produce independent deductions of these, as well as a demonstration of the completeness of his list.

However, all of those deductions are alleged to be deductions of the necessary transcendental conditions of a certain experience of the temporality of
the consciousness of the association of ideas such as Hume considers to be
ultimate in the psychological account of necessity he expounds. Now even if
Kant's deductions from that are valid, they can claim to be necessary conditions of human knowledge only if all human beings experience temporality
in the manner described by Hume. Werner Jaeger writes of Aristotle that
"he flings the net of the categories over reality."[10] If there is some excuse for
Aristotle's not flinging his net more widely, there is less excuse for Kant. And
for us. At the very least we should experiment with the possibility that there
is more than one way of experiencing time and that these may be reflected
in and may reflect "functions of judgment" and "functions of understanding" dominant in cultures other than ours, however "ours" is defined. If this
experiment were to lead to the discovery of a multiplicity of dominant
functions and forms, our very idea of dominance would change. The idea of
constriction and entrapment conveyed by the metaphors of the net and the
web would be meta-metaphorized. Inquiry would no longer be seen as impe-
rial imposition and extortive inquisition. Even "standing reserve," *Gestell,*
might become less static and more reserved. Inquiry would become a real
"advancement of learning."

BACON BEFRIENDED

Bacon's title *The Advancement of Learning* reminds us both of what it is to
become again a child and of the words Kant borrowed from him for the
epigraph of the second edition of the *Critique of Pure Reason:*

> Of myself I say nothing; but on behalf of the business which is at hand, I
> entreat men to believe that it is not an opinion to be held, but a work to be
> done; and to be well assured that I am labouring to lay the foundation not
> of any sect or doctrine but of human welfare and capacity. Next, I ask them
> to deal fairly by their own interests . . . to join in consultation for the
> common good, . . . and to come forward themselves and take part. More-
> over, to be of good hope, and not to imagine that this Instauration of ours is
> a thing infinite and exceeding the ability of mortals, when it is in fact the
> true end and termination of infinite error.[11]

The words "foundation . . . of human welfare and capacity" here translate
utilitis et amplitudinis humanae fundamenta. The words "exceeding the ability
of mortals" translate *ultra mortale.* There is no word in the latter Latin phrase
corresponding to the word "power" that is inserted into a standard published English translation of this passage. Further, when that translation
gives "power" as a translation of *amplitudinis* it is little wonder that Baconian
natural science has come to be considered a paradigm case of Enlighten-

ment conceived as domination. When someone has or does not have the ability or capacity to do a certain thing we say too that she or he has or does not have the power to do it. The French *pouvoir* has this sense. But in saying that someone has the power to do something in this sense we are not attributing power in the sense of powerfulness, *puissance, Macht* as distinguished from *Fähigkeit*. These different senses are not always distinguished when it is said that knowledge and power are synonymous. Although of course knowledge is power in the sense of an on/off ability, *a* power, it remains to be argued that it is power in the sense in which one person may have more power than another and so have power over him or her. The latter sense is what Horkheimer and Adorno have in mind when, already in the second paragraph of *The Dialectic of Enlightenment,* they declare: "Bacon's view was appropriate to the scientific attitude that prevailed after him. The concordance between the mind of man and the nature of things that he had in mind is patriarchal."[12] There are many statements by Bacon that support a dominative, inquisitional, and patriarchal interpretation of his method. For example, he writes that nature "exhibits herself more clearly under the trials and vexations of art," to the point that nature is to be "forced out of her natural state and squeezed and moulded," as though, paradoxically, we learn most about nature by denaturing her. Another reflexive reference is made to nature when he writes that

> For every natural action, every motion and process of nature, is nothing else than a hunt. For the arts and sciences hunt after their works, human counsels hunt after their ends, and all things in nature hunt either after their food, which is like hunting for prey, or after their pleasures, which is like hunting for recreation.[13]

What catches the attention here is the inclusion of the human science of nature within the realm of nature itself along with other natural but not human processes. Thus despite the description of scientific research as a "masculine" probing of the hidden "holes and corners" of nature, nature remains on top. Nature or God. *Natura sive Deus.* For any right over nature that the human race may have devolves from decrees reported in Genesis: "Only let the human race recover that right over nature which belongs to it by divine bequest; their exercise thereof will be governed by sound reason and true religion." The exercise of scientific power is the exercise of a virtue commanded by God, whether on analogy with the dominion over nature prescribed in Genesis 1:26, 28, or with the stewardship of serving and safeguarding of the non-human conveyed by the Hebrew terms *abad* and *shamar* in Genesis 2:15. This verse belongs to the Jahwist version of the book, whereas the other two belong to the later Priestly version. This doubleness reflects an ambiguity in the human attitude to nature.[14] It has begun to look as though there are both Jahwist and Priestly texts also in Bacon.

Even if we follow the usual interpretation of Baconian science as human and indeed masculine dominion, a distinction must be made between the acquisition and the application of knowledge. And this distinction is made by Bacon himself in sentences that Horkheimer and Adorno proceed to cite. In a work treating "The Interpretation of Nature," Bacon distinguishes himself from predecessors who have sought knowledge for its own sake. He compares this search for "satisfaction, which men call truth" to sexual intercourse indulged in only for pleasure. Against this prostitution of knowledge he argues for "the true end, scope, or office of knowledge, which I have set down to consist not in any plausible, delectable, reverend or admired discourse, or any satisfactory arguments, but in effecting and working, and in discovery of particulars not revealed before, for the better endowment and help of man's life."[15]

The admission of knowledge sought for its own sake and not used for the betterment of mankind is consistent with Bacon's thesis that power and knowledge are synonymous.[16] Unused knowledge remains usable. This, however, does not license the importation of rules for the application of knowledge into those for its acquisition. And that Bacon is defending a pragmatic definition of truth seems to be excluded by his admission that there are theories that "though true, have the fault that they do not well lead the way to action."[17] Of course, "that which is most useful in practice is most correct in theory," not because there is no distinction between practice and theory, as some readers of Bacon take him to think,[18] but because practice is not going to be most useful in the long run unless the agent takes cognizance of how things are. And the difference between theory and practice is endorsed when, rejecting as analogies of scientific behavior the behavior of ants that collect material into heaps and the behavior of spiders that spin webs from themselves, Bacon prefers the analogy of the bee that "extracts matter from the flowers of the garden and the field, but works and fashions it by its own efforts."[19] Two stages are distinguished in the bee's behavior, so two must be admitted in that of the scientist. Admittedly, it is not immediately clear whether the second stage, the stage of working and fashioning, corresponds to technological and industrial applications of pure science or whether it corresponds to the formation of pure scientific hypotheses on the basis of the observations that have been made. In a broad sense of production, both the production of engines, bridges, medicines, and the like and the production of scientific hypotheses may be described as technological. In that case the technological cannot be equated with what we nowadays call applied, as contrasted with pure, science.

This equation may oversimplify Bacon's view of the relationship of the theoretical to the practical and productive.[20] Bacon himself distinguishes the "production of effects" as belonging to what he calls the operative part of science, in contrast to the "inquisition into causes," which belongs to what he calls the speculative part.[21] The power to produce effects is the power to produce observations predicted on the basis of speculations produced on the basis of inquiry into perhaps unobserved causes. Is what he calls speculation to be equated with the collecting stage of the bee's behavior? The word "speculation" is ambiguous. According to a traditional interpretation of Bacon's philosophy of scientific method it would mean something like a simple mirroring, as though the mind passively received data that it then actively worked up into a theory or hypothesis. But the word also admits the sense of hypothesis or educated conjecture. It connotes a happy coincidence, the same coincidence, it so happens, as that connoted by the words "reflection" and "imagination" as used by Kant: a coming together of the passivity widely considered to be a characteristic of sensation and of the activity commonly considered to be proper to the understanding and reason. This ambiguity is double. It takes in, on the one hand, the givenness of the merely "reflected," "mirrored," or "imaged" data and the processing, "working," and "fashioning" of "reflective" judgment in pursuit of a universal law under which to subsume particulars. On the other hand, this double ambiguity takes in the ambiguity of imagination *either* enabling the universal to apply to particulars *or* searching for an exemplary model that is a singular work with general if not universal significance.

This double ambiguity is a Kantian "good ambiguity" that is in turn itself an anticipation of another one in Hegel and is anticipated in the circularity of the relationship between the ambiguously speculative and the operative in Bacon's account of the logic of scientific discovery. The traditional story according to which the foundation of Baconian scientific method is naked data from which general truths are generated by "induction" is a story that is more fittingly told of the theorists Bacon criticizes. Collection, such as that performed by the bee, presupposes a principle in the light of which selection is made. There has "always already" been speculation in the sense that involves a processing that exceeds the sheerly given. There has always already been induction. But that is the induction of a prescientific habit. Baconian science requires superinduction from that base. From it, beyond it, to an interpretation that is more basic, but one that is not a generalization considered so basic and infallible that no more remains for science to do than to deduce conclusions from it via intermediate axioms.[22] What Bacon's method requires the scientist to seek is not such "theses" that put an end to experiments, but "hypotheses" or "speculations" that demand them:

> the true method of experience . . . first lights the candle, and then by means of the candle shows the way; commencing as it does with experience duly ordered and digested, not bungling or erratic, and from it educing axioms, and from established axioms again new experiments.[23]

The axioms are established only in the sense that they are supported by experience, not in the sense that they are infallible. They remain vulnerable to refutation by new experiences made possible by further experiment. The progress of scientific discovery is an alternation of experience and hypothesis corresponding to the two stages in the behavior of the bee.

In the light of this distinction between two stages, the dominative, manipulative, and patriarchal elements in Bacon's outlook will be seen to occur in the part of his doctrine that deals with application and its technology, a different attitude being displayed in what he says in those places where he is concerned with the acquisition of knowledge and the advancement of learning.

Such a different attitude is indeed apparent in the very sentences of "In Praise of Human Knowledge" upon which Horkheimer and Adorno base their contention that the concordance between the mind of man and the nature of things that Bacon had in mind is patriarchal. The "concordance" to which Bacon refers in those sentences is "the happy match between the mind of man and the nature of things," which has been prevented by "facility to believe, impatience to doubt, temerity to answer, glory to know, doubt to contradict, end to gain, sloth to search, seeking things in words, resting in part of nature." That is, a happy marriage between the mind of man and the nature of things has been frustrated by, as Descartes might have said, man's over-fondness for confused and obscure terminology, prejudice in favor of tradition, and precipitancy for the sake of vainglory. What Bacon calls for is appropriate humility. And humility is certainly appropriate when scientific discovery or invention is our immediate aim:

> the sovereignty of man lieth hid in knowledge; wherein many things are reserved, which kings with their treasure cannot buy, nor with their force command; their spials and intelligencers can give no news of them, their seamen and discoverers cannot sail where they grow; now we govern nature in opinions, but we thrall unto her in necessity; but if we would be led by her in invention, we should command her by action.[24]

Natural necessity is the mother of invention. Human invention enables us to achieve shelter from the wind and the rain and to turn the wealth of nature into the wealth of nations. However, mankind gains the upper hand only if it lets nature lead it. We must become as little children.

Now little children are of either sex. And it is at mother nature's knee that Bacon calls them to learn their ABC. He advises

> that they should humbly and with a certain reverence draw near to the book of Creation; that they should there make a stay, and that on it they should meditate, and that then washed and clean they should in chastity and integrity turn them from opinion. This is that speech and language which has gone out to all ends of the earth, and has not suffered the confusion of Babel; this men must learn again, and, resuming their youth, they must become again as little children and deign to take its alphabet into their hands.[25]

When the simile of becoming again an innocent child is recalled, we have at least one Baconian trope that does not "give a male content to what it is to be a good knower." And, incidentally, where the sexual analogies for knowledge are operative, as they often are in Bacon's works, these go back at least to the Hebrew and Greek Bibles. "Adam knew (*vayeda*) his wife" (Genesis 4:25). And *ginōskō* (or *gignōskō*), to know, is cognate with *gennaō* and *geinomai*. But these last terms mean either to beget or to give birth, so that it is not only the male partner in sexual intercourse who is said to have carnal knowledge. "How shall this be," Mary exclaims at the Annunciation, "seeing I know not a man" (Luke 1:34).

The metaphor of becoming a child again serves to make the point that the languages of Babel must be unlearned. It does not mean that language must be replaced by babble. Nor does it mean that the born-again scientist must learn an Adamic language the lexicon of which is made up of proper names for raw data. When Bacon refers to "simple natures," an expression Descartes uses too (as we have already had reason to remind ourselves), it is not to raw sense-data that he refers. Natures are essences or properties, and as such exceed the immediacy of sensation. If it is asked whether simple natures may be the immediate objects of rational intuition, it must be replied that the very rationality of such intuition implies that what is intuited holds of a possible plurality of things. If we take seriously Bacon's statement that the alphabet of nature is the alphabet of a book, then the pursuit of science will be, as the title of a work by one of his contemporaries, Jacob Boehme, has it, an inquiry into the *signatura rerum:* the signature of all things, showing the sign and signification of the several forms and shapes in the Creation. The erasure of the languages of Babel does not result in arrival at a mental *tabula rasa.* "On waxen tablets you cannot write anything new until you rub out the old. With the mind it is not so; there you cannot rub out the old till you have written in the new."[26]

The new that the rejuvenated seeker after the advancement of learning is in the first place to acquire is a new language. And that can be learned only through an obedience. "For we cannot command nature except by obeying her."[27] To obey is to listen. The new language can be learned only by listening. But a language is already a hypothesis. With language we are already *in medias res,* but the things, the *res,* are no less in language. In the beginning there is no beginning if by beginning is meant an absolutely fresh start.

There is a fresh start only where there is already a historical deposit. Freshness and newness arise when that inescapable historical sediment is regarded as something that can be stirred up, where infallibility gives way to the idea of a certainty of hypotheses that can be increased only by a repetition of experiments on what has not previously been tested, and where experiment—as is indicated by the active-passive ambiguity of the word "experiment" as between experience and test—oscillates in the manner described by Bacon when he writes my course and method, as I have often clearly stated and would wish to state again, is this, — not to extract works from works or experiments from experiments (as an empiric), but from works and experiments to extract causes and axioms, and again from those causes and axioms new works and experiments, as a legitimate interpreter of nature.[28]

The alphabet of nature is already an interpretation of nature, in the sense that "simple natures" always come laden with theory and speculation, where speculation has the active-passive ambiguity already alluded to and where the same ambiguity haunts the theoretical; for although theory is commonly contrasted with looking and seeing, it is seeing and looking that is meant by *theōria*. This being so, there is no need to attempt to dissociate Bacon's notion of the alphabet of nature from his account of inductive method for fear that the latter will be weakened by the assumption of theory-free simples.[29]

However, since Bacon says that we obey nature only to command her, how can there be any doubt about the validity of Horkheimer's and Adorno's remark that Bacon's scientific attitude is patriarchal? There can be some doubt for two reasons. First, as we have seen, much depends upon where one makes the distinction between what Bacon calls the speculative and what he calls the operative parts of science. We have noted that the distinction is not clear-cut. This is because there is a dialectical relationship between the speculative and the operational that an ambiguity in the word "speculative" brings out. And if the operative part is understood to be technology, that too can be taken either as internal to pure science or as industrial, medical, political, etc. application. Suppose, with the author of *Being and Time,* that theory understood as contemplation of present-at-hand ideas or concepts or models or hypotheses is a modification of a prior operative mode of being in the context of a world with things as ready to hand. The ideas, concepts, models, and hypotheses will still be products of the reflective or pre-reflective operations. They are inventions, in more than one sense of that ambiguous word. They are productions, but if they are true or valid, they are also discoveries — findings, in both senses of that word.

Further, more important than the gendered descriptions of Bacon's scientific method is his characterization of it as pediatrics. To respond to Bacon's invitation to become again a child is to learn again how to play, to learn how to learn by trial and error. His stress upon the variation of tests is a stress on the importance of exposure to refutation by the negative instance. "To learn" is a verb that less-educated speakers of English use with the meaning of "to teach"; in Welsh one word serves to express either sense, according to context, as though to learn were to teach oneself; in Hebrew the words for to learn and to teach have a common root. And the "in" of "intuition" signifies tuition both as reception and as the penetration we call insight.

Play is impossible without a degree of regularity, but it also implies a margin of error and chance. A game with as many rules as chess leaves a space defined by its rules in which the player must rely on judgment and skill. Its texture is open. So too, on Bacon's account, is the texture of good science. So too, consistently, is the texture of his own scientific methodological text. Navigating a middle course between too extreme a partiality for the novel and that idol of the cave consisting in too rigid a respect for the ancients, Bacon would have his readers acknowledge that scientific knowledge is, as he puts it, broken, meaning by this that it is always open to wonder.[30] This leads him to express an antipathy toward a certain understanding of the idea of method. (Would he have been more comfortable with the word "way"?) This leads him to join the tradition to which Pascal, von Lichtenberg, Nietzsche, and Wittgenstein belong by adopting a broken, aphoristic style: "Aphorisms, representing a knowledge broken, do invite men to inquire farther; whereas Methods, carrying the show of a total, do secure men, as if they were at furthest."[31] Bacon wants to save insecurity.

Therefore, when the patriarchal character of Bacon's scientific method is stressed, one should ask to what this is being opposed. Matriarchy? Is a patriarchic and patronizing attitude any more domineering than that of the matronly matriarch? Granted, following an ancient stereotype, Bacon refers to nature as "her," as we have referred to Gaia. But in doing so he says that if we are to command her she must be obeyed. The metaphor implies that nature too commands. Again, when we turn from the relationship between the natural scientist and nature to the analysis of the scientific mentality, the word "matrix" would be a fitting one to use of the mindset from which Bacon wishes to break away. He draws up a list of idols from which we are bidden to cut free: idols of the nation or tribe, idols of the palace, idols of the cave, and idols of the theater. Among the idols of the theater — so called because we are taken in by them as by what is taking place on the stage — are the Aristotelian categories. They purport to constitute the matrix of the world. Notwithstanding all the emphasis Aristotle puts upon observation and experiment, his practice, Bacon writes, was

> not to seek information from unfettered experiment but to exhibit experience captive and bound. He did not introduce a wide impartial survey of experience to assist his investigation of truth; he brought in a carefully schooled and selected experience to justify his pronouncements.[32]

Whether we call Aristotle's catalogue of categories a matrix or a patron (and a patron can be a customer or the boss), it is clear that Bacon aims to break that mold. Even if Aristotle's — or Kant's, or anyone else's — categorial frame were claimed to be an a priori deep structure, Bacon demands, like Chomsky, that there must be good empirical evidence for it. Aristotle's social and linguistic anthropology was too parochial. He should have looked further afield. Let us.

PARTICULARS

Wittgenstein writes in the *Tractatus:*

> If good or bad acts of will do alter the world, it can only be the limits of the
> world that they alter, not the facts, not what can be expressed by means of
> language.
> In short their effect must be that it becomes an altogether different
> world. It must, so to speak, wax and wane as a whole.[33]

It is particular deeds that move the horizon nearer or further away. And it
may be to the particulars that we must look if there is to be any chance for a
geoethics, an ethics that embraces the natural world.

To the *scientific* particulars? The particulars of natural science? Not according to Wittgenstein, who says, "We feel that even when *all possible* scientific questions have been answered, the problems of life remain completely
untouched."[34] Untouched by scientific questions, according to him, are any
ethical, aesthetic, or other normative questions, such as those with which we
are engaged.

In section 15 of *Being and Time* a distinction is made between the present-
at-hand nature of the material out of which tools are made, the ready-to-
hand nature of the tools themselves (which reveals itself in our using them),
and the power or force of nature (*Naturmacht*), nature which " 'stirs and
strives,' which assails us and enthralls us as landscape." In a later text dated
1933 entitled "*Schöpferische Landschaft: Warum bleiben wir in der Provinz?*" he
remarks "*Ich betrachte die Landschaft gar nie,*" "I never view the landscape."
That remark can be heard as an autobiographical distancing of himself
from sightseers who do view the landscape and are enthralled by it. Or it can
be read as a grammatical or categorial remark to the effect that a fecund or
creative (*schöpferisch*) landscape is not the sort of thing that allows of being
contemplated, considered, or viewed, whether or not all landscapes are
schöpferisch. That perhaps they all are might follow if *schöpfen* is echoed by
schaft. I shall return in the final chapter to this *schaft*. But let me return first
to the scientific particulars, and this time, not to those of Galilean mathematical physics, the repercussions of which upon the world of everyday life
since the Renaissance have until recently been emphasized at the expense
of the biological, medical, agricultural, geographical, and geological sciences. Pressing the just-mentioned distinction made in *Being and Time* between the manifold natures of nature, Heidegger goes on to say there: "The
botanist's plants are not the flowers of the hedgerow; the 'source' which the
geographer establishes for a river is not the 'springhead in the dale.' " If the
expressions Heidegger places in quotation marks here are meant to represent modes of expression we should expect from a poet, not from a scientist,
let us take note that it is a scientist, the botanist and biologist Barbara

McClintock, who, having confessed that she has not much time to read poetry, says that we must find the time to look, the patience "to hear what the material has to say to you"; "let it come to you"; cultivate "a feeling for the organism," where, she explains, "Every component of the organism is as much of an organism as every other part." She describes her "scientific method" as follows: "I start with the seedling, and I don't want to leave it. I don't feel I really know the story if I don't watch the plant all the way along. So I know every plant in the field. I know them intimately, and I find it a great pleasure to know them."[35] This sounds very much like getting to know a human being. Polanyi's title *Personal Knowledge* seems to fit. And it seems to fit also knowledge in the mathematical sciences of nature as described by, for example, Einstein when he writes that even the laws of the mathematical sciences are discovered through "intuition, resting on sympathetic understanding."[36] Sympathetic understanding is the feeling intellect, "that grace which dwells between one possibility and another, perceiving and revealing a pattern beneath the surface of experience without wishing to impose a style on it."[37] Pascal would call this the reason of the heart. Einstein again, speaking of his "method," says that "the daily effort comes from no deliberate intention or program, but straight from the heart."[38] And it is he too who declares, "Knowledge is wonderful but imagination is even better." Imagination is better because it is the phenomenological antecedent to the scientific methodology of hypothesis and testing in terms of the data: the precondition of hypotheses and data. Straddling the ambiguity of discovery and invention that the Latin word *invenire* names, imagination is the point of intersection of feminine *anima* and masculine *animus,* the pineal point at which the right and the left hemispheres cooperate with each other and the sinister and the dexterous cross.

As the building-into-one of the many and the manifolding of the one, imagination corresponds to the regulative ideal of science described by Kant as the minimum of theory covering the maximum of data, a minimax structure that is imitated in turn by the imitation — the *mimēsis* — of the moral law by actions mediated by the practical maxims. Here the Ideal of the ordered natural world serves as schema, type, and archetype for the practical imagination's ideal of an intelligible world ordered by the moral law. Typification is a natural-worldy and so in part human-bodily concretization of the purely formal law of reason. The schema provides a model, a diagram, facilitating the application of the formal moral law, via contentful maxims, to the behavior of carnate human beings. The direction is "downward," the direction of determinant judgment. But the direction is "upward" with the reflective judgment. The latter seeks the natural or moral principle or law, whether the ultimate principle or law for the intermediate law or maxim or the intermediate law or maxim for the singular action, event, or entity. Imagination is reflective and determinant judgment, alternatingly or simultaneously upwardly and downwardly mobile. It is judgment not in the sense of predication, but judgment as procedure, skill, and *phronēsis,* where the Greek word is to be understood not as only prudence, but as altruistically moral. As skill, *technē* and art judgment is mother-wit (*Mutterwitz*) with reference to which, in a footnote to B 172 of the first *Critique,* Kant says that deficiency in it is stupidity (*Dummheit*). Coming from the pen of someone who believes that the capacity for moral behavior is distributed democratically, to the point where it is proper to follow Hume in calling it humanity, this is a dark saying if Kant also believes that judgment is a procedure of a moral imagination. He goes on to say in his note that "it is not unusual to meet learned men who in the application of their scientific knowledge betray that original want, which can never be made good." Although that original want cannot be made good, might it not be made at least a little less bad, not by more learning indeed, but by more practice? But it is to Kant's footnote description of this want as stupidity that I wish to add a footnote of my own.

In the book citing the statements made by Barbara McClintock reproduced above, Evelyn Fox Keller quotes Schrödinger's assertion: "our science — Greek Science — is based on objectification. . . . But I do believe that this is precisely the point where our present way of thinking does need to be amended, perhaps by a blood-transfusion from Eastern thought." She cites Niels Bohr's statement that "when trying to harmonize our position as spectators and actors" Western atomic physicists could well attend to "those kind of epistemological problems with which already thinkers like the Buddha and Lao Tzu have been confronted."[39] She also reports Robert Oppenheimer's observation that although these problems shape Buddhist and Hindu thought, they play some part in our own culture.[40] Reverting to her account of McClintock's view of biology, Keller writes:

> The "molecular" revolution in biology was a triumph of the kind of science represented by classical physics. Now, the necessary next step seems to be the reincorporation of the naturalist's approach — an approach that does not press nature with leading questions but dwells patiently in the variety and complexity of organisms.[41]

As the words she quotes from Oppenheimer and her own word "reincorporation" indicate, and as has been argued in this chapter, a place is already prepared in the classical Western scientific methodologies, even in the methodologies of those arch-pressers of leading questions, Descartes and Bacon, for patient dwelling, for (to incorporate a word from Keller in one from Polanyi) "indwelling," for (to reincorporate a Greek word) economy in the sense of *oikeō,* to dwell, to abide and to bide one's time, and in the sense of *oikeiō,* to make a person one's friend. Friendship, *philia,* takes time. And it takes attentive and listening receptivity. How can you have a conversation with someone unless you listen to what she or he has to say? Persistent pressing of clever leading questions will only drive a person away. This much is

acknowledged by Bacon when he employs his male-female metaphor leading to the metaphor of the infant, meaning one who does not speak, in order
to make the point that learning what question to frame is conducive to new
knowledge only on condition of a certain stupidity, a dumb-struckness that
lets things have the chance to speak for themselves. As R. G. Collingwood — a
practicing archaeological scientist as well as a philosopher — maintains, a
proposition is an answer to a question. But before there can be a question
there is wonder, *thaumazein*, that stupefaction which has been recognized as
the beginning of *philia-sophia* since its beginning. And this holds for philosophy understood not only in the sense of what at the University of Edinburgh
is called mental philosophy, but also in the sense of what is called natural
philosophy there. Science, whether it be what at Cambridge is called moral
science or what is called there and generally natural science, begins in a
certain *Dummheit*. It begins, still repeating Kant's words, with a *stumpfer oder
eingeschränkter Kopf*, a kind of narrow-mindedness, thick-headedness, and
slow-wittedness. But mental philosophers as various as Heidegger, Derrida,
and Wittgenstein have preached and practiced the slowness with which
philosophy must be done if it is to be a process of learning to think otherwise. So too the natural philosopher Barbara McClintock makes a plea for
what her biographer calls "slow technology." Modifying the first line of the
jingle that serves as a mnemonic of which forms of syllogistic inference are
valid, one might well quip that *Barbara non celarent:* Barbara is in no hurry.
One of the rules of her method is "take the time and look." It is a rule that
is endorsed by Bacon. It is endorsed also by Descartes, who, while requiring
the scientist to run rapidly backward and forward through an implicative
catena, also requires that this process be repeated patiently again and again
and again.

We are talking about a technology different from technology understood
as application distinguished from pure science. We are talking about a technique and an art at the heart of pure science, about the phenomenological
method understood not as reduction but as a production in the sense of the
production of a theatrical play, as the variation in imagination practiced by
the phenomenologist according to Husserl, and as the oscillation between
sense and sensibility that takes place and makes time in the *Spiel-zeit-raum* of
something like the Kantian imagination, which we have discovered is anticipated in the rationalism of Descartes and the empiricism of Bacon. Something like the Kantian imagination, furthermore, as this figures in various
guises in all three of the Critiques. It operates as epistemic schematism. It
operates as aesthetic schematism and typification, in the widely acknowledged "aesthetic" norms invoked in the construction of scientific models.
Less widely acknowledged and commonly denied is what it makes some
sense to call an ethical dimension in science. For the "aesthetic" relates not
only to the economy and grace of the model or theory or law, not only to the
beautiful. It relates also to the *aesthesis* of the particulars or, as I would prefer

to say, of the singulars. Aristotle notwithstanding, science as study of universals must respect the singularity in which universality begins. It must be open to being struck by the absurd, the *surdus,* that which momentarily cannot be understood or heard. This opening is an opening of the scientist's self, a subjection of the scientist's subjectivity to mathematical or other sublimity, the moment of the responsiveness of imagination that exceeds its power to synthesize, the defeat of dexterity by something that is sinisterly difficult to handle. Is not this responsiveness ethical, perhaps also religious? Between, on the one hand, the interest in making use of the environment that may motivate scientific research and, on the other hand, the application of so-called pure science in which that desire is fulfilled, comes the moment of the exercise of a technique reminiscent of the techniques of self-control by which the Eastern sage seeks salvation in enlightenment. This could be called the mystical moment of science. Scientific objectivity is first the sacrifice of subjectivity. It can be said of science what has always been said of philosophy, that it begins in astonishment.

4

ON THE SAYING THAT
PHILOSOPHY BEGINS IN WONDER

GREEK GREEKS

"Wonder is the only beginning of philosophy," Plato has Socrates say at 155d of the *Theaetetus*. And at 982b of the *Metaphysics* Aristotle says, "it is owing to their wonder that men both now begin and at first began to philosophise."

"Wonder," *thaumazein,* is one of those wonderful words that face in opposite directions at one and the same time, like Janus and the androgynous creature of whom Aristophanes tells in the *Symposium*. It seems possible to use it in opposite senses at once; *thaumazein* both opens our eyes wide and plunges us into the dark. It is both startled start and flinching in bewilderment. Reflection on it might well have made Theaetetus's head swim as much as do the aporias Socrates leads him into in the pages culminating at 155 in Theaetetus's exclamation: "By the gods, Socrates, I am lost in wonder (*thaumazō*) when I think of all these things. It sometimes makes me quite dizzy." His condition would be well described by analogy with the stunning effect of the stingray to which Meno likens the effect Socrates has on those he approaches. Theaetetus and Meno—and, according to the response he makes to Meno's comparison, Socrates himself — are perplexed by aporias. Theaetetus, for example, is puzzled at the suggestion that six dice can be both fewer than twelve and more than four. And Meno is paralyzed by the less readily solved problem of how to define virtue. Despite the greater depth of Meno's problem, he too suspects Socrates of performing conjuring tricks, *thaumato-poios* being puppetry, juggling, and suchlike acts of prestidigitation that dumbfound. Likewise, at the beginning of the *Meditations* Descartes is so stupefied at not being able to identify any sure mark by which to distinguish waking from dreaming that he can almost persuade himself that he may be then and there asleep. *Obstupescam,* he says. His Latin also speaks of *stupor,* for which the French gives *étonnement,* astonishment.

Thaumazein, astonishment, Aristotle says, is provoked by aporias. According to him the difficulties that arose for the early philosophers were first to do with matters close at hand but later concerned remoter questions, questions about the solstices, for example, and the genesis of the universe, *peri tēs tou pantos geneseōs* (982b 17). As with Plato, the aporias often have the form of apparent contradictions, such as the prospect of dolls at a puppet show behaving as though they were alive, and the idea that the diagonal of a square is incommensurable with the side. When the cause of the puppet's movements has been revealed and when we have learned a little geometry our astonishment disappears. What would astonish us then is the suggestion that what we now believe to be possible is not. These are two cases that Aristotle regards as ones that might give rise to astonishment with anyone at some stage. He mentions them immediately after stating that "all men begin, as we said, by wondering that all things are as they are," *archontai men gar, hōsper eipomen, apo tou thaumazein pantes ei autōs echei* (983a 12). The "as we said" refers back to a passage that attributes wonder to any beginning philosopher. It appears to follow that any puzzled person is a philosopher provided that he seeks to remove that puzzlement and that his desire to achieve the knowledge that will remove it is a desire for knowledge for its own sake, not just for the sake of removing the puzzlement and not as a means to some further end. As support for his analysis Aristotle appeals to what he sees as the historical fact that it is only when man's economic needs are secured that he begins to seek knowledge for its own sake, to indulge in what we have found Bacon describing as the prostitution of science.

Given the triviality of some of the aporias Aristotle has in mind, it might seem that a further condition would be required to distinguish knowledge from the specific kind of knowledge called *sophia* for which philosophy is the *philia.* Such a further condition is stipulated. It is that the knowledge sought should be of the universal, knowledge ultimately of the first cause. This condition is compatible with philosophy's beginning with perplexity over "obvious difficulties," that is to say, over aporias that can be explained away by the discovery of causes that are not far to seek. For these difficulties and their removal may be on the way to knowledge of first causes, divine science, the science of being. So we have the picture of a teleological progress of inquiry from proximal causes to the ultimate cause, a cause being for Aristotle one of the four kinds distinguished in the *Physics*. This suggests an Aristotelian parallel to Heidegger's assertion that existing as *Da-sein* is to be already concerned with being. If there is a parallel here it implies that already in our concern with the problem of earning our daily bread we are taking our first steps in philosophy. This would be an awkward implication for Aristotle at least, because it would endanger his thesis that philosophy is not concerned with production, that it is *ou poiētikē*. How could this danger be met?

It could be said that in his absorption with solving the problem of his biological survival man is only potentially a philosopher. However, this still clashes with Aristotle's thesis if the potentiality just mentioned means that man has already begun to philosophize, though only in an undeveloped way. On the other hand, if the potentiality is no more than a possibility, all we shall be saying is that concern with the immediate problems of survival and comfortable living is consistent with going on to become concerned with seeking wisdom for its own sake. Heidegger is not himself faced with the particular difficulty that confronts Aristotle, because he says that Dasein's world is everyday only *zumeist*, that is, not always, but only as a rule.[1] Although Heidegger is not himself giving a genetic account, what he says leaves room for anyone wishing to give one to say that there is philosophy as soon as there is Da-sein. It is not only because his account is not historical (*historisch*) that Heidegger would refrain from saying that where there is Dasein there is philosophy. If philosophy is an articulated theory of being, an ontology, Da-sein's pre-theoretical concern with being does not make him a philosopher.[2] Of course there is an Aristotelian parallel to this distinction, and it is this that provides Aristotle with the best defense against the danger mentioned at the end of the preceding paragraph.

We shall come back to the German Greeks and to what they say about the saying that philosophy begins in wonder. Meanwhile, what else can we learn from what the Greek Greeks say relative to this, for instance about the idea that philosophy seeks knowledge for its own sake?

This idea sets philosophy apart from sophistry. But does it not let into philosophy the solving of crossword puzzles, provided the solutions are not sought for the prize or for the self-conceit that may follow? Not if solving crossword puzzles and suchlike activities are indulged in to pass the time or to relax so that, as Aquinas puts it in the *Summa contra Gentiles,* "we may afterwards become more fit for studious occupations" (3, 26).

As for the collection of facts, even facts about natural causes, just for the sake of having them in one's collection, we shall postpone mention of one of the reasons why this is not philosophy. A reason that may be mentioned forthwith is that insofar as philosophy is what Aristotle means by metaphysics, it comes after physics conceptually, whether or not it is called metaphysics on that account or on grounds of bibliographical history. Philosophy is not only a search after *epistēmē* and, where possible, *nous* concerning causes, but also that pursuit given direction by the hope of wisdom, *sophia,* the knowledge that is deemed to be of the most honorable kind. This ultimate aim is what impresses the stamp of philosophy on the humbler questions with which it begins. It is important that this be remembered as we pursue the question of what Aristotle means when he says that philosophy begins in *thaumazein.* Does it go without saying that a hierarchical structure analogous to this must be kept in mind when we ask what Plato means when he says this?

On Aristotle's conception of philosophy, but not on Plato's, philosophy keeps its roots in "the things we see." But is it true to say that the *thaumazein* from which philosophy springs according to the *Theaetetus* has, at the beginning, its roots in the Forms? The following passage of the *Parmenides* could be taken to suggest that the answer to both of these questions must be no:

> if anyone sets out to show about things of this kind — sticks and stones, and so on — that the same thing is many and one, we shall say that what he is proving is that *something* is many and one, not that Unity is many or that Plurality is one; he is not telling us anything wonderful, but only what we should all admit. But, as I said just now, if he begins by distinguishing the Forms apart by themselves — Likeness, for instance, and Unlikeness, Plurality and Unity, Rest and Motion, and all the rest — and then shows that these Forms among themselves can be combined with, or separated from, one another, then, Zeno, I should be filled with wonder. I am sure you have dealt with this subject very forcefully; but, as I say, my astonishment would be much greater if anyone could show that these same perplexities are everywhere involved in the Forms themselves — among the objects we apprehend in reflection, just as you and Parmenides have shown them to be involved in the things we see. (129c–e)

From this it would appear, perhaps to our astonishment, that Platonic *thaumazein* is of less noble birth than the Aristotelian kind. The down-to-earth Aristotle would seem to allow for *thaumazein* over the ultimate causes of things, whereas the otherworldly Plato would seem to limit *thaumazein* to our questioning about "the things we see." Is Plato not saying through Socrates that we can be astonished at the idea that a stone can be both many and one, but not astonished at the idea that Unity is many? On closer inspection we find that this is not what Plato is saying. Since he goes on to tell Zeno that he would be astonished if it could be shown that the Form Unity taken separately from the counted things was also many, he cannot be contending that the Forms are not appropriate objects of wonder. Someone who had not made the distinction he has just made between the Forms considered in themselves and the particular things in which they are unsubstantiated might well be astonished at the propositions Zeno advances.

What Plato is denying is that such *propositions about* the Forms considered in themselves can be proper objects for *aporetic* wonder when we understand their logical and ontological status. Aporetic wonder about such propositions would suffice to show that we had not understood this status.

Once we do understand the status of the Forms and the ultimate causes, is wonder at an end? Is *thaumazein* only the beginning of philosophy? Is its *telos* its own end, the end of philosophy? All we have shown so far is that neither Aristotle nor Plato denies that there may be a place for *thaumazein* when aporetic, interrogative *thaumazein* is superseded. But do they argue positively that a kind of *thaumazein* may persist? Or do they show any signs of recognizing that aporetic *thaumazein* has a positive side that may be capable of surviving the solution of a problem, surviving into *sophia*? Interpretable as such a sign perhaps is the suspicion Aristotle evinces that it may be blasphemous to entertain the thought that one might attain *sophia*, or at least that others might think so, this "might" becoming articulated a few sentences later into the disjunction that only God can possess *sophia* or, at any rate, God will possess it in a degree above others. Knowledge of the highest kind of the final cause may be beyond human capacity. This is something Aristotle admits, speaking for himself. But it is only speaking as a mouthpiece for the poets that he brings in the idea that divine wrath might descend on those who supposed *sophia* to be within their reach. And there is no explicit statement by Aristotle that the separate and permanent objects of the divine science, if not of mathematics and physics, may be objects of such *Bewunderung* as Kant confesses to experiencing when he contemplates the starry sky above. Plato too avoids the word *thaumazein* when he speaks of the separate and unchanging Forms. Also when he refers to the gods, as at *Republic* 379, though there, as in Aristotle, the language of the traditional myths is used self-consciously. Perhaps this is a clue. The myths have lost their hold. Invocation of a god has become a mere stylistic device, and the invoked god a *deus ex machina* before which the only wonder possible is of the lowly sort caused by the puppeteer. That this is so for Aristotle is borne out by his remark that "even the lover of myth is in a sense a lover of wisdom, for the myth is composed of wonders." Here still the wonder is provoked by something one cannot explain, an aporia before which one has the feeling of being trapped, of there being no way out, no way out of the fly-bottle.

Interrogative or aporetic wonderment is based then on a sense of one's ignorance, where the ignorance is not any absence of knowledge, but an ignorance that challenges us to dispel it because it is presented dramatically in the form of an apparent contradiction or dilemma and is therefore difficult to live with. The object of the wonder is incredible. The stupidity we feel before it is not the stupor of dull indifference that Hegel speaks of when in connection with Aristotle's dictum that philosophy begins in *thaumazein* — for which Hegel's word here is *Verwunderung* — he writes in the *Philosophy of*

History: "the Greek spirit was excited to wonder at the natural in nature. It does not maintain the position of stupid (*stumpf*) indifference to it as something existing (*als zu einem Gegebenen*)."[3] This *Stumpfheit* is not that of being stumped for an answer. It is not just failure to hear an answer. It is failure to hear a question. Ignorance of ignorance, alogicality, it is below the threshold of mental laziness, since laziness does rise to the level of perceiving that there is something that calls to be done, for instance a question that demands to be answered. But the stupidity of *Stumpfheit* is unquestioning. However, it is neither of this blank look nor of the stupidity of interrogative *thaumazein* — the puzzled look — that Aquinas can be speaking when in his comments on Aristotle's dictum he writes in the *Summa Theologiae*:

> What laziness is to outward behaviour, amazement and stupor are to mental effort. One who is amazed refrains for the moment to pass judgement on the object of his amazement, fearing failure. But he does look towards the future. When stupor envelops a man he is afraid either to form a judgement here and now or to look towards the future. Hence amazement is a source of philosophising, whereas stupor is an obstacle to philosophical thinking. (1a2ae, 41, 4)

The stupor of which Aquinas speaks here is not the stupor of dull unquestioning indifference. The latter is consciousness of a state of affairs, and it has an intentional object; therefore it is not so thick a stupidity regarding something that nothing regarding that thing enters our ken. The thing is not something of which we are unconscious. But our consciousness of it does not include consciousness of any question it poses. The stupor of which Aquinas speaks has an intentional object, but the person's attitude to it is not one of indifference. He sees that a question is raised, but he is afraid to even seek an answer. He buries his head in the sand. He wants nothing to do with the question, hoping that if he diverts his eyes from it, the question will go away. Aquinas therefore rightly distinguishes this *stupor* from what he calls *admiratio,* concluding that wonder or amazement motivates philosophy whereas stupidity is an impediment to it. It will be recalled that our proposal in the present chapter is that there is a kind of *stupor* that is intrinsic to *thaumazein.* We are pursuing the idea that "wonder" is a wonderful word in something like the sense of the "speculative" word *Aufhebung,* which delights Hegel because it incorporates opposite meanings, and like the sense of the antithetical words Karl Abel claims he comes upon in Ancient Egyptian, words that he finds as astonishing (*erstaunlich,* he says) as one would find it if "in Berlin the word 'light' was used to mean both 'light' and 'darkness.' "[4] We are wondering whether this may be how it is with at least one of the varieties of *thaumazein.* So far we have been addressing ourselves mainly to its dark side. Now we must turn toward the light, return to the question of whether astonishment can be sustained in wisdom.

GERMAN GREEKS

Can astonishment be sustained when we issue from the cave into the light? As we emerge, the light blinds us. This confusion by bedazzlement of which Plato speaks at *Republic* 515f is the counterpart of the confusion by dizziness that comes over us as we make the passage from seeming understanding (*Schein*) into the darkness of aporetic wonder. As we move into the light of real understanding the object of our vision is, in the words of the hymn, hidden by the splendor of light. Our eyes cannot accommodate themselves to its brilliance any more than our darkness can comprehend aporia. Aporetic astonishment persists as long as there is aporia, lack of passage, as long as the puppeteer or geometer has not administered the aperient. Paradoxically the laxative that is a *pharmakon*-remedy is at the same time a *pharmakon*-poison insofar as aporetic astonishment is a healthy state compared with blank indifference.[5] It is the very source from which philosophical inquiry springs, the springboard of its *Satz vom Grund*, the point from which its spirit spurts. Astonishment is the *pathos* of philosophy, as Plato says, and as Heidegger says, its *Stimmung*, the very timbre of philosophy's voice.[6]

This being so, how can we contemplate with equanimity the prospect that contemplative wisdom promises or threatens? How can we face its apparent lack of dis-ease? We shall perhaps be happy with the satisfaction of *sophia* if we ever reach it. Who knows? One thing we do know here and now is that we do not value highly the satisfaction of pre-aporetic indifference. How then can we with consistency value highly here and now post-aporetic bliss conceived as satisfaction of all our needs, including the need for philosophy? Can Paradise be paradise unless it continues to have something like the shortcomings of existence in Purgatory? It is not simply that heaven threatens or promises to be uneventful and *ennuyeux*. Presumably the gods are not bored up there on Olympus. Nor are we bored at the peaks of, say, aesthetic ecstasy. But would we not here and now prize their and our experience less if it lacked a sense of wonder? Theologians at least since Heraclitus have recognized this. It is recognized in what one reads about the experience of mystical union being at the same time an experience of feeling apart: feeling oneself apart and feeling oneself a part. It is manifest in the apartness that is a part of love, in what is wanting in love, as this is recognized by Levinas when he writes:

> Intersubjectivity is not simply the application of the category of multiplicity to the domain of the mind. It is brought about by Eros, where in the proximity of the other the distance is wholly maintained, a distance whose pathos is made up of this proximity and this duality of beings. What is

presented as the failure of communication in love in fact constitutes the positive character of the relationship; this absence of the other is precisely his presence qua other. The other is the neighbour — but proximity is not a degradation of, or a stage on the way to, fusion.[7]

As well as this Judaic fissionist tradition there is a fusionist tradition. To this latter Hegel belongs. This is the tradition of belonging and of longing that ends in belonging, the tradition announced in Hegel's remarks on the way wonder is the origin of philosophy among the Greeks. The Greeks, as Hegel reads them, are a home-loving lot. They are home-builders and cultivators of *Heimatlichkeit,* and their gods are really all gods of the hearth.

> It is this veritable homeliness, or, more accurately, in the spirit of homeliness, in this spirit of ideally being-at-home-with-themselves in their physical, corporate, legal, moral and political existence; it is in the beauty and the freedom of their character in history, making what they are to be also a sort of Mnemosyne with them, that the kernel of thinking liberty rests; and hence it was requisite that philosophy should arise among them. Philosophy is being at home with self, just like the homeliness of the Greek; it is man's being at home in his mind, at home with himself. If we are at home with the Greeks, we must be at home more particularly in their philosophy.[8]

And in a passage of the *Philosophy of History* from which we have already had occasion to cite, Hegel says:

> According to Aristotle's dictum, that philosophy proceeds from wonder, the Greek view of nature also proceeds from wonder of this kind. Not that in their experience spirit meets something extraordinary which it compares with the common order of things; for the intelligent view of a regular course of nature, and the references of phenomena to that standard, do not yet present themselves; but the Greek spirit was excited to wonder at the *natural* in nature. It does not maintain the position of stupid indifference to it as something existing (*als zu einem Gegebenen*), but regards it as something in the first instance foreign, in which, however, it has a presentiment of confidence, and the belief that it bears something within it which is friendly to the human spirit, and to which it may be permitted to sustain a positive relation. This *wonder* and this *presentiment* are here the fundamental categories.[9]

Here we are at the beginning of a history in which the foreign gradually becomes the friend, the *fremd* the *Freund,* to the point that in the end the distance between philosophy and the *sophia* it loves vanishes away completely in an infinite consciousness of its loved self, Hegel's version of Aristotle's *noēseōs noēsis.*

> Philosophy proper commences in the West. It is in the West that this freedom of self-consciousness first comes forth; the natural consciousness, and likewise mind disappear into themselves. In the brightness of the East the individual disappears; the light first becomes in the West the flash of

thought which strikes within itself, and from thence creates its world out of itself. The blessedness of the West is thus so determined that in it the subject as such endures and continues in the substantial; the individual mind grasps its being as universal, but universality is just this relation to itself. This being at home with self.[10]

Compare this view of the history of philosophy with the history as Heidegger sees it issuing from the same source, the *thaumazein* experienced by Heraclitus and Parmenides. We quoted earlier Aristotle's statement that "all men begin by wondering that things are as they are." That is also how Hegel sees the beginning. He sees both the end and the beginning in an Aristotelian light. And that, in Heidegger's view, is how philosophy tends to see itself. But this is only one aspect of philosophy as Heidegger describes it in his lecture "What Is Philosophy?" — to bring to thought philosophy's hidden side, wonder that things are as they are must be supplemented by wonder that things are. That is what astonished Heraclitus and Parmenides in their astonishment that things are as they are. The seven or seven million wonders of the world of which the poets sing are set within the context of the wonder of all wonders, *das Wunder aller Wunder, that* that which is *is*.[11] What Heidegger might at one time have called fundamental ontological wonder, the *thaumazein* of the thinking of being, prepares the way for another beginning in which man is not only the preserver of the unconcealment of beings but also the guardian of the openness of being.[12]

No attempt will be made in the confines of this chapter to interpret what Heidegger says at different stages of his work on the question how the tasks of the *Wahrer, Wächter,* and *Wegbereiter* are related to those of the scientist and the poet understood in the wider and the narrower senses of *Dichter*.[13] Nor will any attempt be made here to determine how far either of these is helpmeet of the other and how the wonder of the thinker bears upon the ontic wonder of the *Dichter* whose task it is to name the holy. However, picking up the thread of the immediately preceding chapter, it is important to note here that although the wonder of the scientist is the wonder of the *se demander,* the demand for an explanation, it can coexist with a wonder of a different kind: the wonder expressed by the zoologist who named the *sabella magnifica,* the *aranea mirabilis,* and (with less Greek) the *thaumetopoea processionea*.[14] The last-named is the caterpillar to be seen trailing across the Mediterranean countryside head-to-tail in processions up to eight meters long. The accounts that Fabre and more recent naturalists have given of the behavior of these creatures are studded with words such as "remarkable," "singular," "puzzling," and "extraordinary." On the basis of what was said at the end of the final section of the last chapter, I am inclined to believe that these natural scientists could have used the word "sublime." However, in the final section of this chapter it will be relevant to remember that it is not only the puzzling and extraordinary that the natural scientist explains.

THE GODS ARE ALSO EVEN HERE

In this final section we apply to questions raised in the first and second some of the distinctions Heidegger makes in the *Grundfragen der Philosophie*, his most detailed treatment yet published of the saying that philosophy begins in *thaumazein*. So far we have rung the changes on the various ways this Greek word may be translated into Latin, German, French, and English. Within limits that I shall not attempt to make precise the terms are often interchangeable. There is therefore some arbitrariness in the choice of terms Heidegger uses to indicate the outlines of a thaumatology, and this *Spielraum* must be allowed for in translating those terms into English.

Heidegger distinguishes *Verwunderung, Bewunderung, Bestaunen,* and *Er-staunen* with a hyphen, the unhyphenated *Erstaunen* being employed usually to range over all four of the notions he distinguishes. The first three he regards as the ordinary terms for the unordinary. He examines what they mean with a view to eliciting clues to the meaning of *Er-staunen,* ontological *thaumazein*.

Verwunderung (and *Sichwundern*) is marvel at what one finds surprising, remarkable, what one cannot explain and does not want to have explained. It is a manifestation of a craving for novelty, a cult of the unusual and unique that turns its back on the ordinary.

Bewunderung is admiration. What is admired, like the object of marvel, is the singular as contrasted with the ordinary, but, in contrast to the marvelous, what is admired is *recognized as* unusual. Instead of being swept off his feet by it, the admirer stands back and appraises it. To the extent that he gives it marks he achieves a kind of mastery, however lacking he may be in the competence being judged.

Bestaunen, amazement, like marveling, recoils before its object. But it does not evaluate or patronize. Admiration, however wanting in the skill or talent it assesses, assumes it has critical gifts of its own that confer authority to evaluate. Amazement does not grade. Furthermore, what amazes me does not stand out only as unordinary. By comparison with the ordinary it is extraordinary, so surpassingly extraordinary that the very idea of putting a value upon it would never enter my head.

In all three cases so far considered there is some particular thing that causes surprise. And all three involve comparison of the ordinary with what is out of the ordinary to a lesser or greater degree. *Er-staunen,* ontological astonishment or wonder, on the other hand, is wonder at the most ordinary itself. The utterly ordinary in everything strikes us as utterly unordinary. The most commonplace overwhelms us, like the common place, the common where, of which, in the anecdote told by Aristotle and more than once retold by Heidegger, Heraclitus says to his slightly disappointed visitors, "The gods are also even here (*kai entautha*)," here being the humble kitchen where the daily bread is baked. The gods are everywhere. There is no place that they do not haunt. As Aristotle in his way puts it, when he is about to tell this story in *De Partibus Animalium: en pasi gar tois phusikois enesti ti thaumaston,* "every realm of nature is wonderful" (645a 17). As Heidegger puts it, wonder knows no way out from the unordinariness of the most ordinary. There is no escaping it, because the attempt to escape by explaining the unfamiliar presents us with something familiar in its stead, which however is again utterly strange. Nor does ontological wonder know any way in. Whichever way it turns, it is always already faced by the superlative unordinariness of the ordinary. There is no transition to or from wisdom here, since the wisdom of ontological wonder is an ontological between, a *Zwischen.* It is a passage, and it is only in this moment of passage, *poros,* from the most ordinary to the most unordinary that ordinariness and unordinariness as such are highlighted. In that moment dawns the wonder that and what the totality of being is, the wonder of what elsewhere Heidegger calls the ontological difference and here the *Spielraum* of the between of the being of beings. Here too in the *Grundfragen der Philosophie* we come upon the stunning statement that our wonder before the totality of what is is wonder "*dass es ist* und das ist, *was es ist*": that it is, *and that is to say,* what it is.[15] This points up strikingly the betweenness of the ontological difference and the near-farness of the *Denker* and the *Dichter,* who, in one of the images Heidegger borrows from Hölderlin, "dwell near to one another on mountains farthest apart."[16] There is a complicity between them, but also an abyss. How that can be is the mystery of this "und das ist."

Returning to the Greeks, Heidegger quotes from the first chorus of Sophocles' *Antigone:*

> There is much that is strange, but nothing
> that surpasses man in strangeness.
> He sets sail on the frothing waters
> amid the south winds of winter
> tacking through the mountains
> and furious chasms of the waves.

"Here," Heidegger says, " 'sea' is said as though for the first time."[17] The dialogue between thinking and poetry is the dialogue of the between. The between "is" man's transitivity before the totality of what is, his displacement, *dépaysement,* before the question of the ground, the wonder at there not being nothing. Hegel too speaks of the totality:

> The position of hearkening surmise, of attentive eagerness to catch the meaning of nature, is indicated to us in the comprehensive idea of *Pan.* To the Greeks Pan did not represent the *objective* Whole, but the indefinite that is at the same time connected with the moment of *subjectivity;* he is the inexplicable frisson (*der allgemeine Schauer*) that comes over us in the silence of the forests; he was, therefore, especially worshipped in sylvan Arcadia (a "panic terror" is the common expression for a groundless terror).[18]

It would be precipitate to identify this *grundlose Schreck* with the objectless "*Angst* in the sense of terror," *Angst im Sinne des Schreckens,* of the postscript to "What Is Metaphysics?,"[19] notwithstanding that Heidegger there and Hegel above are describing a stance with regard to totality. The meaning of nature of which the Greeks have a presentiment will turn out to be the overcoming of terror and outlandishness when the Greek spirit finally comes home. When at last it is fully *bei sich* in its *Wohnung,* everything about it is *gewöhnlich.* The ordinary has no trace of the extraordinary.

Heidegger's *Heimatlichkeit* is otherwise, as is his reading of the Greeks. Provoked by his reading of *Antigone,* a work that gropes in vain for a way out from the tragic aporia of the between of the *heimlich* and *unheimlich,* he writes, referring to the violence (*deinon, Gewalt*) with which man is enabled to break open new paths, as when the *Dichter* for the first time discloses the sea *as* sea, the earth *as* earth, the animal *as* animal:[20]

> Immediately and irremediably, all violence comes to nothing in the face of *one* thing alone *(Nur an einem scheitert alle Gewalt-tätigkeit unmittelbar).* That is death. It is a term beyond all termination, a limit beyond all limits. Here there is no breaking out or breaking up, no capture or subjugation. But this strange thing (*Un-heimliche*) that banishes us once and for all from everything in which we are at home is no particular event that must be named among others because it too ultimately happens. It is not only when he comes to die, but always and essentially that man is without exit in the face of death. In so far as man is, he stands in the exitlessness of death. Thus being-there (*Da-sein*) is the very happening of strangeness.[21]

Strangeness, *das Unheimliche,* on Hegel's interpretation, is alien to man's final home. On Heidegger's interpretation it is the very finality of man's being at home. No wonder that Freud, in his paper "Das Unheimliche," like Karl Abel before him, exclaims that "*heimlich* is a word the meaning of which develops towards an ambivalence, until it finally coincides with its opposite, *unheimlich.* "[22] No wonder, therefore, that we should find that "wonder" is a word that points in opposite directions. No wonder, therefore, that we find Descartes writing in Article 53 of *The Passions of the Soul* that

> When the first encounter with some object surprises us, and we judge it to be something new, or very different from what we knew previously or from what we took it to be, this means that we wonder at it and are astonished by it; and because that can happen before we have any idea whatsoever as to whether or not this object is agreeable to us, it seems to me that wonder is the first of all the passions; and it has no contrary, for if the object that presents itself has nothing in itself that surprises us, we are not moved at all and we contemplate it without passion.[23]

The word I have translated here by "wonder" corresponds to Descartes's *admiration,* but he is using that word more in the sense of what we earlier called amazement (Heidegger's *Bestaunen*) rather than of what we called admiration (Heidegger's *Bewunderung*). Given the ontological priority he ascribes to God over the *ego cogito*, and given the way in which the argument of the third Meditation is broken off so that the reader may join the author in a hymn of praise to the majesty of the Creator, it would appear in order to say that his seventeenth-century French word *admiration* has in this article the sense of ontological wonder, Heidegger's *Er-staunen*.

For Heidegger ontological wonder is wonder over the between of the *heimlich-unheimlich*, over the *entre* of the exit, death's entrance, death's *entrée*. It is a *Grundbestimmung*. There are at least two ways in which we can get wrong what Heidegger means by this. In *Vom Wesen des Grundes* he warns that *Begründung*, founding, "should be understood, not in the narrow and derivative sense of proving ontical or theoretical propositions, but in a basically primordial sense. Founding is *that which makes the question 'Why?' possible in the first place.*"[24] The *Bestimmung* is a ground base attunement of temper and disposition that is a dis-position in that it is a displacement of man from the condition in which he sees things in an everyday light to the condition in which he sees this seeing as blindness, now that it is disclosed to his astonishment that everything as thing is *phusis*, and that *phusis* is *a-lētheia*, unconcealment, as Heraclitus saw at the very same time that he saw that *phusis* loves to conceal itself, at the first beginning of philosophy and when history first began. The first beginning of philosophy and history (*Geschichte*) is the happening (*Geschehen*) of word, work, and deed. It is incalculably rare, *das Seltenste*.[25] *Geschichte ist selten.*[26] The astonishing passage between the ordinariness of beings and the unordinariness of the being of beings is utterly and unutterably unordinary. It is therefore inexplicable, whether in terms of the causality of beings outside man or of the agency of man himself. The *Grundbestimmung* is not a psychological *Erlebnis*, a passion undergone, nor is it an act of will. It is a way in which one deports oneself. It is an *Erfahrung*, a displacement. It is not a mental state in which Da-sein luxuriates, but a luxation beset with risks: a *gefährliche Erfahrung*.

In posing the *Grundfrage der Philosophie*, "Why are there beings, not rather nothing?"[27] man finds himself disposed toward another beginning of philosophy. This disposition is a being possessed by a *question-savoir*[28] that recognizes that first philosophy is more fundamental than it is conceived to be by Plato and Aristotle, who begin to bring the first beginning to its end when the latter conceives philosophy as the quest for the most universal causes underlying the secondary causes of physical phenomena, and the former, through his doctrine of ideas, prepares the way for a conception of truth as adequacy and correctness and conceives *logos* as assertion that can be repeated and passed on, no longer as gathering, *legein*, *sammeln*.

Before Plato and Aristotle, Parmenides, with whom, as Hegel says, philosophy proper begins,[29] is wonder-struck at the belonging together of gathering thinking with being that at once makes possible inquiries demanding answers and runs the risk of being forgotten on account of such inquiries.

Following Aristotle, Alexander of Aphrodisias speaks more truly than he knows when, in his commentary on Aristotle's dictum that philosophy begins in *thaumazein*, he says that wonder precedes inquiry.[30] But meanwhile *technē*, which at the first beginning is neither passive suffering nor active exercise of will, but receptivity toward *phusis*, a disposition of disponibility, *Bereitschaft*,[31] is on the way to becoming technical control, and the "for its own sake," which Aristotle identifies as a mark of philosophy and Bacon identifies as the prostitution of science, comes to be interpreted as theory opposed to practice, instead of what that distinction presupposes. Paradoxically, the conception of philosophy as quest for wisdom understood as knowledge of the first cause or Ideas imposes upon philosophy the means-end structure of *praxis*, so that Plato sometimes gets perilously close to regarding philosophy as a machine for producing statesmen. Paradoxically too, this peril is what keeps open the possibility of philosophy. If philosophy is the desire for the possession of knowledge, if its *philia* is represented as the *Symposium* represents erotic desire, then the attainment of *sophia* will be the attainment of a *petite mort*, the substitution of indifference for wonder.

If, however, *philia* is not a variety of *epithumia*, if it is being possessed by love that does not seek to possess, but to let being be, wonder will belong to *sophia* as to the beginning of philosophy. The *archē* of philosophy that is *thaumazein* is not just a beginning that is left behind. It remains its ground and guide. *Das Erstaunen trägt und durchherrscht die Philosophie.*[32] The lecture in which Heidegger says this was delivered in 1955. In it, as in the lectures entitled *Grundfragen der Philosophie* given in 1937–38, the word "philosophy" covers metaphysics and what will be called essential thinking in the "Letter on 'Humanism' " of 1946 and "The End of Philosophy and the Task of Thinking," a lecture given in 1964. However, what he earlier calls the coming philosophy, *die künftige Philosophie*,[33] and what he later calls the thinking of another beginning is a thinking of and a thinking on the first beginning, a remembrance of it:

> The preparatory thinking in question does not wish and is not able to predict the future. It only attempts to say something to the present which was already said a long time ago precisely at the beginning of philosophy and for that beginning, but has not been explicitly thought.[34]

What was said at the first beginning but not explicitly thought (*nicht eigens gedacht*) is what Parmenides and Heraclitus named *alētheia*, unconcealment. They also experienced *lēthē*, oblivion, as a dispensation of concealment.[35] But they did not think this explicitly as such, and so did not think explicitly what Heidegger calls *Lichtung*, opening or clearing, as in a forest: the complicity of concealing and unconcealing, which makes possible the opposition and play of darkness and light in which things appear and disappear; which makes possible the language of Platonic and indeed all metaphysics.[36] To stress the irresolubility of this complicity, Heidegger says, not without poignancy, that self-concealing belongs to light. It is not a simple supplement, not *eine blosse Zugabe*.[37] It is because concealment, *lēthē*, is a syncope at the very heart of unconcealing, *a-lētheia*, that Heidegger says that philosophy understood as love toward wisdom cannot be superseded by *sophia* understood as absolute knowing.[38] If indeed there is necessary concealment, then philosophy understood as *zukünftige* philosophy and as essential thinking will never cease being underway. This means that in principle wonder will never cease, even though its aspect as awe before the sublimely stupendous may from time to time give way to its aspect as stupor so dark that it forgets its own oblivion. The very interplay of concealment and unconcealment will be "what is ever and again worthy of wonder and is preserved in its worth by wonder."[39] But, to pose a question to which our final chapter will return, if what this *denkende Er-staunen* wonders at is the ground of the distinction between darkness and light, must not our own characterization of wonder be itself replaced by one that is no longer framed in the language of chiaroscuro, the language of Platonism, the language of metaphysics? Can this be done? Can Heidegger himself describe the *Zwischen* of concealing and unconcealing except by the light and the shadow cast by the idea of the interplay of darkness and light? That we do not yet see how this can be done is perhaps what Heidegger is wishing to bring out by employing the ambiguous word *Lichtung*. But whether or not thinking at the beginning of another beginning can accomplish the task of thinking beyond the language of the end of the first beginning, it will be, as we have seen, a thinking on that first beginning. It will therefore inherit the *thaumazein* that is the only beginning of philosophy — but that is not only the beginning of philosophy or only the beginning of only philosophy, but also the forgotten beginning of science.

5

BELONGINGS

FOOTWEAR

Although Hannah and Jack were obviously a devoted couple, *zutraut* to each other,[1] it was less obvious whether they were formally an *Ehepaar* or were joined by a *mariage pré-contractuel*.[2] For she went by her pen name and he by his brush name, and several years ago her wedding ring was lost. Like Meyer Schapiro and Kurt Goldstein, they had a more or less direct association with Columbia University, but they frequently traveled in the opposite direction to that taken by Schapiro and Goldstein, to work in a rented *mas* just over the Alpilles near Saint-Remy and the road to Arles, not all that far from Le Thor and the Chemin des Lauves.

It always seemed a shame that Jack painted by artificial light even during the day, drawing the curtain across a window from which he would otherwise have seen a landscape of olive groves, almond trees, vines and dark cypresses backed by white crags reaching up to the immaculate Provençal sky. I now understand that he was drawing the curtain between himself and the danger presented by van Gogh. I came to understand this better after beginning to write these words in a *Hof* just over the hills of the Black Forest from Todtnauberg, near a window from which, if I had dared to look, I should have seen the dangerous *Holzwege* and *Feldwege* whose mud clings to one's shoes. The danger of these *Wege* is not that they may be *chemins qui ne mènent nulle part,* finishing up in the unfrequented, *im Unbegangenen.* The danger is that they may lead to the shelter of a certain hut that is by now as *begangen* as the temple of Artemis and the kitchen where Heraclitus baked his daily bread. Their danger is that in following them to that destination there may be no *wëgen,* no opening up of new tracks.[3]

This danger can be exaggerated. Heidegger would have been the last thinker to welcome callers who identified with him, imagining they could put themselves in his shoes. And the danger will be reduced if, following Jack's example, I draw between myself and the work by Heidegger entitled "The Origin of the Work of Art" the curtain of Derrida's *La vérité en peinture,* in particular the fourth part, which is entitled "Restitutions." This part devotes itself to the question of belonging raised by Heidegger's essay and by an exchange of letters between Heidegger and Meyer Schapiro about whether van Gogh's painting of shoes referred to in that essay is the one numbered 225 in the catalogue compiled by J. B. de la Faille. This precaution presents its own danger, that of being drawn to draw the drawn curtain, to reproduce mechanically its filigraph, rather as in some of his work Jack multiplies an initial design with the help of graph paper, a method van Gogh never followed, as far as I know, in multiplying his versions of his paintings of shoes.

This second danger too can be exaggerated. First, for a reason analogous to the one already given. The only way to follow either Heidegger or Derrida is not to follow them. To turn one's back on the book, as the author of *The Fruits of the Earth* asks of its readers.[4] Heidegger's much-visited rectoral address speaks of "the self-limiting self-affirmation," *die sich begrenzende Selbstbehauptung,* of the university. What limits the self-affirmation of the university is not the Führer, as some readers have taken Heidegger to say, but the things themselves that call for thought and give both leader and follower the guidelines in the critical vicinity of which Martin Heidegger is no less a follower than any of his students.

> All leading must acknowledge the power that followers have in their own right. Every following indeed bears resistance within itself. This essential opposition of leading and following should be neither obscured nor ever blotted out.[5]

There is a second reason for not being overanxious about the risk of being dragged along in the wake of either Heidegger or Derrida at the cost of losing one's own identity. The very notion of identity as classically understood is, they both argue, not as fundamental as philosophers have maintained. It is a derivative of belonging together, Heidegger holds in *Identity and Difference,*[6] and both the traditional notion of identity and some of Heidegger's remarks about belonging together are called into question by Derrida.

Reflection on what Heidegger and Derrida say about identity and belonging together may result in our anxiety over losing our self-identity to them being replaced by anxiety over never having had any self-identity of the kind we used to like to think we had. It may be some comfort to tell ourselves that old-style self-identity can no longer be attributed to Heidegger and Derrida either, so that neither of them is in a position to be our master. Even so, this consolation can hardly amount to a waxing of *Das Rettende auch*[7] if it means that all one is left with is one, *das Man,* where no man is his own man and no woman her own woman. But the corollary does not have this implication. Its implication is rather that a certain philosophical picture of authenticity and self-belonging must be seen in focus. In the present discussion we approach no nearer to that picture, however, than is permitted by the decision to view "The Origin of the Work of Art" through the fourth part of *La vérité en peinture,* and by the fact that this fourth part is, as Derrida puts it, a " 'poly-logue' (à n + 1 voix—féminine)" where there is an ambiguity between a dash that adds and a minus that subtracts femininity and where we are not told the names of the persons to whom the voices belong.[8] Not one of those voices nor all of them, therefore, can be attributed to Jacques Derrida, and we — I, you, and the owners of those voices — are indebted to him for screen-ing us from any threat that he and the author of "The Origin of the Work of Art" might present to our own self-presence.

Specifically, without what one hesitates to call external evidence, we can-not attribute to Derrida the several times repeated phrase *tirade pathétique,* applied with some feeling by one or more of the participants in the poly-logue to two paragraphs of Heidegger's essay that are reproduced in part by Schapiro but not reproduced in "Restitutions." There the two paragraphs in which Heidegger describes shoes such as those van Gogh depicted are represented by three dotted lines standing for readings of Heidegger's de-scription in German, French, and English. We shall not make restitution of that description here.[9] Nor shall we reproduce the unsigned and unas-signed description of this description given in "Restitutions,"[10] except for the following sentences:

> All that is classical, an affair of class, of pedagogy also and classicity. Pro-fessor Heidegger, as Professor Schapiro says in homage to Professor Gold-stein, is projecting a lantern-slide. By means of this illustration he wants to rivet the attention of his audience from the beginning of his lecture. For "The Origin" was first, at a very significant date, a series of lectures given to a *Kunstwissenschaftliche Gesellschaft* and then to a *Freie Deutsche Hochstift;* and it shows it.[11]

One of the reasons why one of the speakers in "Restitutions" is put out by Heidegger's description, why he or she finds it "imprudent,"[12] is that there appears to be no basis for assigning the shoes to a peasant, whether male or female, rather than, as in Schapiro's reading of the internal and external evidence, to the person whose signature, "Vincent," seems, on the well-known canvas F225, to be tied to the shoes by the shoes' untied laces. Note too that attached to this question of ownership, an implication of it, at least on Schapiro's reading, is the question as to whether the shoes are those of someone who lived in towns and did a good deal of traveling intercity, or those of a Bauer or Bäuerin who moved no further from his or her hearth than the distance of the field from which he or she walked with slow, toilsome tread as evening fell. This question is the question concerning technology. And when that question is raised, so also is the foot that can too quickly make the *faux pas* toward the conclusion that Heidegger is opposed to technology and simply opposes technology to art and to the windmill, the well and the stove, the *Kachelofen,* that constitute the peasant's world. We must therefore listen more closely to Heidegger's construal of worldhood, to how he spells out the belonging together of world and earth, and to the so-called *tirade pathétique,* in order to catch the sound that may explain why those two fateful paragraphs strike at least one pair or couple of ears as not merely imprudent, but lamentable,[13] the sound of footsteps, not just those of someone on his or her way home from the darkening fields, but of Kurt Goldstein and Meyer Schapiro on their way into exile at Columbia University, and of soldiers marching in the Rhineland while a rectoral address is being delivered by a professor of philosophy who—

Schwer verlässt,
Was nahe dem Ursprung wohnet, den Ort.[14]

—within two semesters will turn a deaf ear to a summons to make the journey from Freiburg to Berlin, and within another two will be delivering the lecture that closes with those words of Hölderlin's and includes the two paragraphs that are felt by one or n + 1 of the *dramatis personae* of "Restitutions" to be ridiculous,[15] a descent from the sublime to the ridiculous. Here is this great thinker pondering the lofty issues of truth and the origin of the work of art when, all of a sudden, he is to be heard talking about van Gogh's and/or the peasant's shoes in a manner that bears witness to what is surely an *effondrement pathétique, dérisoire, et symptomatique, signifiant.*[16] The pathos is a bathos, a coming down to earth. For *the effondrement pathétique,* the pathetic lapse, is also an *effondrement de terrain,*[17] a subsidence of the soil that compels us to ask what Heidegger heard in "the call of the earth,"[18] and how we are to interpret his *idéologie terrienne et paysanne.*[19] Is this ideology no more than a *nostalgie de la boue?*[20] There is more than a trace of such nostalgia in Heidegger's ideology, but it cohabits with a fairly shrewd respect for the relevance of town and technology not only to the conduct of everyday life but to the thinking of that difficult-simple kind to which Heidegger tells us we are called, and called not least by technology.

So Meyer Schapiro has another think coming if he imagines that, in the article on van Gogh's shoes, which he dedicates to the memory of Kurt Goldstein, he is, as an interlocutor in "Restitutions" suggests, restoring those shoes to the place where they belong: the streetwise feet of migrants to the New World, rather than those of "the common enemy" who professed to be content with wandering the field-paths of his native soil.[21] For, despite the itchy feet that took van Gogh to towns as far apart as Amsterdam and Arles, there is evidence, cited in "Restitutions," that at heart he was not so much a devotee of cities as Schapiro makes him out to have been. In a letter to his brother Theo he writes: "I am telling you the plain truth when I say that I am a painter of peasants, and you'll come to appreciate better that it is in painting them that I feel myself at home."[22] Conversely, as Schapiro knows on the best possible evidence, Heidegger too traveled as far as Amsterdam, where he saw at least one of van Gogh's paintings of shoes, perhaps Faille 225, even if he did not follow Goldstein as far as New Amsterdam. And, forsaking the silence of the hills, he was a regular commuter into the nearest city. True, he says in 1933 that he is *heimisch* only when he is back among his hills and their people.[23] However, as one of the speakers in "Restitutions" observes, town shoes would have served as well as peasant shoes to enable him to achieve the purpose he has at the point when he first mentions van Gogh's "famous painting."[24] Multipurpose shoes suited to the suburban life of Zähringen would have done. So the matter lies deeper than the superficial difference between types of terrain over which shoes are used to walk. Deeper than use. Deeper than the kind of terrain. As deep as the earth itself irrespective of the terrain. As deep as the earth that simultaneously discloses itself and closes over itself in an *effondrement de terrain,* in a *faille.*

We have this earth under our feet not only when the gods inhabit the temple but also when they are absent, in the time of our greatest need and forgetfulness. Heidegger's geology or Gaia-ology is at once an extension of and a step back beyond the Ptolemaic phenomenology of ubiquitous earth hinted at in Husserl's "Umsturz der kopernikanischen Lehre: die Urarche Erde bewegt sich nicht," in his *Crisis* and in Schapiro's phrase "our inescapable position on the earth."[25] It is because for Heidegger earth is the foothold of every category, one and all, *hen kai pan,* that for one member of the cast of "Restitutions" it threatens a new crisis, a crisis not only of European sciences but of European *Dichten* and *Denken,* such that the danger prevails most of all when that *Dichten* and *Denken* dwell nearest to the *Ort,* and the gods and the people are restored to each other. The name of this danger is *Verlässlichkeit,* reliability or fiability.

FIABILITY

This essential and "full" fiability makes possible — makes restitution of — not only the most "critical" and most "profound" regression this side of the philosophemes matter-form, utility, production, subjectivity, objectivity, symbol and law, etc., but also the most naively archaic regression into the element of ingenuous trust of the kind that can allow itself to be had, to be exposed to the most rudimentary of traps, the primordial trap, the trap that precedes all traps. To the possibility of temptation constituted by the mirror-play of the world, its *Spiegelspiel*.[26]

Doch gemach, pas si vite. Hold your horses. This disquieting passage covers a lot of ground swiftly, from "The Origin of the Work of Art," whose first version dates from 1935, to the lecture "The Thing" delivered in 1950 and on to the *Spiegel Spiel* of 1966 that retraces some of the ground traversed in the report about his year as rector that Heidegger wrote soon after the war and asked his son to publish when he thought the time was right. Let us therefore go over some of this ground more slowly. And let us begin a step or two further back, on page 70 of *Being and Time*, where we read:

> The shoe to be produced is for wearing (footgear, *Schuhzeug*); . . . A work that someone has ordered is only by reason of its use and the assignment-context of entities which is discovered in using it.
>
> But the work to be produced is not merely usable for something. The production itself is a using of something for something. In the work there is also a reference or assignment to "materials": the work is dependent and focussed on (*angewiesen auf*) leather, thread, needles, and the like.

The shoe is a *Zeug* and the needle is a *Zeug* in the sense of something produced, *erzeugt*, in order to fulfill a certain purpose. Leather, like timber and rock, is *Zeug* in the sense of raw material, *Stoff*. The pragmatico-semantic *Spielraum* between these two senses of *Zeug*, *Zeug* as ready to hand and *Zeug* as present at hand or extant (Welsh *defnydd* means material, *defnyddio* means to use), is one of the chief topics explored in *Being and Time*, the *topos* that is the *Lebensraum* of the everyday world that Da-sein occupies for the most part and as a rule.[27] But on the same page of *Being and Time* reference is made in passing to nature, not as raw material or natural product or wherewithal, but as "nature which 'stirs and strives', which assails us and enthralls us as a landscape . . . the flowers of the hedgerow . . . the 'springhead in the dale,' " which, rather than being "the 'source' of a river as established by the geographer," is closer to the source of the work of art. It would be misleading to say that this transition from *Being and Time* to "The Origin of the Work of Art" is a transition from understanding, *Verstehen*, and project, *Entwurf*, to disposition, *Befindlichkeit*, mood, *Stimmung*, and thrownness, *Geworfenheit*, since the former and the latter belong to each other. This interlacing is brought out by "The Origin of the Work of Art," because it is especially where we are treating of the so-called aesthetic and the so-called *objet d'art* that we are inclined to separate off and privilege feeling or mood, posited as a supervenient state of consciousness. For the same reason it would not be misleading to say that special attention is given to *Stimmung, Bestimmung*, and *Geworfenheit* in the Origin essay and the essays dating from the 1930s on Hölderlin, though *Stimmung* is a key notion too in the rectoral address of

1933 and the *Grundfragen der Philosophie* of four to five years later. Perhaps the danger sensed by the speaker of the disquieting sentences cited from "Restitutions" could be characterized as the danger that the *Stimmung* of "The Origin of the Work of Art" may turn into what in the more or less contemporary lectures on Hölderlin's hymns *Germanien* and *Der Rhein* Heidegger deems to be a *Miss-stimmung* or *Ver-stimmung*.[28]

Verstimmt, discordant, are each of the three classical accounts of what it is to be a thing that are reviewed and found to be wanting, though not incorrect, in the section of the Origin essay subtitled "Thing and Work." It might be objected that Heidegger's treatment of each of these accounts is wanting. His discussion does not seem to furnish sufficiently persuasive reasons to seek an alternative account. Thus, in what he says about the account of the thing in terms of *hypokeimenon* and *symbebēkota* it is not entirely clear whether the account he has in mind is one according to which the thing is "that around which the properties have assembled" or one according to which the thing is this *Kern* together with the properties. Furthermore, it might be objected that in his discussion of the thing as "nothing but the unity of a manifold of what is given in sensory experience" too little is said about the different explanations that could be and have been offered of the unity in question. Heidegger simply observes that it might be conceived as sum, totality, or form. He leaves it at that. No attempt is made to examine the credentials of an analysis that interprets this unity as the unity of a law implying subjunctive conditionality and what is contrary to fact. If he had considered such an analysis he might have been less ready to say that whereas the account of the thing as bearer of-or-with traits locates the thing too far off from our own body,[29] the account of the thing as the unity of a manifold of sensations puts it too near. An interpretation of that unity which makes room for the counterfactual subjunctivity of law seems eminently suited to place the thing at a distance intermediate between the purely sensory and the purely non-sensory.

As for what Heidegger says about the account of the thing as formed matter, his reason for finding this inadequate appears to rest solely on how the hylomorphic model applies to utilitarian artifacts such as axes, jugs, and shoes, the *Zeug* as product contrasted with *Zeug* as stuff. Admittedly, he does mention this contrast, for as well as referring to manmade articles he refers to "the self-contained block of granite" that is "something material (*ein Stoffliches*) which has a definite though unadapted form or shape." The block of granite here mentioned is undressed stone whose form is the way its parts are distributed in space without any necessary dependence on human intervention. But Heidegger leaves it at that. Instead of moving forward immediately from his reflections on the relevance of the hylomorphic pattern of analysis to the *Zeug*-product-gear, should he not have demonstrated the inadequacy of that analysis to *Zeug* as stuff, for example a quantity of granite? Otherwise, how can we be sure that the hylomorphic interpretation will not work for a volume of undressed granite, and that this interpretation could not be extended to a utilitarian artifact and even to a work of art? True, the Origin essay is not directly concerned with thingliness in general, but with the thingliness of the (great) work of art. So it might seem legitimate for Heidegger to shelve questions not arising from within the frame of the work of art itself. But how can this manner of proceeding be justified if one of the suggestions, not to say conclusions, that the essay moves toward is that the question of the thingly character of a thing cannot be approached, let alone presented, directly, but must be mediated by the question as to the workly character of the work of art? Might the argument not have taken on a different complexion if more direct attention had been given to the mountain that is not a quarry for rock, the wood that is not a supply of timber, the flowers of the hedgerow, the "springhead in the dale"?

The response that "The Origin of the Work of Art" gives to these questions is prepared in the statement on page 70 of *Being and Time* that nature discloses itself in the use of natural resources but that in this case nature is discovered neither as what is present at hand nor as, for instance — if these can be called instances — the springhead in the dale or the flowers of the hedgerow: the power of nature, nature that stirs and strives and that — translating Heidegger's *webt* literally — weaves.[30] This nature as *Naturmacht* and as *phusis*, appearing, remains hidden. That may begin to explain why the van Gogh painting Heidegger appeals to, in order to bring out what he wants to say in the Origin essay regarding truth in painting, is not one of his landscapes, not, in particular, a painting of the wild Alpilles as distinct from a landscape depicting a plantation of almond trees or an olive grove alongside the road to Arles. This can be no more than the beginning of an explanation, however, if the essay purports to say something about art, or at any rate great art, in general. The explanation must go on to show why the choice of van Gogh's painting of shoes is a natural one for Heidegger to make. It is natural because it is made in the context of his argument, developing the argument of *Being and Time*, that it is a predisposition of our historical epoch to think that thinghood is typified by the utilitarian artifacts that dominate Western culture, and that it is because of this that we are prone to conceive the essence of thinghood in terms of the opposition of matter and form. For us manufactured gear is first in the order of discovery by which we attain what we believe to be a grasp of what it is for something to be a thing. Hence it is understandable that Heidegger should set out from a consideration of shoes in order to bring us around to perceiving that "Matter and form and their distinction have a deeper origin."[31]

A well-known painting of shoes by van Gogh is invoked to invest the createdness of the work with the intuitive concreteness that would be more difficult to achieve by a merely verbal description of shoes. In the Middle Ages it would have been more natural to achieve this intuitive concreteness by looking out through the window toward, say, the limestone cliffs of the

Alpilles or the granite blocks of the Black Forest. For in that epoch the world was not primarily *Umwelt* at the service of man, but Creation, the handiwork of God. Nature itself was an artifact, a one-off masterpiece whose "that it is" and design were due to the more than sufficient reason of the most gifted Maker of all, "the Maker of the world" to whom Dürer refers in the third of his *Four Books of Human Proportion,* the Maker, thanks to whom "art is to be found in nature, and he who can wrest it from her has it." However, after citing this statement, Heidegger goes on to say that this art is found only through the work, which is where art finds itself originally. In saying this Heidegger is not repeating the familiar idea that our thinking of God is thinking by analogy with the human artist and that our notion of the Creator is shaped by our notion of the creator, Dürer, or van Gogh. Heidegger is making a distinction between aspects of human createdness. It would not be incorrect to say that van Gogh created his painting of the shoes, but a piece of equipment too has a creator in this sense. The aspect of createdness Heidegger is alluding to is something that distinguishes the work of art from the piece of equipment. What distinguishes the work of art is that its createdness (its that it is rather than is not) is itself created into the work created, stands out in it, whereas that a piece of equipment has been made is lost sight of in its role, used up in its use. It will be recalled that, according to *Being and Time,* only when the serviceability of gear is suspended, when the gear is out of gear and itself needs servicing or supplementing, as when the hammer (or, we might add, the word) breaks, and as when the shoe (for example, the upturned shoe in Faille 332)[32] wears out, only then do we become aware of the totality to which it belongs. This kind of totality is the totality of a world, but of the everyday world. It is not all there is to worldhood. That this is so is brought out by a painting of gear that is at two removes from use. Van Gogh's painting is of shoes that are not being worn, although perhaps they are not worn out. Although they may still be fit for wearing, they must first be put on and laced up. An actual pair of shoes needing some adjustment in order to be worn could serve as well to bring our attention to their equipmentality and to the nature of the raw material needed to keep them in repair. When they are further detached from daily use by being depicted in a painting, however, we can come to see that both the use of gear and the stuff on whose shape and texture that use relies rely on something that underlies them both, namely, the reliability or fiability concerning which "Restitutions" expresses anxiety.

"Restitutions" also draws attention to the way these abilities and liabilities are interlaced, like the Celtic interlace motif (*plethyn*) that emerges from the author's mouth on the jacket of the Harper edition of the volume containing "The Origin of the Work of Art." No one in the no less recursively interwoven polylogue is, as far as one can gather, especially anxious about these circles. They are not condemned as vicious. The worst that is said of them is that they are "inequalities to itself of the discourse," *inégalités à soi du discours.*[33] But is there anything at all that is equal to itself? When Heidegger, in attempting to explicate the reliability on which the service-ability of shoes relies, has recourse to the family of notions that includes those of the ground and the bedrock under the soles of our shoes, he is turning in a hermeneutic circle, as he would put it, disclosing, as Derrida would prefer to say, that discourse is always unequal to itself. The question at issue between these two writers is whether the hermeneutic circle is one that truly comes back to itself, whether it makes full restitution. At least one of the interlocutors in "Restitutions" questions whether this particular herme-neutic circle is decentered, in the sense that although the plantedness of the shoes on the soil may at first look like a metaphor for a common root or primary etymal point of origin, namely the earth, it cannot be a metaphor since it is already inscribed within the alleged *etymon,* and the *etymon* itself turns out not to be itself, but already tropical. The peripheral is central and the center of the circle is its circumference. Heidegger's apparent meta-phors, and perhaps not only his, are the point of departure for his thinking. "Thinking thinks *on the basis of* them." *La pensée pense* à partir *d'elles.*[34]

To what extent is the questioning that goes on in "Restitutions" a ques-tioning of Heidegger's right to say what he says in "The Origin of the Work of Art"? Although certain "symptomatic contradictions" are unearthed in what Heidegger says by participants in the polylogue, one of the participants takes it upon himself or herself to defend Heidegger against Schapiro.[35] Of course, even if that defense succeeds, Heidegger will not have been shown to be invulnerable to other attacks. As someone in "Restitutions" observes, to judge Schapiro wrong in his attribution of the shoes to a city dweller does not suffice to show that Heidegger is right in attributing them to a peasant. To assume that it does is to be guilty of committing the fallacy of undistributed and unattributed *Mittel.* Someone, perhaps the same one, also says in "Res-titutions" that no one in this discussion is being accused, condemned, or even put under suspicion. However, that comment is made following a refer-ence to the position that, in no uncertain terms, Heidegger is charged with occupying in the two paragraphs that are so embarrassing to the participants in the discussion that none of them wants to cite them, paragraphs that bear witness to Heidegger's subscription to the ideology of the soil and to the principle of reliability that supports it: reliability in general, *Verlässlichkeit überhaupt* and, one might add, in anticipation of what will be said in our next chapter, *unterfuss,* "the first and last condition of the concrete possibility of all reattachment, of the product to its utility, to its use and wear, to the subject wearing or supported by it, to its belonging *in general.*"[36] So the dispute as to whether Heidegger and van Gogh are at home in the city or among the peasants is neither here nor there. As the Origin essay itself makes clear at one point, it is of shoes in general that it treats. When those in the painting by van Gogh are attributed on insufficient grounds to a peasant, this may be a contradiction symptomatic of Heidegger's attachment to the soil and to what in the essay of 1933 entitled "Creative Landscape: Why Do We Stay in the Provinces?" he designates as the *Treue* of the remembrance of the peasant — to whose work he says his own work belongs.[37] But this contradiction is a slip of the pen that could just as well and without contradiction have been a slip of a typewriter or word processor as far as the question of the underlying subsoil in which town and country have their common root is concerned. The question we have to ask now is, granted that there is a superficial *effondrement de terrain* that may lead to an accidental *faux pas* on the *Feldweg*, is there a fault in the supporting stratum beneath — not to say in the substratum or *hypokeimenon*? How solid is that? How much weight will it take before it gives, gives way?

Someone or other in "Restitutions" remarks that it will not do to translate *Verlässlichkeit* by "solidity." Solidity fits in well with the notion of *Ruhe*, rest and supportive repose, but, as "Restitutions" does not fail to note, for Heidegger this *Ruhe* is not simply opposed to movement. It is at the same time a *Be-wegung*. To employ the expression of Hölderlin's that Heidegger reproduces in his essay of 1934–35 on Hölderlin's hymn *Germanien*, it is a *lebendige Ruhe*.[38] This *lebendige Ruhe* is not a neutral suburban compromise between activity and passivity. It is not the medium mesmeric state that can be exhibited in gustatory intuition with the help of Messmer tea on the packet of which we are advised that "Nach 3 minuten Ziehdauer hat der Tee eine belebende, nach 5 Minuten eine beruhigende Wirkung," so that after being allowed to draw for the intermediate time of four minutes the effect of drinking the tea would presumably be neither sedative nor stimulating. Quite different is the *Wirkung* that the work of art exhibits. This is a repose that is "an inner concentration of motion, hence a highest state of agitation."[39] This *innig, widerstrittige Einklang*,[40] neither only rest nor only motion but both, harks back to the *Grundbestimmung* of which Hölderlin says that it is *Innigkeit* and *Harmonischengegensetzung*.[41] This is what in *Being and Time* Heidegger refers to as the power of nature and seven years later calls the power of the earth upon which from time to time man lives poetically "according to his particular historical Da-sein."[42]

Yet once we name earth we must also name world. Although earth is both opening and closing and world is both clearing (*Lichtung*) and concealment (*Verbergung*) as refusal (*Versagen*) or dissemblance (*Verstellen*) there can be no worlding clearing and concealment, no truth, no *a-lētheia*, without earth. Contrariwise, "The earth cannot dispense with the open of the world if it is to appear as earth in the liberated surge of its self-seclusion."[43] The inwardness of this polemic between earth and world is so simple, *einfach,* that one is tempted to say, not merely that when earth is named world must be named too, but that in naming the one the other is thereby named, so that it could be said not only that *Welt weltet* and (though I do not recall Heidegger's saying this) *Erde erdet,* but also *Welt erdet* and *Erde weltet*. The risk run in saying this is one we have already been alerted to, the risk of a pact that brings earth and world together in a (Messmeric) "insipid agreement,"[44] instead of en-suring that the strife remains an *Aus-einander-setzung,* as does the great work of art. In words that suggest that the earth is not only a mother earth[45] but, by conventional classifications, masculine too, and that the world is not without the traditionally assumed female attributes, in words that suggest a plus-or-minus femininity-masculinity, Heidegger writes:

> The world grounds itself on the earth, and the earth juts and towers through (*durchragt*) the world. But the relation between world and earth does not wither away into empty unity of opposites unconcerned with one another. The world, in resting upon the earth, strives to surmount it. As self-opening (*als das Sichöffnende*) it cannot endure anything closed. The earth, however, as sheltering and concealing, tends always to draw the world into itself and keep it there.[46]

The power of art is that of bringing into the open this power of the earth as self-concealing, its power to rise up as self-closing. "To set forth the earth means to bring it into the open as the self-closing (*als das Sichverschlies-sende*)."[47] It is because being can be brought into the open only as the being of what is that we are liable to see only what is. Hence, as we noted in the last chapter, there occurs in the *Grundfragen der Philosophie* (1937–38) the phrase *Dass es ist und das ist, was es ist.*[48] And in the Origin essay Heidegger speaks of the work of art as one of the ways through which we are primed to be struck by the that-it-is of an entity as that entity. The work of art displaces us out of our usual condition of being lost in the what and how of things, therefore to the worldhood of the world. And lost to the thinghood of the thing.

The lecture entitled "The Thing" (1950) seems on first reading to turn inside out the already complex relationship in which world and earth belong to each other. We have only begun to gather how complex that is. For we have not so far mentioned the curious way in which the clearing, *die Lichtung,* which in the Origin essay enables us to see the wood for the trees, is itself both an open center, *eine offene Mitte,* and a circumference that embraces every thing. In the happening of truth

> there is a clearing, a lighting. Thought of in reference to what is, to beings, this clearing is in a greater degree than are beings. This open center is therefore not surrounded by what is; rather, the lighting center itself encir-cles (*umkreist*) all that is, like the nothing which we scarcely know.[49]

Earth is inexhaustible, the *Unerschöpflich* out of which arise the beings in which, thanks to the artist, to the *Schöpfer,* the protecting and concealing presencing of earth is revealed.[50] Thus far the Origin essay is rewriting what in *Being and Time,* "What Is Metaphysics?" (1929), and "On the Essence of Truth" (1930, 1932) Heidegger tries to say in the language of being, be-ings, nothing, world, and truth. The Origin essay continues to employ this abstract language, but much more than the earlier pieces it also draws upon "unphilosophical" words such as are to be found in the poems of Hölderlin. Hölderlin prepares the way for Heidegger by retrieving and rejuvenating the words of Heraclitus that, although still *dichterisch* for Heraclitus, had lost their force in the philosophical tradition into which they were absorbed. Heidegger's recourse to these unphilosophical words is even greater by the time of "The Thing," as is reference to temples, sculptures, poems, paintings, and other works of art (though rarely to music). Heidegger's *Denken* becomes increasingly *dichterisch*, and the Origin essay explains why. That essay already promises a more thorough articulation of what it is to be a thing. When that promise is kept in the essay entitled "The Thing," the unity (*Einheit*) of the world, an important topic in the *Critique of Pure Reason* and a topic Heidegger had already explored in *Being and Time* and *Kant and the Problem of Metaphysics*, is interpreted as the onefold or *Einfalt* made possible by the thing, which is the meeting place of the four regions: earth, sky, mortals, and the godlike messengers of the gods. *Das Ding dingt Welt.* In this foursome each region belongs to the others so intimately, with such *Innigkeit*, that it would appear that we mortals, in listening to the call of the thing, are listening to a call from ourselves: a self-belonging and self-hearing that is a self-affection reminiscent of the hearing of the call of conscience as treated in *Being and Time*. Yet, rather as the call of conscience comes from ourselves and also from above or beyond ourselves, *über uns*,[51] so in the mirror-play of the foursome the call of the thing comes not only from ourselves as belonging to the thing but also from the three other regions and from other mortals who belong there.

How serious is the danger of our being suffocated by the closeness of this belonging, suffocated now not by a too close self-affective belonging to oneself, but by a too intimate other-affected losing of oneself that presents itself in the Origin essay as a *Be-erdigung* and in "The Thing" as a betrothal and entrusting of each region of the fourfold, and therefore of us mortals to the other regions, an entrusting that is anticipated in the *Verlässlichkeit* appealed to in the embarrassing paragraphs felt to be such an ominous threat by one of the anonymous contributors to "Restitutions"? Into how dire a plight are we plunged by this pre-contractually plighted troth, *Treue*, that underlies originary truth?

SAFETY FROM SAFETY

The gravity of our plight can be exaggerated. "Restitutions" refers to a "possibility" that in his description of the shoes in van Gogh's painting Heidegger may have fallen into a trap, and this suggests that the trap can be avoided.

It is noteworthy also that no one in "Restitutions" gets worked up about the other main "illustration" made use of in "The Origin of the Work of

Art," the one that corresponds to the reference to the temple of Artemis in the Heraclitus lectures as the description of the shoes corresponds to the reference to the secular oven in those lectures. Perhaps Heidegger would have agreed that it could be said of the shoes what Heraclitus says of the bakehouse: that the gods are also there.[52] But if the gods are there in the way that they are there in the temple, the "security" or *Geborgenheit* of the peasant woman's world is security of a not entirely restful kind. For even if the god has not forsaken the temple, we cannot be complacent about his being there, *da*. In being there in the temple or the sculpture he runs a lively risk of being deposed, of being *fort*. But whatever Heidegger may have believed about the secure world of the peasant, with the temple it is as it is in the tragedy, where the battle between the old and the new gods is being fought, the battle that "puts up for decision what is holy and unholy, what great and what small, what brave and what cowardly, what noble and what ephemeral, what master and what slave."[53] A few pages after these words in "The Origin of the Work of Art" a decision is said to be based on something that we do not have securely in hand, something hidden and confusing. The repose of gear such as shoes,[54] which may ensure a kind of security in the world of the peasant woman despite her uncertainty as to when and where she will get her next loaf of bread, is disturbed once the shoes are shoes in a painting. Any repose there may be in the painting cannot be that of naive fiability. It can be the repose only of judgment in suspense while the battle rages. The work of art is the safeguard against safety. However closely the regions of the foursome belong to each other, the gods and goddesses, who cannot be compared with beings that are fully present,[55] are never more than *vorbeigehend*, passers-by. "Passing by is the mode of the presencing of the gods, the fleetingness of a scarcely perceptible wave of the hand that in the moment of passing can portend every blessing and every terror"[56] (such terror as reigned in the region of other ovens at which God was a passer-by). The regions (*Gegenden*) of the foursome are very toward (*gegen*). The glimpses of the gods vouchsafed through the work of art are not premonitions of safe haven. The proper time (*kairōs*) is a time of *wirkliches Nachfragen*,[57] a time for decision, a time of loose ends (*kairos*), thrums, which Webster's dictionary defines as the fringe of warp threads left on the loom after the cloth has been removed. This time of cutting off is a time of grief and mourning, *Trauerspiel*. So it is a time of irreligion, not of religion, if by religion is understood unquestioning reliance, *das bloss nachhängende Nachsinnen*,[58] such as one might think one detected in Heidegger's description of the life of the peasant, a life where, it would seem, *Gott erst Gott* is dead.

The *Wirkliches Nachfragen*, the questioning work of the work of art, may well bring to light the *lebendige Ruhe* of the war among the gods that gets hidden under the everyday wearing of laced-up shoes. But when the *dichtende Denker* permits himself to use a painting of unlaced shoes or a description of a sacred place, the work of art becomes an instrument, and the living word, the *wesentliche Wort*,[59] is exposed to the danger of which Heidegger was the last person to be ignorant, the danger of incorporation into propositions in order, *meine Damen und Herren*, to communicate a point. Then, fortunately, accidents may happen. Something may go awry. A symptomatic contradiction may prevent the example that the work of art has become from fulfilling the purpose for which it is employed. We may find Heidegger saying that although the sculptor does not, except when the work miscarries, use up the stone in creating the figure that is to be housed in the temple, the mason does, in spite of the fact that the mason is making the house of god that stands as one of the examples of a work of art that Heidegger uses in the essay on the origin of such a work. Or, when Heidegger asks us to recall the other chief exhibit to which that essay refers, we may find, as does at least one unnamed speaker in "Restitutions," that a possible accident becomes actual. Such accidents will happen. They are an occupational hazard when *dichtendes Denken* becomes professorial — in order to point with a long stick at examples, cases, and illustrations.

Is there a possibility of finding rescue from this danger by retracing our steps to the Chemin des Lauves and the *gedachtes Dichten* that is not about Cézanne, not about his gardener Vallier, nor about Vallier's muddy shoes?

> Das nachdenksam Gelassene, das inständig
> Stille der Gestalt des alten Gärtners
> Vallier, der Unscheinbares pflegte am
> chemin des Lauves.
>
> Im Spätwerk des Malers ist die Zwiefalt
> von Anwesendem und Anwesenheit einfältig
> geworden, "realisiert" und verwunden zugleich,
> verwandelt in eine geheimnisvolle Identität.
>
> Zeigt sich hier ein Pfad, der in ein Zusam-
> mengehören des Dichtens und Denkens
> führt?[60]

Notice, ladies and gentlemen, how in the last strophe the word for "belonging-together" belongs and does not belong to itself, being broken by a hyphen where one would expect it least, and at the interval between one line and the next, as if to commemorate the nearness to and the farness from each other of the *Dichter* and the *Denker* who, as Hölderlin says in *Patmos* and as Heidegger-Hölderlin says in the postcript to "What Is Metaphysics?":

> Nah wohnen, ermattend auf
> Getrenntesten Bergen.

6

A FOOTNOTE IN THE HISTORY OF *PHUSIS*

BETWEEN A ROCK AND A HARD PLACE

Is nature a part of the environment, our surroundings, or is the environment a part of nature? Is neither a part of the other? The environment, the surroundings in which human beings live, contains things that human beings have made or made different. But things that human beings have made or altered are made from or are alterations of raw material. When the adjective "natural" and the definite description "the natural" are used with senses directly cognate with the noun "nature" or "Nature," and not as directly cognate with "the nature" in the sense of "the essence," they are being used with the sense of the raw, as opposed to the processed. What is natural is literally or metaphorically uncooked. It is metaphorically, if not literally, "untouched by human hand." We would say without hesitation that we are surrounded by natural things, for instance animals, trees, and stones, as well as by artifacts, for instance zoos, tables, and walls. In the evaluative sense of the word "natural," with which we shall be only secondarily concerned in this chapter, we would find it natural to say that the natural and the artificial are part of our environment (though we might not find it as natural to say plurally that they are *parts* of it). The realm of nature includes things that are part of our surroundings. Among these natural things, things "untouched by human hand," are our own hands. But my own hands are not normally things that form part of my surroundings. Nor, normally, is my body. Nor is that nature or Nature of which my hands and my body as a whole form a part. Neither my body nor part of my body nor the nature of which they form part is touched or touchable by my hand in the sense in which nature touches me, my body, my hand — or my foot.

Take a human artifact, for example a spade or a garden fork. The shapes of these tools correspond to the different textures of the material that is to be worked on. Heavy clayey soil is handled best by a spade with a point, stony soil by a fork. A fork will be useless for shifting dry sand. For that task a sided shovel copes best. But there are ways of coping with raw material that are more "hands-on" than are digging and shoveling, as when with our bare hands we shove a stone from where we find it lying to a new position in which it is to become the foundation stone of a temple or an altar. The stone itself becomes part of an altar without being altered. It has not been hewn or otherwise changed in shape. No one has contravened the precept "And if thou wilt make me an altar of stone, thou shalt not build it of hewn stone: for if thou lift up thy tool upon it, thou hast polluted it" (Exodus 20:25). In that sense it "has not been touched." It has been touched only in the sense that it has been handled. And, although it has not thereby undergone any change in its qualities, its position has been changed. Although it has not been worked, it has now become part of a human work. But it could be put back where it was originally found and nobody other than the person who moved it need know it has been moved. However, it will have been moved. This fact is not enough to entitle us to say that the stone, now back where it was found, is an artifact. It was not that even when it was part of an artifact, part of the altar. For us to be entitled to say that it is part of an artifact it will have to be put back in the altar or made part of something else we have built or formed, *gebildet*.

Suppose that, without any other stones being moved, the stone is adopted as a high altar (etymologically speaking, all altars are high, *altus*). It is now *used as* an altar. But *is* it an altar? Well, it is now a *natural* altar. Here high human culture seems to be closer to nature even than basic agriculture that makes use of the spade. For it is as if, without what is found at hand having to be changed, it is handy for founding an altar. It is as though there is a pre-established harmony between the way the world is disposed and a practice of human culture or cult. Indeed, speaking again etymologically of the altar and cult, there may be a pre-established harmony between the altar table's height and the lowliness of the stone on which it is established. Unless the Brothers Grimm are telling a fairy story lacking historical foundation, there is in the very word *Boden*, through its connection with *Bodem*, a hidden connection with the connection between the Latin *fundus* from *fundare*, to found, and *fundus* from *fundere,* to pour, as when the priest officiates at the altar in offering libation. The Septuagint uses the words *basis tou thusiasteriou.* The Grimm dictionary notes that a common ground of the concepts of founding and libation is the notion of the bottom of a bottle or vat. Other philologists observe that this notion is part of the history of the word "body." The antecedent of this word was lost when its work was divided between *Leib* (cognate with *Leben,* "life") and *Körper.* English was fortunate to retain a word incorporating the ambiguity between these two senses, the animate body and the inanimate body, the stone and the corpse, an ambiguity celebrated at altars and other tables.

Although one may say, as has been said, that it is as if there is a pre-established harmony between the way the world is disposed and a practice of human culture or cult when a stone is naturally suited to serve as a step or as an altar, such a match is local and dependent upon the choice that human beings have made of a site. But their choice of it is in part a response to the lay of the land. The topography lends itself to their practice. Where the match is not at first complete, practice may have to bend to the topography. If the stone is adopted as an altar, one's practice may have to be adapted to it. The consequence of not changing the former may be that a change in the latter must be made. Because we have not moved it, we have to move our-selves in a different direction. For instance, instead of approaching the altar at right angles as was customary, one may have to be allowed to approach it obliquely. The extent to which one has to adapt one's behavior may be more than can be accommodated by some practices. One can imagine a practice in which the altar must lie exactly on an axis such that in approaching it one is facing toward Jerusalem, Mecca, or the point at which the sun rises at the winter solstice. Or the natural lay of the slab and its weight may oblige us to seek an alternative location. But whether we adapt our practice to accom-modate what we find at hand, to hew the slab into a different shape, to change its position, or to change our position and seek a suitable slab else-where, nature provides. Nature provides, whether or not it is the ultimate provider, whether or not it provides only thanks to the Providence of God. Nature provides in its own good time, its failure to do so at one moment of history being remedied at another time out of its own resources, rather as God's wrath is made good by his mercy, and as in the name Hari-hara names of the jealous god Siva and of the saving god Vishnu are combined.

THE OUTCAST

Phenomenology suspends metaphysico-theological questions such as those just raised. It is therefore not able to take sides on the questions of whether nature is God or God is nature, whether we are entitled to speak with Spinoza of *Deus sive Natura,* and whether *Natura* in this non-exclusive alternation is to be understood as *Natura Naturans* or *Natura Naturata*. Nevertheless, we find that what Merleau-Ponty says about nature from the phenomenological standpoint is what some would say about God, and that the natural and the supernatural are in some important respects phenomenologically one. For, reporting and/or following Husserl (it is not always clear which), Merleau-Ponty describes nature as *the primordial condition and support of human life.*

Non-constructed, non-instituted, nature, Merleau-Ponty writes,[1] may be for us an object, but it is never only over against us. Rather is it beneath our feet, the bedrock or the soil on which we stand, hence "concealed. Like stone."[2] It is like stone unworked by human hand, a slab that may be used by human beings as an altar. However, to say that the stone is in its natural state is to say that its visibility and tangibility are supplemented by an invisibility and an intangibility. The natural object is enigmatically more than its perceivable qualities. It is these plus something hidden, for at least some of its perceptible qualities do not befall the natural thing from outside. They are not matters of accident, but emerge from within.

Just as in phenomenological description the Spinozan metaphysics of God as Nature is suspended, suspended too, because all metaphysics is suspended, is the Leibnizian metaphysics according to which the phenomenal qualities of a thing are logical entailments of its interior essence. Although the opposition of nature to culture and that of the natural to the artificial retain a connection with the opposition of essence to accident, the task that Husserl and Merleau-Ponty and Heidegger take up is that of describing all these notions without making assumptions or claims about metaphysical or empirical fact. The aim of phenomenology is not metaphysical truths, causal explanations, or empirical descriptions. It is concerned with meaning, and not merely the meaning of words.

Merleau-Ponty is readier to appeal to empirical evidence than is Husserl. Is he relaxing the phenomenological attitude when, like Heidegger, he comments on the meanings of *phuō* and *natura*? Rather than being phenomenological descriptions, do these comments not fall within the field of empirical lexicography? Not if, despite being as unreliable on such occasions as some of those that will be cited below, the lexicographical can be a guide to the phenomenological, and if what he seeks with the help of the lexicon is access to the primordial phenomenological meanings beyond the lexical significations of these terms, as Heidegger does. Heidegger wants not to be bound by lexicography. Indeed, he comes to want not to be bound either by a narrow conception of phenomenology, for example a conception centered on consciousness. To give priority to consciousness is to concentrate on only one epoch in the history of being. When he takes up the task of exposing the history of being in its many variations, he is exposing the history of language, since language is "the house of being." A historical dimension accrues to phenomenological ontology, if we may continue to employ this latter phrase. But this historicality is primarily *Geschichtlichkeit.*

So Husserl and Heidegger agree that any history of language and linguistic meaning that is a chronicle of an objective etymological succession, *Historie,* has to be "understood back" (*rückverstanden*) to inhabited tradition if meaning is not to be truncated. It is because Merleau-Ponty in turn agrees with them on this that he agrees with Lachelier that "The words of a language are not tokens and have a *phusis* of their own," adding that where there is life there is meaning, even if there is not necessarily thinking.

Is this assimilation to life of nature, which has already been assimilated by Merleau-Ponty to Roman *natura* and through that to Greek *phusis,* the reason why the inorganic — despite the above demonstration that a stone may be literally and phenomenologically the bedrock, the *harte Fels,* of a human practice — tends to get treated only cursorily by him, as cursorily as by Husserl, and as cursorily as in *The Fundamental Concepts of Metaphysics* Heidegger treats the rock and the plant? In his *Notes de cours* Merleau-Ponty writes that "History [is] to be understood not as acts, but as an institution that produces and re-produces itself, to be conceived in the sense of *phusis* (that *phusis,* which, the Greeks thought, comprised men, gods, and not only animals and plants)."[3] But not rocks and stones? Do the Greeks admit these lowly things into *phusis* only by surreptitiously promoting them to a higher rank in the chain of being by calling prime matter *hule,* wood? Or are they admitted only when the stones are Deucalion's and Pyrrha's, stones turned into human beings? Do stones have to become human beings before they can become subject matter for phenomenology? Or, for *phusis* to comprise stones, do we at least have to be able to ask sensibly what it would be like to be a pile of stones? And must it not be sensible for us to ask this if a pile of stones or something very like it — a handful of dust, ash, earth — is what all of us are destined by nature to become? What all of us already are, according to the tombstone exhortation

> O earth, O earth
> Think of this well
> That earth in earth
> Must come to dwell . . .

It is not directly and simply of this clayey or stony earth that Husserl and Merleau-Ponty are speaking when they write of the earth (*Erde*) or ground (*Boden*) that we take with us when we travel on the surface of this planet or in a spaceship to another planet, or anywhere in our imagination. Yet one may ask in passing whether the phenomenological earth of which they write accompanies the traveler who takes off for the destination imagined when the epitaph goes on to predict

> And earth in earth
> Must there remain
> Till earth from earth
> Shall raise again.

The phenomenological earth of which Husserl and Merleau-Ponty write is the phenomenologically Ptolemaic world that neither moves —*Eppur* non *si muove*—nor remains still in the way that things within my world do.[4] It is the ultimate condition of such movement and rest. If it be said that it moves with me or that it remains at rest, it must be said also that it moves and is at rest at the same time, in the sense that its movement-rest is the absolute condition of the temporality of my world, its ultimate support. That is to say, according to Merleau-Ponty, it is Nature, *Natura* or *phusis*.

And, according to the note of his referred to above, nature means history, though "History to be understood not as acts, but as an institution that produces and re-produces itself, to be conceived in the sense of *phusis* (that *phusis*, which, the Greeks thought, comprised men, gods, and not only animals and plants)." The Greeks referred to here cannot not include Aristotle. His *Physics* states that living beings are those beings whose principle of motion and change is contained within themselves. Non-living beings derive their motion from something else. This holds even for what he considers to be the natural motion of a thing, for instance the downward motion of an earthy thing, like a stone. If a stone is caused to move upward, its motion is, in a factual and secondarily evaluative sense of the term, unnatural (*Physics* 254). That is not its normal behavior, even though its abnormal upward motion can be explained by natural laws. So, even if there are no besouled things lower than vegetables, an *inanimate* earthy thing can behave unnaturally without this meaning that it does not belong to nature. Even an animal, something that unquestionably does belong to nature, can also behave (*sich benehmen*) unnaturally—though it may not be able to comport itself (*sich verhalten*) thus or in any other way,[5] for example when the material of which one of its limbs is composed is made so light by disease altering the degree of heat and cold that it moves up instead of down, as it would naturally do. Faced with the challenge insectivorous plants pose for the thesis that the classical chain of being is in synchrony with the food chain, a stickler for simple hierarchies might say that such a plant is behaving unnaturally. For it is as though here a vegetable, which ought to be pedophage, dependent on the earth for its nourishment, or, at worst, a vegetarian cannibal, consuming its own kind, is trying to move up in the world, to rise beyond its station in the natural order of things.

But what of the idea that the realm of nature is the realm of things born, *res nata*? Are we to say that earth, air, fire, and water, Aristotle's four elements, are born? Is a stone or the minerals of which it is composed? Lalande's *Vocabulaire technique et critique de la philosophie* comments upon this etymology, noting that also the terms "foetus" and "fecund," not to mention *felix*, are associated with *phuō* and *phuton*, that is to say, with the plants on which Aristotle, unlike Heidegger, wrote a treatise. The notion shared by these expressions is that of "spontaneous development of living beings according to a determinate type." Lalande reports failure to find examples of this fundamental notion in Greek texts. He notes that Bailly's *Dictionnaire grecque* has an entry "*Phusis galaktos,* the formation of milk in the breasts; Aristotle, *De generatione animalium,* II, 2." On two counts Lalande denies that this is an example of the alleged fundamental notion. "First, Aristotle's chapter is not about milk but about semen. Second, his phrase *tou spermatos phusis,* the nature of semen, which occurs twice there (at 735a29 and 736a19), designates the physical and chemical constitution of semen" (*désigne la constitution physique et chimique du sperme*).[6] Here and in other places he mentions, the word *phusis* refers, he maintains, to the body's being constituted by one or other of the elements: water, earth, and so on. Although to describe this constitution as chemical and *physical* is question-begging if it assumes that chemistry can be reduced to physics, it is clear that what Lalande is saying is that the Greeks used the word *phusis* in a way that allows it to cover not only what we now would call the physical as opposed to what we would call the biological, but to cover also this latter. This wide coverage is claimed also by Heidegger, when in the *Introduction to Metaphysics* he writes that "*phusis* originally encompassed heaven as well as earth, the stone as well as the plant, the animal as well as man, and it encompassed human history as a work of men and gods; and ultimately and first of all, it meant the gods themselves as subordinated to destiny."[7] What did it not cover? Among the Greeks its range later narrowed so that it became opposed first to *ethos,* human culture and rule-governed social practice, then to *technē,* the knowledge that makes possible production of institutions and artifacts. Now these two areas, which the Greeks came to contrast with *phusis,* are retained within its scope in the above-cited statement by Merleau-Ponty. Even human history is retained within its scope, as it was for the early Greeks. But not the stone. The stone is cast outside

ANIMATION

The stone is still an outcast when Husserl writes "the biophysical . . . , but also the biopsychical," adding in a footnote: "But also the purely psychic, unalloyed 'monadic,' here not understood transcendentally."[8] The passage in which these words occur is one in which the contexts of the human and the animal are being compared, ultimately the context of the organic in general. The inorganic goes unmentioned here by Husserl and in the sentence cited from Merleau-Ponty because their researches begin with the topic of life, and branch out from that. So their discussions of the world of everyday human life, the *Lebenswelt,* lead them to make comparisons with the life of other animated beings, and they frequently refer both to human beings and to beasts as animalia. Heidegger's descriptions are aimed at calling into question this Aristotelian tradition for which man belongs to the genus animal and is differentiated from other animals by rationality. Hence, for Husserl, for Merleau-Ponty the psychologist of *The Structure of Behaviour,* and for Merleau-Ponty the Husserlian phenomenologist of *The Phenomenology of Perception,* as distinguished from the more Heideggerian Merleau-Ponty of parts of *The Visible and the Invisible* and from the more Heideggerian Husserl of some of the Husserliana that postdate *Being and Time,* a key notion is *psychē* understood as life or the soul as the seat of life, whether as sentient *anima,* or as *animus,* that is, as consciousness, mind, or spirit. Although Heidegger sometimes uses or ambiguously mentions-uses the terms "mind" or "spirit," *Geist,*[9] he generally prefers to steer clear of these terms. He prefers to steer clear also of the term "man," favoring instead the term *Da-sein,* and stressing that the bedrock of Da-sein is the complex being-in-the-world. Taking this complex as fundamental, that is to say as unanalyzable into independent elements, Heidegger stands more chance of avoiding the problems that threaten Husserl when, not content with describing concrete ways of conducting oneself in the world in which we live our daily lives, he has recourse to the classical terminology in such places as §62 of *Ideas II.* As many problems are posed as are elucidated by Husserl's analysis in this section. They arise in part from his conducting that analysis in a nominal syntax, not in the verbal and adverbial syntax adopted in Heidegger's concrete descriptions of being-in-the-world or worlding, where, even when *Da-sein* is used to refer to an individual, it is Da-sein's ways of being (*Seinsweisen*) that are being described. Our view of these problems will turn on what we make of the fact that the midpoint of Husserl's otherwise nominalist analysis is the conjunction "and."[10]

Despite warnings Husserl gives in other places that his talk of levels and hierarchies should be taken as only a pedagogical device, and despite his insistence that he is not doing metaphysics, classical metaphysical puzzles are posed by his placing at the core of his account a conjunction of body and soul, *Leib und Seele.* Husserl's "and" inherits the dilemmas posed by the task his hero Descartes expects to be performed by the pineal gland. They are, as it were, a postultimate residuum of what he refers to as "the last residuum of the Cartesian theory of two substances."[11] These arise notwithstanding that the body Husserl conjoins with the soul at the center of his scheme is the *Leib,* the body as lived subject, not, as in Cartesian dualism, the *Körper,* the body as object, the object of physical science. Now the "and" could in theory stand for an identity of lived body and soul, but that is not how Husserl intends it. The hyphen of the phrase "psycho-physical," a phrase to which he has frequent recourse, may suggest a more dynamic relationship between conjunction and identity, a relationship that would be neither simple unity nor simple duality. This could lead us to read Husserl's "and" in the manner of Merleau-Ponty, as the sign of an irreducibly ambiguous *corps propre* or flesh (or an irreducibly metaxic, betwixt, chiasmic, gl-and-ular, and hypocritical imagination).[12] It is in this direction that we are pointed by

Husserl's own statement that the lived body and the soul are two-sided or double or Janus realities or poles, each of them having two aspects or faces. The two faces of the lived body are, first, the body in its aesthesiological aspect as "dependent on" the material body as appearance and part of the personal surrounding world or environment (*Umwelt*), and, second, the body as subject to being moved by the will. As for the soul, in one respect it is conditioned by the lived material body, and in the other respect it is conditioned by *Geist*, spirit or mind.

In what he says about both sides Husserl uses the language of conditioning and dependence. But the dependencies so far noted hold within the sphere of the lived body and the soul. He goes on to place these dependencies of body and soul between what can be called pure spirit and purely physical nature. Purely physical nature is nature in what he calls the first sense, nature in relation to which body and soul are "nature in the second sense," though, he adds, "properly speaking only according to the side turned toward physical nature." So, to return to Merleau-Ponty's statement that nature is what we are ultimately supported by, this description fits both physical nature and "nature in its second sense," the lived body and soul, but it holds for each of these in different senses. Body and soul are ultimately supported *causally* by physical nature — and indeed in that relation are themselves regarded as objectively physical realities. But physical reality is *phenomenologically* dependent on or supported by nature in its second sense, the lived body and soul (or the lived-body-and-soul).

At the limit in the opposite direction (unless God *is* Nature) Husserl provides for a parallel duplicity of ultimate reliance, phenomenological and causal, though here causality would be that of God's will in relation to the lived body and soul. In this direction the *corps propre* faces a limit that, following Merleau-Ponty's description of nature, we might call a supernatural nature or *natura sepernaturans* — or, with Kant, the intelligible kingdom of ends, or, with Levinas, illeity, nature denaturalized. Husserl seems to license us to say that the purely spiritual would be a secondary surrounding world or environment, a *sekundäre Umwelt*, though he uses this phrase to describe only the physical world. The latter is secondary in relation to the phenomenological primacy of the environment as appearing to and inhabited by the body and soul (or the body-and-soul — or the person). The phenomenologically secondary but causally primary physical environment will contain rocks and stones. Not, however, rocks and stones appearing as parts of a wall or an altar. Nor rocks and stones as the "rocks and stones and trees" sung by the poet, with which we are "rolled round in earth's diurnal course."[13] Rather, rocks and stones as the embodiments of whatever concepts a particular science favors at a particular stage of its history: sub-atomic particles, waves, earth, air, fire, water — in which case reality at the physical end of the chain of dependency could be dust or ash or mud. Opposite (assuming still that there is opposition here) the *limes* of nature as supernature of the spirit and the sublime, the *limes* of physical nature may be *limus,* primordial primeval slime. If this is *Natura naturata,* it is nonetheless the origin of life.

Of course, what is ultimate for one science will not be ultimate for another. But when one science, say physics, sees itself as more fundamental than another, in forming its explanatory terms it will depend either on the language of the discourses of the sciences it claims to found or, although it may translate them into Greek, on the untechnical homely terms of everyday speech. So in "particle" physics or "wave" mechanics these qualifying terms have a metaphorical sense. Causally ultimate first nature may be lexically dependent upon the less fundamental sciences from which terms are transferred and, ultimately, upon "nature in the second sense," the second nature of the world in which we live our diurnal lives. It has already been noted that causally ultimate nature is dependent upon and supported by the phenomenologically ultimate nature that Husserl and Merleau-Ponty call "earth" and "ground" or "floor" (*Boden*). Is this phenomenologically ultimate Earth a metaphorical earth? Yes and no. Lexically yes, but phenomenologically or phenomeno-ontologically no. The word "earth" is transferred to it from its cosmological, mineralogical, or hortological contexts, but the Earth to which the word is transferred is itself the condition of all transfer, so of semantic transfer, no less than, as explained earlier, of transfer in geographical or extra-terrestrial space.

While granting that the two words "world" and "earth" sometimes coincide, Kant uses the former for the sum total of appearances regarded as the topic of mathematics. This totality is called "nature" when it is regarded as the dynamic whole of appearances for the changes in which physics seeks the causes (*Critique of Pure Reason* B446). Nature is a "self-subsistent whole" (*bestehendes Ganzes*). Although Husserl sometimes prefers to say that the world of nature studied by mathematical physics is objectified rather than abstracted, he observes that, since this world is an abstract from the world we inhabit in our daily lives, it cannot be self-subsistent. It follows that he would have to deny self-subsistence also to what we have called supernature, pure spiritual nature, *actus purus,* God. It or He, the Father, or She (*sive* Mother Nature?) is phenomenologically dependent on Man or Woman or Da-sein. Here is a phenomenological parallel to the Kabbalistic teaching that God has need of the human being and contracts his own power in order to leave room for that need to be met, a contraction of power that only seems to be inconsistent with the divine nature if we overlook the possibility that power may not be the only thing God needs. One of God's strengths may be God's "weakness," God's need to love, his-*sive*-her-*sive*-its need to be needed. And God's need of the human being is not inconsistent with the human being's need of God as that on which the human being ultimately relies. Nor does it mean that the human being ultimately relies on itself. The reliance is not self-reliance. Further, this interrelationship is not one of mutuality, since the need in one direction is phenomenological, whereas in the other the need is spiritual or religious, a call for help, grace, or salvation. We call upon the non-subsistent so that we may be subsistent. Our need is a need for sustenance, very much like a need for food. And when we eat God, we experience the need to render grace. Whether at the altar table, at the communion table, or at the table in our homes where we eat the daily bread baked in the oven in the environs of which, Heraclitus says, the gods are even present, we are nourished and nurtured by nature in one form or another, by what we ultimately rely on. And, in the food chain, that means the rock and the stone or the minerals of which these inorganic things or stuffs are composed. Man may not live by bread alone, but without bread he will not live to enjoy for long whatever else he may deem to be something or someone without which or without whom he cannot live.

So he breaks oven-baked bread and puts it in his mouth, or someone does it for him. Someone handles it. It touches my lips and my tongue. I swallow it. Unless I take it out of my mouth to give to another, handle it again in a gesture of gift, whether or not this be also a transaction of *Handel,* trade, economic exchange, or householding. Not even the Presence, *parousia,* or appearance of God in the environs of an altar is vouchsafed without work of the hand, without the cooperation of surgical liturgy.

METAPHYSICS

Appearance and operation. If we restrict our readings of Husserl to those pages — pages in the *Crisis,* for instance — where he is preoccupied with the problem of the relation between the primary mathematical qualities of the invisible Galilean world and the so-called secondary qualities of the world in which we live, we may draw the conclusion that he is a transcendental idealist and an empirical realist, despite the differences that distinguish his methodology from the philosophical methodology of Kant. We cannot draw this conclusion once we attend to those pages where the intentionality of the notions of appearance brought in with the terminology of idea and idealism is shown to be inseparable from the operative intentionality of our handling of the materials and products of that world. And given the priority of readiness to hand over presence at hand in Heidegger's descriptions of the world of everyday life, it is only with reference to the dependent zone of at-handness that we can say that he is a transcendental idealist and an empirical realist.[14] Provided that that restriction is imposed, the Kantian analogy is not entirely without justification as a paraphrase of Heidegger's joint assertion that "World is only, if, and as long as a Da-sein exists" and, in the next breath, "Nature can also be where no Da-sein exists."[15] Nature understood as the realm of enduring objects that move according to Newton's laws is causally independent of Da-sein. It is not a contradiction in terms to say that we think of Nature treated by mathematical physics and kinematics as independent of thinking. It is part of what Newton and Galileo mean by Nature that it is a realm of substantive objects in themselves independent of people or Da-sein. However, their independence is not independent of Da-sein, or of the world understood in the sense of Da-sein's being-in-the-world. To understand independence or indeed anything else is to be a Da-sein whose being is worldish. Still, because Heidegger is speaking of Da-sein and being, including the being of objects in Nature, we are in danger of missing the point of the fundamental ontology he claims to be expounding if we attempt to formulate it in terms of idealism and empirical realism. Readiness to hand is more fundamental than presence at hand in our everyday world. But it is not clear what could be meant by the question whether an empirical realist, a transcendental realist, a subjective idealist, or a transcendental idealist account should be given of what is ready to hand.

READINESS TO FOOT

Other than readiness to hand and presence at hand is a category or quasi-category that has less to do with the hand than it has to do with the foot. To be able to handle things or to have them at hand, we must have a foothold. When a climber reaches out for a handhold it is as well that at least one of his feet be planted relatively firmly. All handling and surveying have a plantigrade pre-sup-position or pre-sub-position. This peduncularity is metaphorical. It is metaphorical in that it is the condition of our moving ourselves from one place to another or moving a limb. It is metaphorical also in that the foot's function of providing a foothold may be transferred to another part of the body. Somewhat as the face in the way it is spoken of by Levinas may be an arm or the nape of the neck, so our peduncularity, in the sense intended here, may manifest itself in sessility. Our base in the world may be a seat. It will be what supports the hand when the hand holds firm in order to allow a foot to find a new position. Then, when the foot is feeling around for a safe place, the foot is feeling for something that is ready to hand in Heidegger's sense, though what is being felt for in this pedipulation is something that is, speaking literally, ready to foot, a *Fussboden*. This interchangeability illustrates the thought that things are handy for us not because we have hands, just as we see things not because we have eyes, but because we have vision.[16]

Both hands and both feet may be peduncular when the climber is taking a rest, splayed out like "the lizard basking in the sun on its warm stone."[17] The climber is stretched, but not stretching his biceps (*lacertus*) to take himself higher up the rock or higher up the great chain of being. The climber is now totally taken up by the rock, *benommen,* be-had by it for a space of time rather than be-having, held rather than holding, halted, *unterhalten,* rather than *verhaltend.* Momentarily without movement, not going anywhere yet, yet the climber is all feet and all earth. Omnipedunculate and omnipodunculate, because the step from Greek *pod* to Latin *ped*, both standing for the foot, brings with it a reminder of the Greek *ped*, meaning earth. The climber now is all earth because, like the work of Galilean science according to Heidegger, she is disworlded, *entweltlicht*,[18] a state that implies a previous state of *Weltlichung.* But the climber sprawled on the rock is at the same time unlike the work of Galilean science, because, like the work of art according to Heidegger, she is not *enterdet*, not deprived of earth. The *Be-erdigung*, earthing, of the climber's body is an *Entweltung*, a deprivation of world not to be confused with the worldlessness (*Weltlosigkeit*) Heidegger attributes to the rock. Nor is it to be confused with the poorness in world (*Weltarmigkeit*) he attributes to the lizard. Therefore it is a deprivation of both *Zuhandenheit* and *Vorhandenheit*. The climber is entirely captive to *Zufussenheit*, the premiss that both of these presuppose.

This premiss about a hidden premiss does not get passed over in *Being and Time*, but Heidegger does pass on from it without eliciting its implications. He does not bring out all its implications. In §15 of *Being and Time* he draws the reader's attention to "Nature," in quotation marks. As much could be said about these quotation marks, perhaps in a book entitled *Of Nature*, as Derrida says in a book entitled *Of Spirit* about the quotation marks with which Heidegger protects the word *Geist* and himself. It must suffice to record here that "Nature" stands for such raw material as is not ultimately dependent upon Da-sein for its production, such material as ore taken from a mine, rock taken from a quarry, or leather taken from an animal, for instance the leather of which a climbing boot or a shoe is produced and upon which that shoe depends, as does its wearer, who may be a peasant woman like the one of whom Heidegger speaks in connection with one of van Gogh's paintings of shoes. So the leather is ready to hand in the way of raw material, rather than in the way of the shoe. It is ready to hand at one remove. If we abstract from that readiness to hand it does not necessarily become present at hand, the modality it has for a natural scientist, for whom it is a source of theoretical knowledge. Nor is it part of Nature as source of awe and poetry. It is part of Nature as resource co-discovered by the wearing of the shoe, *mitentdeckt durch*—and, it may be added, co-thought, *mitgedacht* through the treble meaning of *Zeug*: *Zeug* signifying stuff or raw material; *Zeug* signifying particular products like tools, things that have been *erzeugt*, produced; and *Zeug* standing for the latter collectively. Here Nature is *Umwelt* or *Umweltnatur* where the *Um* indicates not only our surroundings, our environment, but Nature as *for* Da-sein's use, whether or not Nature be thought also as created for Da-sein's use by a Designer.

What has just been described as readiness to hand at one remove comes under what has been referred to earlier as readiness to foot. It covers what we ultimately rely on, what, to revert to Merleau-Ponty's phrase, ultimately supports us. However, without being ready to hand, what we ultimately rely on may be as close to us as what is immediately ready to hand, as close as the rock underfoot, whether or not the foot is shod. And this *Zufussenheit* corresponds to a certain existential or quasi-existential tonality that gets mentioned in *Being and Time,* but without Heidegger's noticing the correspondence. Twice in this book Heidegger mentions joy, *Freude.* It is mentioned once along with other affects, hope, enthusiasm, and gaiety, where hope is given much more attention, in particular in relation to the achievement of a future good, but in order to show also that this futurality goes along with the idea that the person who hopes is hoping for something for himself. By this Heidegger must be understood to mean not that one doesn't ever hope for a good for someone else, but that hoping presupposes that the hopeful person is taking himself along with the hope, and that that presupposes his having previously in some sense and degree taken possession of himself.[19] Joy is also mentioned in relation to *Angst,* but again the future is stressed, namely as the "unshakable joy," *gerüstete Freude,* in the possibility of the individualized potentiality for being we are brought before by sober *Angst.*[20]

In the first-mentioned of these two contexts, *Being and Time* treats joy alongside fear, which is not, according to Heidegger, a fundamental mode of attunement. In the second context, as has just been observed, joy is paired with *Angst.* Therefore, since *Angst* is a fundamental tonality, one might infer that so too is joy. Whether this is so or not, joy merits more attention than it receives in *Being and Time.* In giving it a little more attention here, emphasis will be put not only upon the way in which any reference it may make to the future goes along with a reference to the past, as with hope, but also upon the way in which the references to the past and the future are founded upon a reference to the present.

The word *gerüstete,* used to qualify joy, is rendered in both published translations of *Being and Time* by "unshakable." A more accurate translation would be "prepared" or "fore-armed." These translations preserve the reference to the future and past. They suit Heidegger's existential analysis. But perhaps they do not give the present its due. This is done if his word is understood following the hint of a connection with *Rüste,* roost or rest, to mark that in her state and place of rest, her *Ruhestatt,* the climber is enjoying life to the full, enjoying just being here, *da-seiend* in the lower case. Her attention is absorbed in what she lives from; not, however, because she is attending with the intentionality qualified by Husserl as straight-ahead (*gerade, geradeaus*), but because that intentionality is absorbed away. So the present that is enjoyed is not that of presence at hand, which is a present of such straight-ahead intentionality. If there is any intentionality left, it is the intentionality qualified by Levinas as inverse.[21] This inverse intentionality of the present that is enjoyed is the intentionality of a present that is a presented present, a gift. Something is presented, something is given, but these past participles stand not solely for the pastness of the gift's having been given but for the how of what is given here and now. The temporal relation to the past becomes almost fully absorbed into the climber's absorption in enjoyment of the *nunc stans*. Almost fully absorbed in this absorption also is her concern for the morrow. Almost fully. Not fully fully, because although the relational property of reference to the future, like the relational property of reference to the past, is on the point of becoming a physiognomic quality of what is enjoyed, a quality borne on its face, the quality, precisely because it is a quality of what is enjoyed, has implicit in it a reference to something due. Implicit — hidden — precisely because of the absorption. Due in two senses at one and the very same time: due as on the way and due as owed. These two senses are implicit in Heidegger's thinking of the gift and the giving of the *es gibt*. They are explicit in his thinking of thinking as thanking. Nevertheless, as Levinas and others have said, his thinking thinks too little the enjoyment of today.

Heidegger's neglect of the enjoyment of Da-sein's today in favor of concern for tomorrow is of a piece with his seeming to other commentators also to imply that Da-sein does not have (a) sex. In a quite broad interpretation of Levinas's remark, Da-sein is never hungry.[22] But since hunger, like any other need, want, or wish, implies an inclination to grope for and grasp, and these operations are surgical, that is to say, they imply readiness to hand in a positive or defective mode, it is more important to underline that what Heidegger's enthymemetic syllogism needs is affirmation of the taste of life, *Genuss* (Hegel), its joy, *Freude*, and enjoyment, *Vergnügen* or *jouissance* (Levinas). All of these are to be distinguished emphatically from happiness. Why this is so is a question that will only be touched on here. Suffice it to say here that whereas one may be overcome and surprised by joy, one is not overcome or surprised by happiness.[23] Another question that will be only touched on here is whether it can be assumed, as the lexicon suggests, that joy is, phenomenologically, always the internal accusative of enjoying. Because it is convenient to have a verb and a verbal noun formed from the noun "joy," that assumption will continue to be made in this chapter. An equivalent assumption is made seemingly without qualms by Levinas when he equates *bonheur*, happiness, with *jouissance*, enjoyment, or with *joie*, joy, or with both.[24] But Schiller's "Ode to Joy" is not an Ode to Enjoyment. And although one jumps for joy, one does not jump for enjoyment. Again, although joy is something by which one can be overcome, enjoyment is not. English and French may induce us to forget this on account of the historical and lexicographical circumstance that they lack expressions that are etymologically related to the German *Freude*, joy, and *sich freuen* or *frohsein*, to rejoice. *Frohsein* is "more than" *vergnügen*, to enjoy, Grimm asserts, doubtless thinking of *vergnügen* as *ver-genug-en*, a mode of enoughness. But Grimm does not answer the question: more what? As indicated by the translations just risked, English makes do with words deriving from a single root to express the senses for which German has words deriving from two distinct ones. The same holds for Levinas's French. Despite the questionability of the idea inculcated by French and English that whatever is enjoyed is enjoyed under the aspect of joy, Levinas is unquestionably right to distinguish joy and enjoyment from satisfaction. What is satisfied or gratified are needs or desires. Now, although joy may be "more than" enjoyment, and although what one needs or desires, for instance food, may be what one enjoys, the enjoyment of it is more than satisfaction or gratification. In anticipation of what will be said in the final paragraphs of this chapter, it can be said that enjoyment is not gratification because, rather as joy is not, phenomenologically, the internal accusative of enjoyment, so grace is not the internal accusative of gratification. Grace is, however, the internal accusative of gratitude. And among the things we are not gratified by but graced with is joy. This chapter's final remarks will return to this.

RAISINS AND ALMONDS

Returning first to the rockface and the foot planted thereon, it has to be re-emphasized that what is *zufussen* may, anatomically speaking, be either under the hand or under the foot. Further, both *Zufussenheit* and *Zuhandenheit* can relate simultaneously to a single hand, as when the hand's "heel" is in a fixed position and the climber, like a female lizard (*lézarde*), stretches her fingers toward a fissure (*lézarde*). *Zufussenheit* and *Zuhandenheit* can relate simultaneously to a single foot when the foot's "palm" is secure and the heel is swiveled round to gain additional support. Nevertheless, *Zuhandenheit* and *Zufussenheit* are as phenomenologically distinct as the future is from the past and the present. Through its correspondence with the complex existential of care (*Sorge*), the Heideggerian category *Zuhandenheit* is linked primarily with the future, the *Zukunft*, the acoming. *Zufussenheit* is linked to the past, Da-sein's bethrownness, from the basis and in the light of which its future is envisaged and projected, this projection in turn being a hermeneutic and historical (*geschichtlich*) recycling of how Da-sein finds itself thrown. The past ecstasis is caught up in the future ecstasis. But *Zufussenheit,* although it occurs in this circle of ecstasis, is a moment of sabbatical stasis. It is the *carpe diem* interrupting them that adverts to the fleetingness of time, and indeed to mortality, but does so by dwelling on the enjoyment of the now.

The enjoyed now may be simple, as the rear foot firmly held in its place is simple in relation to the stride. Or it may be complex, as when the stride or the movement of reaching up the rockface or some other operation becomes condensed into a moment that is enjoyed for itself in abstraction from the purpose of the performance. Then becoming ceases to be becoming and becomes the non-becoming of finding yourself collected at a new home base from which to make another move. You can seize seconds, minutes, as much as, if you are lucky, an hour or even as much as a day or a night (*carpe noctem*). But however extensive and however simple or complex it may be, the moment seized on and lingered over is not enjoyed without the retention and protention of the unreflective glance forward and back. For retention and protention are implicit in the enjoyment's wish to retain itself, to save itself from evanescence. Not a desire for something else, but an attachment to itself, enjoyment, if it could have its way, would arrest time. As for joy (and here is another reason for not collapsing joy utterly into enjoyment), it would be an ecstasy *out of* the existential ecstases, an exit from ecsistence. Joy, like *jouissance* in its specifically sexual sense, would implode the re- and the pre- of preoccupied concern. It would love to bring time's flow to a standstill. But the forwardness and backwardness of time still stand. They belong to the very experience of the *joie de vivre* and the enjoyment of the moment of dwelling, the moment that is marked in Levinas's analysis with a certain femininity and in the present chapter's phenomenological analysis of climbing by the climber's double gender. For to enjoy that moment to the full is to experience it and its instantaneity against the horizon of its and our own comings and goings.

So to this dwelling in the enjoying of the held moment there adheres the bittersweet pathos of lingering (*Verweilen*), the raisins and almonds of the Passover song. However, since this moment is held as a foothold against the possibility of an engagement with something ready to hand, not present at hand, our lingering in it, although it may be kinesthetic, is not the respite either of aesthetic contemplation or of the detached theoretical observation of what is present at hand. The lingering in the *nunc stans* pertains in the first place to the moment of rest. But again, the moment of rest is not to be confused with the pause (*Verweilen*) in one's "having-to-do with the world concernfully" when one "holds oneself back from any manipulation or utilization," and when "the *perception* (*Vernehmen*) of the present-at-hand is consummated," perhaps with a view to formulating scientific propositions and principles about what one has perceived, perhaps with a view simply to an aesthetic appreciation of the view.[25]

The platform beneath the hind foot of passage is held at a site lost to sight, out of *Sicht,* not surveyed in the *Blick* of the *Augenblick.* Hence, it is liable to be passed over in circumspective concern, however prospectively cautious (*vorsichtig*), and in retrospective meditation. Out of view, this *nunc stans* is also out of time. However, it is out of time not because it is atemporal, but because it is born, *natus,* out of time in the sense that "out of" has in the parlance of equine genealogy. It is the now of the instant that is not seen in the moment of vision because it lies beneath it, supporting its vision of the future until we are out of time in the sense that our time has run out.

Zuhandenheit as understood by Heidegger has positive and defective forms. There would be such defective forms when the crack the climber reaches for is too far out or rendered greasy by damp moss. Are there defective forms of *Zufussenheit*? The defective forms of *Zuhandenheit* just mentioned would turn into defective forms of *Zufussenheit* if they affected the holds from which we are seeking to perform an operation with another hand or foot. Handiness and its defective forms of unhandiness affect the next step or manipulation. Footiness and its defective forms affect the step or pedipulation already effected. They refer in the first place to an accomplished tenancy, to the present and the past. They refer to the *pied à terre* from which we move on to what will have become another *pied à terre* for a second movement, for another *Satz vom Grund.* The foothold shares with essence or nature — the *to ti en einai* — the idea of what is over and done with. It also shares with it the idea adverted to above in one of our citations from Merleau-Ponty's lectures on *Nature,* the idea of something hidden and the idea of history, ideas encapsulated in the words for essence or nature in many languages, not least, as already remarked, in the Welsh word *hanfod,* the second syllable of which is the verb-noun "to be," the first syllable of which is cognate with *hanes,* "history," the conjunction of the two implying something kept in reserve. *Mae hanfod yn caru'i guddio'i hun.* That is to say, *phusis kruptesthai philei.*

The idea of a foothold as an achieved relatively settled basis from which to make historical progress is presupposed too by *Vorhandenheit,* for *Vorhandenheit* presupposes *Zuhandenheit.* The schema of progression from the peduncular to the manual dramatized in the movements made in climbing a rockface is expressed in various other more or less pedestrian and manual ways of comporting ourselves, for instance in dancing and walking. And in thinking. Heidegger observes that between the first and the second Critiques Kant comes to see that the real nature of the I is doing, *ich handle,* so that the latter is also the real nature of thinking, and Fichte states explicitly that thinking is a *Tathandlung,* literally an act-handling, though in everyday speech the word can imply violence.[26] In *Was heisst Denken?* Heidegger himself maintains that *Hand-Werk* relies and rests on (*beruht in*) thinking.[27] Elsewhere he goes as far as to say that even philosophical thinking is a kind of handling, of the kind practiced by the farmers, foresters, and woodcarvers with whom he sits near the *Herrgottswinkel* at the inn after their day's work. Such *Denken* is *dichtend,* poietic, in the way of the production of baskets and boots to which the philosopher Plato so often refers.[28] But if thinking is a kind of handling, it must also be a kind of footing. And so too must be language if we think because we have language rather than have language because we think.[29]

In this chapter only passing mention has been made of the many chiropractices other than grasping, for instance grasping for a handhold on a rock, that a hand may perform, for instance offering something or somebody at an altar. And we do no more here than merely mention Derrida's handling of these various ways of handling in "La main de Heidegger (*Geschlecht II*),"[30] and what he has written so dexterously and sinisterly (he always writes aptly with both hands) about Maine de Biran's *humainisme,* and about the haptologies, haptographies, and haptolographies of a number of other philosophers, among them Merleau-Ponty and Husserl, members of the trio treated in the present physiographical footnote presently drawing near to its end.[31]

THANKS

The main purpose of this chapter has been, from the basis of Merleau-Ponty's remarks about the interconnectedness of *phusis,* history, and language at the beginning of *La nature,* and from more precarious and less prominent footholds in the writings of Heidegger and Levinas, to show how climbing and as down-to-earth a movement as walking illustrate the nature of being and the being of nature that the Greeks called *phusis.* More particularly, a purpose of this *Fussnote* on *phusis* has been to show how good a metaphor for ontological metaphorization, that is, for the history of being as such, is the status of the foot, which has to conceal the place on which we put our weight if we are going to be able to see our way forward and to handle the tasks we encounter in the world. Being-in-the-world is a movement forward into a lit clearing that relies on something kept in the dark, something that keeps us guessing, something that keeps us divining, something secret, perhaps something sacred, something divine, whether *divus, deus,* or *deus sive natura.*[32] Something or, rather, not a thing, not a being, but being, than which, Heidegger holds, there can be no thing that is more divine.

A further and final purpose of this overextended footnote has been to supply a category that, rather as the rock and the stone are referred to by Husserl and Merleau-Ponty merely in passing, appears not to be given its due in *Being and Time.* Yet it is a category that is required in order to reciprocate a certain existential that he does mention on one occasion, though in lectures first delivered seven years after the publication of *Being and Time,* and without calling it an existential. *Der Ursprung des Kunstwerkes,* a work we treated in our last chapter, and a work in whose title is latent a thought that lies barely hidden in the title *Der Satz vom Grund,* does not refer merely in passing to the rock, the stone, even the stone that has been hewn to serve as an altar. The unnamed existential in question is none other than that implicit in Merleau-Ponty's statement, so frequently cited or alluded to above, that nature, *phusis,* is not an object over against us, but what bears us, *nous porte,* like the soil, the *sol* that is synonymous with solidity. While reference is made to the stone in *Der Ursprung des Kunstwerkes* in connection with the temple and the gods, it is the soil that is mentioned in connection with van Gogh's paintings of the shoes of the peasant.[33] By virtue of being equipment, *Zeug,* and, as Heidegger would have said a few years earlier, by virtue of being ready to hand, these shoes have a usefulness or serviceability (*Dienlichkeit*). But when they become used up, worn out, the using of them (*Gebrauchen*) becomes a misusing (*Vernützung*). Their equipmentality wastes away. This is because the equipmentality is no longer supported. It lacks *Verlässlichkeit*, reliability. Here again is encountered the notion of what is relied on that was invoked by Merleau-Ponty. Here, however, we stop short of what is relied on ultimately, *phusis* as defined by him. The *Verlässlichkeit* is what the usefulness of the shoes is said to rest on (*ruht in*), but it is in regard to ready- (or unready-) to-hand equipment that this category is applied by Heidegger. He leaves us in need of a *Verlässlichkeit* that holds not for the shoe, but for the soil or rock underneath it whose support is enjoyed. He omits to meet this need in *Der Ursprung des Kunstwerkes* and in *Being and Time* because he is pre-occupied with bringing out what defective modes of handiness reveal. Even the later discussions of the various uses of the hand in *Was heisst Denken?* are uses and acts, *Handlungen,* where a part of the body touches something or someone, a touching that is still not far away from the straightforward noetic-noematic intentionality described by Husserl. It is not until we reach Merleau-Ponty's reworking of Heidegger and Husserl, and his reliance on what Husserl writes about passive genesis and about the touching hand and the hand touched, that due attention begins to be given to our being touched ultimately by the earth under our feet, the water in which we bathe and the air that finds its way into our lungs without our having to reach for it: the elements and aliments on which we ultimately rely. This is a reliance on where we stand. And because standing does not require the exertion of pressure on our part, it does not offer reciprocal resistance. Except where the foothold is unsure, what it offers is enjoyable assistance.

We may also be "enthralled," and "overcome" by the joy something brings,[34] but enjoyment of it is already ground for gratitude for it, whether or not that gratitude be unarticulated at the instant of enjoyment, and whether or not (*sive*) this gratitude be directed toward nature itself, toward a being beyond nature, *epekeina tēs ousias,* to being, or simply to our lucky stars. Whatever doubts there may be about the theology or atheology of it, whatever debt we may owe through our finding ourselves not the ultimate ground of our existence, and whatever our debt toward the other human being, the feeling that we owe a debt of gratitude is part of the phenomenol-ogy of the enjoyment of our indubitable dependence on *phusis.* This is gratitude for a grace, for a gift that is as gratuitous as is the debt Levinas says one owes the other human being. It may be a debt of gratitude for the other human being, and a debt even of gratitude for that gratitude.[35] But it will also be a debt of gratitude for the gifts of the earth, the *Erde* that remains the same from one geographical place to another and from one historical epoch to another. Although the dueness of this gratitude will be more than the dueness of the coming or becoming that are dimensions of the time in which Heidegger says being's meaning consists, this temporal dueness will remain part of the dueness of debt. For where there is a debt of gratitude something requires to be done through which that gratitude will be expressed. And where there is a debt there is burden and suffering. The suffering may be the suffering of persecution by bad conscience over my inevitable failure to assist other human beings as much as they call me to do, my unavoidable failure to exercise sufficient care on their behalf. But as well as and before that *Sorge* for other human beings, before their call is heard, the suffering may be that entailed by the debt of gratitude for the uncalled-for assistance I have received from non-human nature, from that on which I rely ultimately and initially either directly or through my progenitors' dependence upon it. Here then, in both Levinas and Heidegger, is recognition of the heaviness of suffering, its *lourdeur* and its *Last*. But where is the lightness of *laetitia* and *Lust*? The latter is acknowledged in the ode to enjoyment that forms part of the second section of *Totality and Infinity*. However, this acknowledgment goes along there with failure to acknowledge the dueness of the debt of gratitude to which that enjoyment gives rise. Conversely, in the pages of *Being and Time* ample acknowledgment is made of the weight of Da-sein's debt to being and beings, but there is no reference — let alone a paean — to enjoyment. If Levinas is justified in saying that for Heidegger Da-sein is never hungry, it is no wonder that Da-sein never enjoys the bread — or the raw or cooked flesh — that is in its mouth, hence no wonder that Da-sein cannot hear the call that enjoyment conditions, the call to sacrifice this enjoyment to another, whether or not on the steps of an altar.

Notwithstanding, *Being and Time* does provide a place at which its author might have found a precarious foothold for the *Befindlichkeit* of our already finding ourselves enjoying the gifts of nature that we live from and of our consequently being already in nature's debt: namely, the unnamable place of the difference between being and beings — so neither being nor a being nor nothing — where being and beings face each other in the asymmetrical ambiguity of *to on* and of *phusis*, and where the being of the being that is the where, Da-sein, finds itself ultimately and initially relying on something as inhuman as a rock beneath its foot, and therefore, neither simply a being nor simply being, but owing, owing thanks.

TOUCHING EARTH

MAXWELL'S MAXIM

On the far west coast of Scotland is Loch Hourn. On Loch Hourn is Camusfeàrna, the Bay of Alders. The Bay of Alders is also a bay of burial. Between a burn and the white sand of the islands clustered at its mouth an unhewn rock marks the position of the room where Gavin Maxwell wrote some of his books, until his house was destroyed by fire. The rock covers Maxwell's ashes. Nearby, and near the pool and the cataract to which he hoped his spirit would return, stands a rowan, the tree that is supposed to bring good luck. By this tree stands a memorial to Edal, the otter who adopted and was adopted by Maxwell along with Mij, whose life and whose death by the spade of a confused human being Maxwell's book *Ring of Bright Water* describes. Edal died by fire. On a brass plate on a stone over Edal's remains is inscribed Maxwell's injunction: "Whatever joy she gave to you, give back to Nature."

How do you respond to this injunction? At the very least with gratitude, at least if by joy is meant enjoyment. Gratitude is due directly for our enjoyment of the fruits of the earth, whether the living things from which we live or the presumably unliving things on which life depends: earth, air, water, and fire. But joy, we have maintained, is not enjoyment. No more than the sublime is joy the intentional object of enjoyment. It comes out of the blue. It is not enjoyment's accusative. Logically and phenomenologically joy is less like an accusative than it is like an accusing. It shares with being accused a directedness from outside. It is not ecstatic. It is instatic. I am, as Wordsworth knew, surprised by joy. I am overcome by it, as I may be overcome by grief — indeed I may be overcome by joy and grief at one and the same time.[1] I am overcome by joy as I may be overcome by a fit of laughter or a paroxysm of rage. Joy is a passion and an affect. It is more than I can think I deserve. What one deserves is usually something one enjoys. But to say one enjoys a joy is to say too little or too much. This is because a joy may be more than one can bear. One can be so full of joy that it hurts. Although a hurt can be a just desert, this is not how it is with the hurt of joy. Joy is outside the field of reward and punishment. Beyond justice and injustice, joy is an absolute luxury. But because humankind cannot bear very much of it, humankind is liable to invoke divinekind to share the load. It throws up its hands or puts them together in a gesture of thanksgiving to a god.

WITNESSING EARTH

Consider a different gesture, the *mudrā*, or that posture which in Chinese is called *Ch'u-ti-yin*, in Japanese *Sokuchi-in*, and in Sanskrit *bhūmisparsha*. *Bhūmi* means earth, *sparsha* means touch. Typically, in images of this posture the seated Shakyamuni Buddha or another Buddha or a Bodisattva is shown touching the earth with the middle finger of the right hand, calling the earth to witness. Various stories are told of what the earth is called to witness. They fall into two main classes. According to one group, the Buddha is about to demonstrate his graduation to full enlightenment from the status of a Bodisattva, that is to say, of one who gives assisting others to attain *nirvana* or salvation priority over the attainment of it for himself. At that moment he is challenged by the demon army of the Satan figure Māra. Shakyamuni's gesture summons and receives the support of the earth. According to another group of stories the earth's support is still accorded, but more emphasis is put upon the claim made by Māra that he is sovereign over the earth and this world, whereas Shakyamuni Bodisattva represents what is beyond this world, and therefore is not entitled even to that patch of earth under the bodhi tree where he is seated in meditation. Shakyamuni's gesture proclaims that he has gained that entitlement through the actions performed in previous lives in selfless service to others. In neither group of accounts is Shakyamuni's enlightenment simply opposed to the earth. It is supported by the earth. Indeed *bhūmi* and *chi* mean earth as "that which may produce," "that which serves as a base," "that on which something relies." Taken from authorities on Buddhist iconography, all of these phrases are almost identical with those used by Merleau-Ponty, following Husserl, as glosses on the Greek concept of *phusis* or, as we and he and Gavin Maxwell say, Nature. For there to be complete identity of import between these phrases and Merleau-Ponty's phrase for *phusis* or nature we have only to add that on his gloss the support constituted by nature is primordial or ultimate and that what that support supports is the life of human beings. Whether or not, as Bodisattva or as Buddha, Shakyamuni is to be described as a human being, he was certainly that as the Buddha-to-be named Siddhartha who was born into the Gotama family in or around 563 BC. Furthermore, as Bodisattva or Buddha represented in the *bhūmisparshamudrā,* his posture proclaims not a forsaking of the tactility of the earth, but that latter genitive's subjective-objective bidirectionality, an ambiguity comparable with that of the lived body as described by Merleau-Ponty and Husserl. In this posture "the right leg stands for the world of the Buddha(s) while the left leg stands for that of Sentient Beings. Placing the right on the left symbolizes that the world of Sentient Beings is gathered (*shōshu*) into the world of the Buddha and also that the world of the Buddha takes refuge in the world of Sentient Beings."[2] As though to emphasize the Buddha's continuing contact with the earth and its minerality the posture is described as adamantine or diamond-hard (*vajra-paryaṅka*), and he is usually seated on a throne also so described. "The term 'adamantine throne' designates the purity and solidity of the support. Without this throne the earth would not last, and He who wishes to be victorious over the demons must sit upon it. The Buddha(s) of the present all attained enlightenment on it. Were the earth to be shaken on its foundations, the throne would remain unmoved."[3] Still, the still throne is made of earth, both the throne represented in the carved image and the image in which it is repeated, the this-worldly work in which the trans-worldly work of the Buddha may find itself embodied and embodhied. Whether or not that embod(h)iment takes place, it is easy to suppose that it is only because it might take place that the raw material out of which the image or icon is made can be honored. Honor gets directed to the person or god honored through it, perhaps to a being deemed to have been its creator. Or, as in the stories that explain the Buddha's gesture of touching the earth, the earth is personified and the forces that challenge the Buddha are embodied in demons. At the very least the roles of the participants in the narratives are allocated to animals in order to guarantee sentience, should sentience be regarded as a minimal condition for what is to be accorded the respect and dignity it would otherwise be denied, and should what we call the physical or material world as opposed to the world of sentient life be deemed to be no more than a resource for the natural understood as what is born (*natus*) or at least for what reproduces itself, nourishes itself, and passes away.

FIGURES AND FINGERS

In Aristotle's scheme of things there is no room for a *psychē* of the mineral. Yet, although we contrast the psychological and the physical, the mineral for Aristotle is a part of *phusis*. This is because for him *phusis* is the sphere of internal movedness (*kinēsis, Bewegtheit*), where movedness includes rest as a limiting case. This movedness not initiated from outside is common to what has a *psychē*, whether vegetable, animal, or rational, and to earth, water, fire, and air. Each of these elements has its distinguishing kind of movedness, and in this respect they are not contrasted with what belongs to *phusis*. They belong to the very same *phusis* as that to which belongs the rational *psychē*, *nous*. However, Aristotle is ambivalent in his treatment of the latter. On the one hand, the term *nous* refers to understanding as contrasted with sensation. On the other hand, *nous* is Aristotle's word for the highest activity of reason, intuition, and as such is attributed also to the gods. Consequently, there arises the question whether *nous* as existing separately in the gods can also be a trace of divinity in human beings. The question arises for Aristotle as it had for Plato, Pythagoras, and other early Greek thinkers, partly on account of the historical fact that they were not unaware of religious teachings originating further east than Greece, teachings we touched on in our remarks on touching the earth, teachings that raise the further and wider question as to the supposed essential Greekness of philosophy and the alleged separateness of philosophy from religion. I say from religion, not from theology, since in Aristotle, for one, first philosophy *is* theology. Indeed, it sometimes seems that in Aristotle philosophy aims to become god's narcissistic contemplation of himself so to speak *de haut en haut*. As distinct from this astro-theological science, religion would be the way the heavenly bodies and-or their ultimate first mover are honored. But this distinction should not be assumed to be so clearly made that this honoring has no influence on the discriminations made by the philosopher or theologian. That this assumption should not be made is rendered all the more urgent when we recognize that in the philosophico-theological writings of the Greeks it is sometimes difficult or impossible to distinguish the god from the good. For to say, as Aristotle does, that god is the *highest* topic of thought is not to speak only about a spatial relation, and the thinking that this topic calls for is not independent of desire, a fact that is encapsulated in the name philosophy gives itself. Of course the *sophia* of this *philia* is grounded in argument, for instance the argument by which Aristotle grounds his account of the order of dependency when he writes:

> We must consider also in which of two ways the nature of the universe contains the good and the highest good, whether as something separate and by itself, or as the order of the parts. Probably in both ways, as an army

does; for its good is found both in its order and in its leader, and more in the latter; for he does not depend on the order but it depends on him. And all things are ordered together somehow, but not all alike — both fishes and fowls and plants; and the world is not such that one thing has nothing to do with another, but they are connected. For all are ordered to one end.[4]

It is not easy to resist drawing the conclusion that this last-mentioned single *telos* and topic, the final "leader," is god, here regarded as separate but as also the source of the good in the world. An analogous conclusion is even more compelling in the case of Plato, particularly on the readings of his doctrine of the good given by Jaeger and Ritter, who stress that the good is power. The case for this reading is improved if, rightly or wrongly, we translate *to agathon* as "virtue," thereby bringing Plato into proximity with Nietzsche's genealogy of morals from *virtù*, strength, notwithstanding Nietzsche's protest against Plato's otherworldliness. Aristotle is no less Nietzsche's target. Like Plato, Aristotle comes to see philosophy more and more as the contemplation of heavenly beings and the inhibition of sensory experience such as the experience of touching the earth.

In the light of Nietzsche's references to "the desire of the Buddhist for nothingness, Nirvana — and no more!," it might be expected that he would criticize Buddhism too for turning its back on this earth.[5] Let us remind ourselves, however, that according to one interpretation of the *bhūmisparsha-mudrā* not only is the world of sentient beings gathered into the world of the Buddha but also the world of the Buddha takes refuge in the world of sentient beings. Whatever may be meant by this taking refuge, it does not take the same direction as the bolder of Plato's cave-dwellers take when, having turned around, they suffer the confusion of discovering that what they have been looking at are silhouettes cast by the light of a fire behind them, and then have this confusion worse confounded by discovering that that fire and therefore the objects on which it shines and the shadows they cast on the cave wall owe whatever connection with reality they have to the light of the sun, that is to say, ultimately to the idea of the good.

Let us remind ourselves too that in the *bhūmisparshamudrā* the earth is called to witness. To witness is, speaking Platonically, already to participate in the idea of the good. It is to perform a deed that is proto-ethical or ethical in the broadest possible sense of the term. The ethical force is particularly stressed when, as in the case of a bronze representation of the Tibetan meditative (*dhyani*) Buddha Akshobhya (for example Royal Museum of Scotland 1955–130), the earth-touching pose is said to symbolize unselfishness. Just as the wisdom of the contemplation of god or of god's visible sublunary mediators, if there are any, is not only *Wissen*, understood as a condition of consciousness, but also *Gewissen*, conscience in a very broad sense of the term, so too the field of consciousness in which the experience of touching the earth takes place is at the same time a field of conscience or proto-conscience.

In two fields, this is the twofoldness of each of the works that Antony Gormley calls *Field, Field for the British Isles, Field for Europe, Field for America,* or, as he would doubtless be willing to say, *Field for the Universe.* In the words of Waldo Williams's poem *Mewn Dau Gae,* "In Two Fields," *Field* is a field "llawn pobl." That is to say, in the words of William Langland's *Piers Plowman, Field* is a "field full of folk." That is why the field is the inextricable twofold of consciousness and conscience expressed in the single French word *con-science,* and in the words of Gormley himself when he writes that the way the physical space of the gallery is invaded and occupied by the figurines is "a kind of physical equivalent for consciousness. The *Field* becomes a kind of conscience."[6] In the case of the Mexican version of *Field* there are forty-two thousand of these figurines, handmade from clay by approximately sixty members of the local community, of ages ranging between sixty and six.

> The procedure involved kneading a ball of clay that felt good in the hand, moulding the body quickly between the palms, pulling up the head, push-ing in a sharp point to form the eyes (at first with a nail, but as the days passed, a wetted, sharpened ice-lolly stick seemed preferable). The pieces were allowed to dry a while on their backs before being stood up, making sure that the heads looked upwards. . . . There were some who rejected the idea that the figures should be laid down for a while and stood them up straightaway, which meant that they sank down and became more portly, or ended up thinner in cross-section. There were others who liked their fig-ures to be taller and would leave them lying overnight before standing them up the next day.[7]

Finally the figures are stood crowded together on the floor, taking up one or more rooms or a corridor of the gallery. Some figures are darker than others because they were nearer the source of heat in the kiln. All have their eyes directed at the eyes of the spectator. The only ones to whom you can get near enough to touch are those at the threshold. Behind the front row, the shorter ones seem to stand on tiptoe lest they go unnoticed. Because of the thickness of the wall many of the figurines are destined not to be seen anyway unless you trample upon those near the door, but we know that in the eyes of every one of them we would be able to read the word "Look." "These gazes look to us to find their place; they have a place but it's a place that we cannot enter."[8] Shades of Husserl's Fifth Cartesian Meditation. But, Gormley goes on, "they are looking to the space of consciousness inside us as their rightful promised land and that's a strange feeling." *Unheimlich.* He continues, "I hope that this work makes the viewers' experience its subject; the experience of looking." Referring to the people who worked with him in Mexico he speaks of another hope: "I explained that what I hope for was to make an image of people yet to be born. I think they liked this idea."[9] Elsewhere he takes this thought further when he speaks of "the primal population made of the earth, where mud takes on the attributes of sen-tience and the evocation of the unborn — those who are yet to come."[10] So that even before the eyes are inserted with those sharpened ice-lolly (Popsicle) sticks, in their rhythmic motions of separating, kneading, and forming the clay the makers were going through the motions of making themselves. Not adamantine, but Adamic, there is here a touching of red earth: "not a touch," says Gormley, "but touch itself." And touch of oneself, if Gormley's hope to make an image of people yet to be born is realized and if in shaping the clay one is in indirect contact with one's progenitors, those on whom one ultimately depends not only genetically but also mnemically. They depend on us to remember them, but we depend on our memory of them. We owe it to them to remember them precisely because we owe to them our existence, just as we naturally hope to be remembered by those whose existence depends on us.

In saying "naturally" here I am thinking both of Gavin Maxwell's bidding that we return to nature whatever joy nature has given to us and of the Aristotelian conception of nature. I am thinking too of the way that in both of these contexts what is natural is not the contrary of what is owing or fit or just or right, but is proper to it — *priod,* as Welsh says with the meaning also of married. Here the "is" of natural factuality and the "ought" of dueness are bound to each other. Doubly bound, because the tie, the religation implied in the idea of dueness, is tied to naturality. So Maxwell's prescription is at the same time a description, as Kant says of rules of skill and counsels of prudence in the realm of human nature and of the moral law in the realm of pure practical reason untied from sensibility. But Maxwell's maxim is reflexive insofar as we human beings addressed by it belong through our sensibility to nature. In order to feel the imperative force of the imperative we need at the very least to distinguish non-human nature from the rational animality that is the Aristotelian definition of human nature. This distinction is implied in Maxwell's imperative. Alongside that distinction is that between dueness or properness derivative from human convention and, on the other hand, agreement on rules and dueness or properness grounded in what we call natural laws. But that distinction is not equivalent to a separation if what is proper in human conduct is determined partly or wholly in terms of the non-conventional, and if what is non-conventional is the natural experienced phenomenologically rather than derivatively from "the natural standpoint" of objective science.

A closer look at this separateness in proximity might discover a way to make sense not only of calling the earth to bear witness that the one doing the calling deserves honor, whether it be a Buddha, Bodisattva, or someone else; it might discover a way to make sense of what is presupposed by such calling witness, namely that what is thus called to witness is itself to be witnessed to and honored in its own right. To show this might be one of the tasks of a Bodisattva. But in order to show this we should also have to make some progress with the difficult philosophical task of demonstrating how what Aristotle calls the rational animal is related to what Heidegger calls Dasein. That demonstration might lead us to consider whether it would have to include a demonstration of the need to acknowledge the indispensability of proto-ethical separateness in proximity along lines drawn by Levinas, but expanded to include our rapport with the non-human.

In the course of this investigation we shall inevitably find ourselves asking whether human beings in their proximo-separate relation to other human beings are in some sense "analogically" related not only to that on which we ultimately depend, which we may call the earth, the base alluded to in the phrase "that which serves as a base" used by our Sanskrit authorities to explain the meaning of *bhūmi*. No less inevitably we shall find ourselves asking whether there is some sort of analogy between those two relations and the relation between, on the one hand, ourselves and the earth and, on the other hand, ourselves and what passes under the word "god." No less inevitably will this second question have to be put, because, even if we say that what passes under the word "god" has passed, the word has not, and will not for as long as anyone wants to say in his heart that there is no god, for as long as there is a fear or a hope of driving god underground, and for as long as anyone mourns his or her or its passing. God is nominated and denominated in such mourning, no less darkly than the word *dieu* is spelled out in the word *deuil*.

Further, rather as the "heavenly bodies" are as earthy as planet earth insofar as they too are made of at least some of the elements earth, air, fire, and water, a denial of god in one direction may lead to an affirmation of god in another, for example when we translate the word "god" as "earth." That translation would be facilitated by the fact that both the earth and the divinity or divinities admit of being described as that which serves as an ultimate base, with the difference that when the noun "base" is used of god it does not usually get exposed to the risk of acquiring the pejorative force it attracts when used as an adjective applied to the earth. The competition between what is to be deemed high and what low turns into cooperation once we recognize that agapeic love and respect are not diminished or divided when directed at more than one being, and once we allow that there can be more than one ultimate foundation or (since there is an interdependence) more than one non-foundational *Ungrund*. This interdependence may be construed causally. It may be construed logically. Our question is whether it could and should be construed ethically or ethico-religiously in any tenable interpretation of these adverbs.

DEPOSITION

We have moved little further toward answering that question than we were when near the outset of our questioning we deduced a debt of gratitude from our enjoyment of the fruits of the earth ("The Fruits of the Earth" is the title of another of Gormley's works). That deduction is facilitated by the fact that a fruit is something enjoyed, *fructus,* and that to enjoy something may be to have the use of it, its usufruct. Enjoyment, it was maintained, is as much something for which we think thanks should be given as enjoyment is, other things being equal, something we think it is good to seek. The question that this deduction leaves unanswered — though an answer was hinted at when we distinguished enjoyment from joy — is whether we can find room for a gratitude that is not tied to the enjoyment of what we depend on because it is something we need.

Enjoyment is the pleasure of satisfaction. Joy, we said, can hurt. This does not mean that enjoyment cannot be accompanied by pain. But the pain of joy is intrinsic to it. Somewhat as what translators of Kant's word *Achtung* call awe, respect, reverence, or veneration is intrinsic to the feeling of the sublime. There is something to be said for each of these translations of Kant's word. "Respect" conveys the sober coolness of the feeling attached to the idea of the moral law. "Awe" mimics the open mouth of dumb-struck wonder tinged with fear. "Reverence" is a bit churchy. "Veneration" also may be too religiose, but it has the attraction that to the resonances of "awe" it adds those of the root *van,* which sends up shoots from its Sanskrit soil into *venustus* (meaning attractive), Venus, *Wunsch,* and "want." In veneration the urge to step back is complicated with the desire to approach, a complication that results in our doing neither. However we translate Kant's word *Achtung,* we should not let go of the force the word has when taken not simply as a noun but as the imperative "Attend," "Be aware," "Look," like the "Look" that cries in the eyes of Gormley's earth-bound, upward-looking figurines.

Gaudeamus igitur. Let us therefore rejoice. Let us rejoice in whatever it is in the eyes of these little folk that deposes us out of our sense of self-centered security. Let us rejoice in a way from which we could be led away if we thought that in rejoicing we were enjoying ourselves, as we might be inclined to think we must be by the fact that in French to rejoice is *se réjouir.* Grammatically reflexive though this verb is, let us try to bend it still further back toward something like what would be called the middle voice in the grammar of Greek. And of Sanskrit, the language of the *bhūmisparshamudrā* where the middle finger touches the earth. By the mediality of this voice I mean that an active-voiced reaching out responds to a passive-voiced approach to the subject on the part of what concerns the subject not because it is in his or her interest, but because the subject is touched by it independently of all such interest, touched ethically, or, if you prefer, touched "ethically," or, if you prefer, touched religiously, or, if you prefer, touched "religiously," provided the religious, with or without quotation marks, is not opposed to the ethical, without or with quotation marks; that is to say, the ethical is not to be understood here in the way it is understood by Kierkegaard; it prohibits "teleological suspension." Only if we can manage to hear this voice can we recognize rejoicing as an expression of joy. To rejoice is to give voice in something like the medial or deponent diathesis. It is to utter a cry or silently express open-mouthed awe at finding oneself and one's self de-posed, stopped in one's tracks by something suddenly seen as something which satisfies no need, but for which we experience the need to thank someone or something.

And with this we come back down to earth. I enjoy the earth's fruits. I enjoy the mineral earth itself on which feeds the vegetation of the earth understood as the planet we inhabit. But let us try for a moment to isolate the mineral earth from its aspect as that on which our life depends. One way of trying to do that is to turn to what Heidegger says about what Aristotle says about earth as *phusis* or, if you will, nature, perhaps that nature to which Maxwell bids us return whatever joy nature has given to us.

DIRT

In his essay "On the Essence and the Concept of *Phusis*" (1939) Heidegger writes in several places of what he calls presencing (*Anwesung*), interpreted by Aristotle as the simultaneous going forth and going back into itself of *phusis*.

Although the word *Anwesung* appears passim in Heidegger's early and late writings and although "presence" or "presencing" is a possible translation of it, the introduction of a notion of presence or presencing in translations of at least this particular essay by him is not entirely convincingly founded on Aristotle's Greek. Not that that should prevent our following Heidegger's thinking, given how he would have us think of thinking. But his thinking takes off from what he claims to find in the Greek words, here those of Aristotle. Among the most relevant of these Greek words are (middle voiced) *hypokeisthai* and *ousia*. At one stage of Heidegger's exposition the latter is glossed through the former and the former gets translated as "lying-present."[11] But what is said by the German word translated by this, *vorliegen*, is no more than to lie before, whereas the Greek says to lie under, *hypo*. What lies under would be just as well or better understood as what is not present, but absent because hidden. The only support for the claim that *hypokeisthai* and its cognates mean presencing is the fact that *ho hypokeimenos chronos* is the Greek grammarians' term for the present tense.

At a later stage of Heidegger's exposition, presencing (*Anwesung*) is said to be a moment of *ousia,* another moment being that of stability, *substantia, Ständigkeit*.[12] Heidegger says that the materialist Antiphon recognizes only the second of these moments. But is not Antiphon right not to acknowledge as a moment of *ousia* what Heidegger calls presencing? Heidegger is not talking of *parousia*, which would give him what he wants, but of *ousia*. As well as meaning substantiality, *ousia* can mean property. Where does Heidegger find also the notion of presencing understood as coming forth into the open? This notion is not to be found in *ousia*. It is to be found, however, in *phusis.* So rather than *phusis* being explained by *ousia* and *ousia* by *hypokeimenon,* it seems that *ousia* is being explained by *phusis.* Unless — and this would be in keeping with Heidegger's frequent statements that the thinking of being is circular — a non-vicious circularity in his analysis is signaled by the bidirectionality of the "of" in this phrase "the thinking of being." Even so, it looks as though one can get back to the starting point of this circle by following the circumference in one direction but not by following it in the other.

Phusis is recession and procession out of itself. In the essay "The Origin of the Work of Art" (1935, 1936, 1956, 1960) recession is the dimension of earth. As already suggested, this may be why the mineralogical earth is so much more frequently bypassed in philosophy than the god, even the god who passes by, even the god thought as absolutely absent, absent even at Auschwitz, it has been said, more absent than the remaining dust and ashes. "And Abraham answered and said, Behold now I have taken upon me to speak unto the Lord, which am dust and ashes" (Genesis 18:27). Why don't we take it upon ourselves more often to magnify not only the Lord but the dust and ashes to which not only Abraham but all of us come? Why do we so seldom magnify the name of the earth? Why are we so begrudging of geology? The problem is already posed by Plato's shamefacedness over admitting to his heaven Forms of dirt, that is to say drit or what could be said in another four-letter word rhyming with it, shamefacedness about saying which is precisely the problem. (Do North Americans, who use this four-letter word with as few inhibitions as they use the five-letter word "stuff," do less or more honor to matter thereby? How seriously are the chances of doing honor to matter reduced by the fact that the word "matter" is sometimes synonymous with the word "pus?")

Through his rethinking of Aristotle on *phusis* (*p(h)us(is)*!) and, to mention it here for the first time, his rethinking of Plato on *a-lētheia,* Heidegger helps us to understand why the earth gets such a bad press in comparison with heaven, Platonic or otherwise. Now it is not of ontic dirt or the mineral that the geologist's or sculptor's or mason's chisel chips that Heidegger is primarily thinking in, say, "The Origin of the Work of Art," where earth makes a twofold with world, or even in a later essay like "The Thing," where earth denotes one of four folds. But, literally or metaphorically, metaphor is there, and that is as bidirectional as the coming and going of *phusis.* So we can as much or as little say that earth construed ontologically is a metaphor of the earth construed ontically as vice versa. Which is the nobler? Earth thought as being or earth thought as a being? Being, Heidegger tells us, is more divine than god understood as a being.[13] So would not earth as being inevitably be more nobly noble than earth as a being? Or is the movement up the same as the movement down? If it were not, how could being be more divine than god and yet the name of being be earth? The movement up and the movement down could be the same if they were also different. How could that be? That could be if there are at least two names for being, the name of earth and the name of god, so that we could call for witness in the name of either — or of both at the same time, as when some of us say "Touch wood." Why then, assuming that the earth as being is more divine than the earth as a being, do we honor god more than we honor earth? The Platonic answer to this is that god is or is closer to the sun, and although we are blinded by the sun, it is by the sun that we see things in the world. In the essay on the work and working of art the world as disclosure is contrasted with the earth as closure.

There is also an Aristotelian answer to the question why we so rarely honor and so commonly dishonor the earth. Aristotle reaches his own conclusion about the relation of form to matter by taking as a point of departure Antiphon's materialism. For instance, although in Greek wood is called *hulē*, which also means "matter," wood may be the raw material for a table or a bed and a host of other things. Wood can be chopped and chiseled and chamfered into a multiplicity of forms, and wood itself is of many forms that differ according to, for example, hardness and grain. These various and variable forms are therefore, Antiphon infers, less than the earth out of which wood is formed. Earth is their common de-nomination. Consequently only earth and the other elements, fire, air, and water, truly *are* as *phusis*. True being belongs only to them.

Put thus, Antiphon's position is in tension with the Greek conceptions of truth and being at least as interpreted by Heidegger, who says "For the Greeks . . . 'being' means: presencing into the unhidden."[14] If this is granted, it follows that the expression "true being" is pleonastic, at least on Heidegger's literal interpretation of the Greek conception of truth as *a-lētheia*, unhiding. From this it seems to follow immediately that there must be something wrong with Antiphon's claim that only earth and the other elements have true being, for his account seems to imply that earth, for example, is hidden. It is hidden because it lacks form. However, if what is formed can in principle be deformed, changed, then Antiphon has a ground for his thesis that only the unformed can remain in principle unchangeable and that true being is therefore matter.

Heidegger's thinking of earth in "The Origin of the Work of Art" may be read as up to a point a defense of Antiphon. It brings out that Antiphon's materialism is not inconsistent with what Heidegger holds to be the Greek understanding of being as presencing into the unhidden. There can only be presencing into the unhidden if there is unpresencing into the hidden. This says again in terms of *alētheia* what is said in terms of the distinctions between *hypokeimenon* and *symbebēkos* or *eidos*, *substantia* and *accidens* or appearance, *hulē* and *morphē*, matter and form. It says what is said in the ambiguity of the Danish word *blive*— but, strange to relate, apparently not by the German word *bleiben*. *Blive* means to remain but it also means to become, therefore to change, as in the change of growth, the idea of which is one of those conveyed by Greek *phusis*. *Blive* therefore seems to be another of those words of opposite meanings that delight Hegel, Karl Abel, Robert Musil, and Freud (and the author of this book). But the opposition here is not a contradiction. For there to be change of form or accident there has to be something persisting through this transformation, even if what persists is no more than the interrelation of the accidents or appearances, as in the third of the classical accounts of the thing to which Heidegger refers in the essay on the work of art. This last "phenomenalist" account of the thing is the most economical of the three (the other two being the account according to which a thing is formed matter and the account according to which a thing is the bearer of properties). It risks little more than is built into the logical truth that a predicate is the predicate of a subject. The phenomenalist denies the necessity to argue from the necessity of a logical subject to the necessity of metaphysical substance. The phenomenological ontology of *Being and Time* and the thinking of being conducted in Heidegger's later writings amount to a non-metaphysical revision of that aspect of Antiphon's materialism that Heidegger's Aristotle can endorse, namely the thought that there is no unconcealing that does not imply a concealing. Thus baldly enunciated, this thought sounds as much like a logical truth as the thought that where there is a predicate there is also a subject, the thought to which appeal is made by the phenomenalist wielding Occam's razor. Given the analyticity of the phenomenalist's principle, which is already in one sense of the term counter-metaphysical, and the apparent analyticity of the truth that where there is truth as unconcealing, *a-lētheia*, there must be concealment and forgetting, *lēthē*, we may be inclined to infer that Heidegger's phenomenological ontology and thinking of being enjoy the beardlessness aspired to by phenomenalism. How can that be, given the emphasis Heidegger puts upon concealing?

What we are calling phenomenalism is, we have noted, but one of the three accounts of what it is for a thing to be that Heidegger mentions in the essay on the work of art. It is an account of the being of beings. And it is precisely as such, as an account of the being of beings, that this very doctrine that nothing is hidden hides the need to think being as such.[15] It is itself a manifestation of hiding, and a hiding of the need to make hiding manifest, to make manifest that the history of philosophy as a story of the succession of one account after another of what it is for something to be is itself a history of being, being's history, happening, and coming to pass. This history cannot be only a historiography, a more or less scientifically objective *historisch* account of past phenomena. That again would be a hiding of hiding, a forgetting of forgetting of being as such, of the *Wesen* or *Anwesen* of the *Erfahrung*, the experience in movement of time, time-travel, time-travail, and its happening: its *Geschehen* and its *Geschichte*. The science of historiography, like all other soft or hard sciences, is partial until earthed in the thinking of being, which is to say earthed in the thinking of earth.

NATURE AND ART

For Heidegger the thinking of earth may be a thinking of the working of history. It may be a thinking of the working of politics. It may be a thinking of the working of art. It may be the thinking of the work of philosophy. It is for Heidegger especially the thinking together of the working of art along with the thinking of the working of philosophy, a cooperation that he calls *dichtendes Denken*. The co-appartenance and co-apart-enance of philosophy and poietry, their "dwelling near to one another on mountains quite separate" (Hölderlin, *Patmos*),[16] can be brought out by bringing together a few sentences from Heidegger's essay "On the Essence and the Concept of *Phusis*" with a few sentences from "The Origin of the Work of Art." We considered earlier whether in the former essay Heidegger interprets *ousia* through *hypokeimenon* or vice versa and whether he appeals to these in order to gloss *phusis* or appeals to *phusis* in order to gloss *ousia*. We wondered whether his interpretations were bidirectional. Without reopening that question now, let us note that still further on in his exposition of Aristotle's argument against Antiphon he writes that "*phusis* for the first time is adequately conceived as *ousia,* a kind of presencing."[17] Without yet pursuing the question of why Heidegger says this, let us note the expression "for the first time," *erst.* This is echoed when a page later he writes of beings that put themselves forth into the appearance of house and mountain "and so first (*erst*) place this appearance into presencing." This first-timeness is heard for a third time when Heidegger goes on to say, "In the Greek definition of the essence of the human being, *legein* and *logos* mean the relation on the basis of which what is present gathers itself for the first time as such around and for human beings," *erst Anwesendes als ein solches.*[18] No doubt the first-timeness referred to on these pages is historiographic, but it follows from Heidegger's thinking of historiography that it must be at the same time historial, a *geschichtliches Geschehen.* This first-timeness of poietic thinking is inseparable from the first-timeness and originarity of thinking *poiēsis* invoked when in the "The Origin of the Work of Art" Heidegger writes, "The establishing of truth in the work is the bringing forth of a being such as . . . places this being in the Open (*ins Offene*) in such a way that what is to be brought forth first (*erst*) clears the openness of the Open into which it comes forth,"[19] and "The emergence of createdness from the work" means that "the simple 'factum est' is to be held forth into the Open by the work; it means that unconcealedness of what is has happened (*geschehen*) here; it means that as this happening it happens here for the first time (*geschehen ist und als dieses Geschehene erst geschieht*)."[20] See also the assertion in the *Introduction to Metaphysics* that in the first strophe of the first chorus in the *Antigone* of Sophocles "sea" and "earth" are said "as though for the first time (*zum ersten Mal*)."[21]

Where does this leave Antiphon's emphasis on the priority of earth? Is what may be read as his attempt to win more honor for the earth defeated by both Aristotle and Sophocles? To say "earth" for the first time is to utter its strangeness. But the first thing that is said in the first strophe of Sophocles' *Antigone* is that although "There is much that is strange," there is "nothing that surpasses man in strangeness." Does this mean that at the very moment the earth is said for the first time it is being made subordinate and subservient to man? There can be no doubt that what we are reading as Antiphon's endeavor to defend the honor of earth in its own right is challenged by Aristotle, at least on Heidegger's reading of him.

Although we may not be able to defend the honor of earth by defending the version of materialism Antiphon advances, an opening for a defense of the honor of the earth can be made by a little levering of Heidegger's words. In a paragraph from which we have already cited one sentence, Aristotle's ontology is located in the space between the ontologies of Antiphon and Plato. Where for Plato the unchanging is the Form, the *morphē*, for Antiphon the stable is *hulē*. The unchanging Platonic form is contrasted with the changing phenomena of the visible world, and the latter are contrasted with unstructured and unchanging matter as described by Antiphon. Aristotle refuses to oppose *hulē* and *morphē* to what is changing. For him *morphē* is *eidos*, what is seen, and "*eidos* is genuinely understood as *eidos* only when it appears within the horizon of one's immediate addressing of a being. In each case the statement immediately addresses a this and a that as this and that. i.e. as having such and such an appearance."[22] Aristotelian *morphē* is, Heidegger says, "*Aussehen*," in quotation marks, or, more precisely, the standing and placing itself into appearance. Further, *morphē* is not an ontic property like the squareness or hardness that would be the *morphē* of a particular table according to both Antiphon and Plato. It is a way of being, a *Weise des Seins*. Because Heidegger's word *Sein* here translates *ousia*, and we have said that this word means substance or property, we could say that *morphē* is for Aristotle an ontological property or propertyhood or belonging as such. What Heidegger himself says, however, as we have been prepared to find him saying, is that *morphē* is a way of presencing. We have also been prepared to find him saying that placing into appearance is movedness, *Bewegtheit, kinēsis*. We saw that, according to Heidegger's interpretation of Aristotle, when movedness is not initiated from outside it is the movedness of *phusis*. There would be a movedness initiated from outside when a carpenter or turner turns wood into a table. But the wood has to be already suited for this production. It has to be suitable or appropriately orderable as a table. In Heidegger's words, it has to be *eignungschaft Verfügliche*. Here *eignen* expresses the belonging of the movedness to itself, *schaft* connotes createdness, and *Verfügliche* alludes to *Fuge*, a joint, and to *Fug*, the word Heidegger uses in his "Anaximander Fragment" to translate the word *dikē*, which is commonly given the legal-moral force of "justice," but which Heidegger uses to refer to the order or jointure of what appears for a while, what presences itself.

We have just learned what Heidegger judges to be the Aristotelian and genuinely Greek notion of *hulē*. It is precisely this appropriate orderability and ordainability that he also calls *dynamis,* and that we glibly call potentiality, obscuring the sense of self-contained movedness connoted by the Greek. We all too easily find ourselves with Antiphon thinking of *hulē* as separate, rather as we all too easily find ourselves with Plato thinking of *morphē* as separate. But *morphē* and *hulē* are united in a *wesensmässige Zusammengehörigkeit,* a togetherness that is essential in the sense that each partner is inherent in the other because their belonging together constitutes *phusis* understood as a way not of a being but of being as such. Both the Platonic conception of *morphē* and the Antiphonic conception of *hulē* are conceptions of beings, not of being that is presupposed by them both.

In tying *phusis* to *logos* in this way, a certain separateness of *morphē* and a certain separateness of *hulē* are lost. It would seem that just as this loss is the loss of a certain holiness and godliness for *morphē,* it is also the loss of an opportunity to secure a basis on which to celebrate matter understood in the manner of Antiphon as the elements of air, water, fire, and earth. But suppose we go back to Heidegger's reference to *logos* as address, and instead of construing this as our addressing the seen thing, or its *eidos,* we construe it as the seen thing's addressing us, and its *eidos* as its looking at us, like the figurines in *Field.* Neither my word "our" nor the word "one's" of the translation of Heidegger's essay as published in *Pathmarks* has an explicit equivalent in the original German, which is quite non-committal as to the direction of address. It says

> das *eidos* ist wesenhaft erst als *eidos* gefasst, wenn es sich zeigt im Gesichtskreis der unmittelbaren Ansprechung des Seienden, *eidos to kata ton logon.* Die Ansprechung spricht unmittelbar je ein dieses und jenes als das und das, d.h. von dem und dem Ansehen an.

> *eidos* is genuinely understood as *eidos* only when it appears within the horizon of one's immediate addressing of a being, *eidos to kata ton logon.* In each case the statement immediately addresses a this and a that as this and that, i.e., as having such and such an appearance.[23]

I suggest therefore that, whatever Aristotle's and Heidegger's intentions, we try to think the *Ansprechung* as at least the thing's addressing of us who look at it, and who no doubt also address it by name or give it a name, for instance the name "mountain" or the name "house." Let us also try to see the *Ansehen* not solely as our looking at the mountain, but also as the mountain's looking at us. If this is judged to be a return to primitive animism, let it be understood that by the mountain's looking at us what is meant is our being struck by the fact that, in George Mallory's immortal words, "it is there," in a mode of existence irrelevant to any it might also have connecting it to human needs or satisfactions. It is as though a thing's so-to-speak beholding us could intimate our being beholden to it. We are talking not simply of a field of consciousness, but of a field of conscience, which could be stirred even if what appeals to us has neither mouth nor eyes, not even eyes made and made wet by wetted ice-lolly sticks. The animism here is our being animated by the proto-ethical affecting of our conscience by the thing, by what, remembering Duns Scotus and the windhover of Gerard Manley Hopkins (of all of whom more will be said in our closing chapter), we could call, for want of a more beautiful word, the thing's ethical or "ethical" or aesthetic or "aesthetic" or aesthethical inscape. The presence and absence of quotation marks, like my words "as though" and "so to speak," betray that it is imagination we are touching on here, imagination understood not simply as a faculty of images and memory, but as the place where the *as* takes place, between the heavenly heights of reason to which we reach up and the earth to which we reach down to touch. Furthermore, imagination understood thus as the *as* or the *how* of our being in a world is imagination understood and experienced as the *as* of our being in the world's debt. In debt not only because we find ourselves lacking responsibility for there being a world for us, not only because a lack is met by things in the world we enjoy, but also because of the gifts of natural or supernatural grace or of good luck or fortune that bring joy.

The things that bring joy are not as restricted as our particular cultural and historical conditions and conditioning lead us to think. So-called aesthetic joy may not be restricted to the beautiful and the sublime as these are widely conceived at least since Kant. Not if we can tune in to the idea Heidegger attributes to the Greeks, that beauty (*Schönheit*) is a way in which truth shines (*scheint*) especially when assisted in its shining through the working of art. Recall too that other thought of Heidegger's, the thought that the creation of the work of art calls for the beholder's taking care, its *schonen*. Heidegger's word is *Bewahrung*, the preserving in truth or truthing, *a-lētheia*, *Wahrheit*, which opens the Open to what it may be difficult at first to experience as a thing of beauty; opens it also to what at first may seem to be too lowly to be experienced as sublime, but which may nevertheless preserve something like the relation to moral respect touched on in Kant's phenomenology of the sublime. So that it may be the good that is being touched and is touching us when, like Bodisattvas in the *bhūmisparshamudrā*, we touch earth and those things for which Plato hesitated to allow there are Forms.

What things we allow there are Forms for, not least the Form of the good, is not unconnected with the specificity, generality, and generosity of our experience. As that is magnified, so too could be the magnitude of our gratitude for the joy with which we respond to the gratuitous gifts of nature. Even if it is unclear whether this thanksgiving *for* these unearned gifts of nature is also a giving thanks *to*, it is at least the beginning of a giving back to nature the joy nature has given us. As keepers of the truth of and of our troth to the earth, directly or indirectly through the work of art, we experience that the truth of being cannot be divorced from the truth of beings. That Heidegger may seem sometimes to forget this is a consequence only of the fact that his primary concern is to bring out how being gets forgotten. The connection between the unconcealing of being and the unconcealing of beings is plainly declared when he writes, "The openness of this Open, that is, truth, can be what it is, namely, *this* [naturally, culturally, and historically conditioned] openness only if and as long as it establishes itself within its Open. Hence there must always be some being in this Open, something that is, in which the openness takes its stand and attains its constancy."[24] He also writes that "truth occurs only by installing itself within a particular thing"[25] and "it is in the nature of truth to establish itself in that which is, in order thus first to become truth."[26] In this last citation the note of first-timeness is struck again. It is struck along with a new note when in the same essay we read, "The establishing of truth in the work is the bringing forth of a being (*Seienden*) such as never was before and never will be again (*und nachmals nie mehr werden wird*)."[27]

So when Sophocles says earth as though for the first time, is he at the same time sounding its knell? After all, the name that is given at one's baptism is normally the name that appears on one's tomb. And first-time naming, baptism, never happens more than once, even if baptism is a second birth. So if Sophocles says earth as though for the first time, should we say he says it as though for the last? And perhaps it is as this *as* or *how* that must be heard the "such as" of the sentence about "the bringing forth of being such as never was before and never will be again." Perhaps. But these words of the published translation are not obviously there in the German. Although the German speaks of "such" a being, "eines solchen Seienden," the clause following it is "das vordem nicht war and nachmals nie mehr werden wird." This says *that*—not *as though*—the thing never was before and never will be again henceforth. Even so, there remains a residual as-ness to the thing despite its not being said that it is as though it never was before and never will be again henceforth, but rather that it never was before and never will be again henceforth. The thing in question is a work of art. This means that the creator and the preserver experience it *as* a work of art and not as a useful device or thing of nature. Similarly, the device is experienced as a device and the natural thing as a thing of nature. Furthermore, each of these three kinds of thing is capable of being experienced as either of the other kinds. Even so, the experiences are different. One difference between a piece of equipment and a work of art, Heidegger says, is that in the former what we call the material out of which it is made, for example the stone or wood or iron out of which an axe is fabricated, disappears into the implement's use. It is what is passed over and rendered intangible even in one's holding of the axe to chop wood. If it weren't rendered intangible and invisible it would fulfill its function less well or not at all. But suppose the axe is used to create a piece of sculpture or a temple. Then the work causes the material

> to come forth for the very first time and to come into the Open in the work's world. The rock comes to bear and rest and so first becomes rock; metals come to glitter and shimmer, colours to glow, tones to sing, the word to speak. All this comes forth as the work sets itself back into the massiveness and heaviness of the stone, into the firmness and pliancy of wood, into the hardness and lustre of metal, into the lighting and darkening of colour, into the clang of tone, and into the naming power of the word.[28]

In creating a work of art a world is created for the first time, but the first-timeness does not belong to the world only in opposition to the material out of which the work is worked, the material that Heidegger calls earth. Remember that it is earth and sea of which he says that in Sophocles they are said as though for the first time. In Sophocles' chorus, in the Greek temple, and in van Gogh's painting of shoes what happens is a coming forth into worldhood of earth whose nature, the nature of nature, of *phusis*, of being, is to withdraw into itself, as we are told by Heraclitus. The work of art unconceals the concealing of nature, reminds us of our forgetfulness of it. It can do this because, as contrasted with the madeness for service of a tool, the createdness of the work of art is brought out in it. Here createdness is the giving (*Schenken*), grounding (*Gründen*), and beginning (*Anfangen*), in a word the *Ur-sprung*, the original leap, expressed otherwise as the coming and coming forth as though for the first time.[29] The work of art, as creation or giving and as preserving or what we superficially call reception, is a working. We are not talking any more about *objets d'art*, but of an initiating event, *Geschehen* or *Ereignis*. So although the temple or the sculpture or the canvas may still be extant, the originarity of its coming is from the beginning destined to pass. As the originary leap, *Ur-sprung* and *Satz vom Grund*, the that-it-isness of the being that is experienced as though for the first time is already on the way to its withdrawal. This withdrawal is the withdrawal of the bringing into the open of withdrawal, the forgetting of forgetting, the *a-lētheia* of *a-lētheia* that is announced in what in *Being and Time* is called *Verfallen*, Da-sein's original ontological falling. It is because this is one of Da-sein's existential ways of being that in the *Introduction to Metaphysics* Heidegger can write this:

> The beginning is the strangest (*Unheimlichste*) and the mightiest (*Gewaltigste*). What comes afterwards is not development but the flattening that results from mere spreading out; it is inability to retain the beginning; the beginning is emasculated and exaggerated into a caricature of greatness taken as purely numerical and quantitative size and extension.[30]

It is as though Heidegger were treating the coming into being that happens in the work of art in a manner analogous to the manner in which he writes of the being of Da-sein; as though the being of the thing in the moment of its just having been brought forth in the work of art is stretched between the joy surrounding a birth and the grief occasioned by a passing away, however much its coming to be and its passing away may differ from a human being's being stretched between its finding itself cast into the world and its running ahead toward its own death. Whether or not this analogy is sustainable, by now we ought not to need reminding that in the case of neither of the poles of the analogy is the coming into and going out of being to be taken simply as ontic generation or causation. What Heidegger is primarily concerned with in what he writes in the essay on the work of art is ontological coming into being of being as such, as this is manifested in the coming into being in the being we call a (great) work of art. We saw that such originary manifestation as takes place in the work of art may also take place in the founding moments of historical, political, and philosophical revolution. Heidegger adds to this list the moment of essential sacrifice and the moment of the "nearness of that which is not only a being, but the being that is most of all." Presumably these could be the same moment, and the same as any of the others. When in the Middle Ages the universe comes to be thought of as Creation, would not the moment in which the truth of being shines forth in the being that is most of all be a moment of or be very much like a moment of such shining forth of truth and being in the work of art? "All things bright and beautiful, the Lord God made them all." But does this mean that in default of a God who created the natural world, what Heidegger says about the work of art is not relevant to the things of nature, and that to assume it is, is as illegitimate as to assume that what he says about the work of art applies to human-made instruments, tools, and other devices? Does this mean that we cannot, as we have been doing, select statements made in the essay on the work of art and assume that what they say holds for natural things, say a kestrel, any more than we can assume that such statements can be applied to utilitarian artifacts like the actual shoes depicted in the painting by van Gogh that is one of the works of art referred to in the essay on the work of art?

Now Heidegger refers to that particular work of art also in his paper on nature or *phusis* according to Aristotle. From what he says about nature there it is clear that although the work of art is created by an agency outside it, and is in this unlike nature, which emerges and returns to itself, what the work of art brings out is nothing other than this natural emergence. Heidegger writes in "On the Essence and Concept of *Phusis*":

> we may say of a painting by van Gogh, "This is art," or, when we see a bird of prey circling above the forest, "This is nature." In such "language use" we take a being that, properly considered, is something by virtue of and on the basis of art, and we call this very thing itself "art." For after all, the painting is not art but a work of art, and the bird of prey is not nature but a natural being. Yet this manner of speaking manifests something essential. *When* do we say emphatically, "This is art"? Not just when some piece of canvas hangs

there smeared with dabs of colour, not even when we have just any old "painting" there in front of us, but only when a being that we encounter steps forth preeminently into the appearance of a work of art, only when a being *is* insofar as it places itself into such an appearance. And the same holds when we say, "That is nature"—*phusis*. Therefore, this way of speaking attests to the fact that we find what is *phusis*-like only where we come upon a *placing into the appearance* (Gestellung in das Aussehen); i.e., only where there is *morphē*. Thus *morphē* constitutes the essence of *phusis*, or at least *co*-constitutes it.[31]

This explains why in "The Origin of the Work of Art" Heidegger cites Dürer's statement "For, truly, art lies hidden within nature; he who can wrest it from her, has it."[32] Both nature and the work of art are hylomorphic, as indeed is the utilitarian artifact—or the natural thing used and enjoyed as a tool, for example a twig used to stir tea, or a branch used to reach a banana. But if nature likes to hide its hylism, it likes to hide its morphism too, and both of these are also hidden when a tool is serving its function well. Where Dürer says that art lies hidden within nature (and, he could have added, within the used artifact) we might say, consistent with Heidegger's use here of the word *Hervorbringenkönnen,* that the thing of nature is potentially—is fitted to become—a work of art. What Heidegger goes on to say may at first sound like the tautology that if the thing of nature is actually to become a work of art the potentiality must be actualized. Although what he goes on to say is not a rejection of what Dürer has said (for Heidegger alludes to him as someone who must have known what he was talking about), it is a clarification. He agrees that art is hidden in nature, but adds that art only and first (*erst*) becomes manifest in the work.

In the work of this chapter an attempt has been made to make manifest that the work of art is one way of bearing witness to the earth understood as the facet of *phusis* or nature that hides itself and thus tends to go unhonored. To bear witness to the earth is to allow to it at least the honor without which it would be impossible to call it to witness. Earth's honor. Nature's honor. God's honor. *Deus sive Natura,* where the *sive* is not exclusive. Primordial truth, the *a-lētheia* on which we ultimately rely, is equiprimordially troth.

SACRILEGE

I went to a mosque for help with a question about the translation of a certain passage in the Koran. In the library, surrounded by the bright faces of thousands of books written in a language it is now too late for me to learn, help was graciously given. On taking my leave, in the fluster of gathering my coat, my bag, my umbrella, and my shoes, I inadvertently placed my copy of the Koran on the ground. Ever so gently, my host chided me. Yet, I asked myself when I had overcome my embarrassment, what place for a holy book is more holy than the earth?

8

SEEING THROUGH GOD

ONLY A GOD

Let us return to an occasion reported at the beginning of our second chapter. If we say *adieu* to the God or god of whom Heidegger says to the interviewer for *Der Spiegel* in 1966, "Nur noch ein Gott kann uns retten," will that be the last goodbye? Quite apart from whether that god might return and so be in a position to be bidden a second goodbye, the god to whom Heidegger refers may be a second god, one of a plurality of immortals. The most common English translation of Heidegger's statement is "Only a God can save us." But the colloquial South German way of saying "only" or "just" in this context is *nur mehr,* and it would not have been uncharacteristic of Heidegger to use that expression if what he meant was what is said in the usual translation or in the variation that says "Only a God can still save us."

In both of the translations considered so far Heidegger's word "Gott" becomes "God" with a capital "G." Although "god" with a lower-case initial might seem to fit better the indefinite article that precedes it, this would not fit all the contexts in which Heidegger touches upon theological questions to do with the gods of the poets or of revelation or both. Those contexts

127

range over atheism, polytheism, and monotheism. And there is more than one monotheism. I therefore write the word "God" with an upper- or lower-case initial according to what in my judgment the different contexts in which Heidegger uses it demand.

Two further interpretations of the pronouncement in *Der Spiegel* deserve mention. It is not impossible for *nur noch* to mean "hardly," "only just," "barely," or "scarcely." If any of these translates what Heidegger intended, the implication would be that the plight was even more dire than the usual translation implies. But perhaps what he said was "Only another god can save us." That interpretation would fit in with his appeal in so many other texts to a pantheon of immortals along the lines of the old and new gods of the Greeks, and to a plurality of immortals incorporated into a partnership of quasi-categories the other members of which are mortals, earth, and sky. The idea would be that where other gods have failed we can only wait for another divinity to rescue us.

Rescue us? Of what sort of soteriology does Heidegger here speak? From and for what are we saved? In what does the *se cura* or *nos cura* of *securitas* consist? Who is meant by "us"? And — and this is the question to which the first part of this chapter will be largely confined, before I conclude with paragraphs relating more directly to Levinas and Derrida — does Heidegger mean that our salvation depends on the reappearance of a god?

From the context of the interview in *Der Spiegel* and from descriptions of the darkness of this age such as one reads in "The Overcoming of Metaphysics" dating from twenty to thirty years earlier than the interview, the "us" can be taken to refer to those who, whether or not they be inhabitants of the geographical West, are beset by the "planetarism" and mania for planning and planing down of the age of Western technology. According to the interview, Heidegger conceived the danger of planetarist technology differently at the beginning of these three decades. Then he took the main need to be need of the political movement called for by modern man and planetarily determined technology. Communism was a god that failed in that task. National Socialism was then the most hopeful recourse. Still in 1966 he is not convinced that any known form of democracy is up to that task. It is not obvious that the task was understood in the early 1930s as one of devising a political *technology*. It is already a political *philosophy* that is thought to be required. But that philosophy was not one, he says, that saw its task to be that of thinking the essence of technology as *Gestell*. Only later, presumably when he began to read Hölderlin more closely, did he come to see that it was the task, the *Aufgabe*, of the thinker, supported by the poet, to think the essence of what he refers to as pragmatism and Americanism. Rilke too speaks of the poet's *Aufgabe*, but when he also speaks of Americanism he is using this term, Heidegger contends, as a name only for a *Weltanschauung*, and he is therefore thinking too shallowly.[1] The preparation for any rescue would be a preparation for a god or goddess like Mnemosyne, the goddess, *thea,* of an *a-lētheia* that would enable us to remember our forgetting of being, thereby opening a way to another thinking, a thinking other than the metaphysical thinking that gives one account after another of the beingness of beings instead of thinking being as such.

This *andere Denken* would be *andenken,* commemorative. This does not mean that it would be a thinking only of the past or of something that had passed. It would be a thinking of passing, but at the same time of arriving. Yet for there to be a chance of salvation no god would need to arrive, not if god be conceived as a being. Indeed, if conceiving of god as a being is conceiving of god as the highest value, the chance of salvation would be even more remote. No higher blasphemy against god can be conceived than to conceive god as the highest value. That, Heidegger writes in the essay "The Word of Nietzsche: 'God Is Dead,' " is the last cut that brings about the death of God.[2] In the "Letter on 'Humanism' " he writes that "To declare 'God' 'the highest value' is to degrade the essence of God. Here and elsewhere to think through values is the greatest blasphemy one can think against being."[3] That is to say, God is diminished when God's essence is diminished. The greatest blasphemy against God is a blasphemy against being. This does not mean that God is diminished by being thought as a being, a being to whom one may pray or before whom one can kneel or dance.

Although Heidegger's thinking of being, beings, and God is supposedly untrammeled by a hierarchy of values, it is made explicit that it depends on a hierarchy when the "Letter on 'Humanism' " says, "Only from the truth of being may the essence of the holy be thought. Only from the essence of the holy is the essence of divinity to be thought. Only in the light of the essence of divinity can be thought and said what the word 'God' should name." Only and perhaps also for the first time, *erst.* "Erst aus der Wahrheit des Seins lässt sich das Wesen des Heiligen denken. Erst aus dem Wesen des Heiligen ist das Wesen von Gottheit zu denken. Erst im Lichte des Wesens von Gottheit kann gedacht und gesagt werden, was das Wort 'Gott' nennen soll."[4] The hierarchy is one of logical conditionality. If one is to name God properly, one must first have access to the essence or essencing (*Wesen*) of divinity; one has access to the essence of divinity only if one has access to the essence of the holy; and one has access to the essence of the holy only if one has access to the truth or unconcealing of being. This order is only partially followed ten years earlier in the sentences "Unsafety as unsafety indicates the track to salvation. Salvation calls up the holy. The holy binds the divine. The divine approaches God." "Unheil als Unheil spurt uns das Heile. Heiles erwinkt rufend das Heilige. Heiliges bindet das Göttliche. Göttliches nähert den Gott."[5] These sentences come from the essay "What Are Poets For?" This is an essay whose middle movement takes its theme from Rilke. One of Heidegger's aims in this essay is to discuss Rilke's claim to be described as "poet in time of need." Its treatment of Rilke is flanked by two brief outer movements treating of Hölderlin, from whose poem "Bread and Wine" this description comes. Hölderlin is described as the herald, *Vor-gänger*, of the poet in the time of need. As such he is not to be superseded or overtaken. This may or may not be a way of saying that in some respect Rilke falls short of Hölderlin. And this respect may be that which is illustrated by the just mentioned incompleteness with which the sequence in the essay tracks the sequence in the Letter. The possibility of this alternative interpretation should be borne in mind as I now proceed to develop an interpretation according to which the sequence in "What Are Poets For?" only appears not to include, and in the same order, every link that is included in the sequence in the Letter.

In the first place, an objection to the assimilative reading I am about to offer is anticipated if one notices that the sentences cited from the essay occur at the point at which Heidegger turns from talking about Rilke back to talking about Hölderlin. So an assimilative reading is not necessarily rendered implausible by the fact that while Hölderlin is par excellence for Heidegger the thinker's poet, Rilke is deemed to have been led astray by Nietzsche. Second, it is noteworthy that these sentences echo the words so often cited by Heidegger from Hölderlin's *Patmos:*

> Wo aber Gefahr ist, wächst
> Das Rettende auch

> But where danger is grows stronger
> Also that which saves.

But does that which saves need to be God or a god or gods? I said that the order of priority of the sentences extracted from the "Letter on 'Humanism' " corresponds only partially to that of the sentences cited from "What Are Poets For?" This is because the truth of being is the ground (or *Abgrund*) of the series unfolded in the Letter, whereas there is no mention of this in the series as laid out in "What Are Poets For?" and, prima facie, not even an implicit reference to being such as is made by the reference to essence or essencing at each step of the sequence set out in the Letter. Yet while in this sense the string in the essay may be said to be shorter than that in the Letter in apparently being untied to the truth of being, it does have a mooring in the salvation, *das Heile,* toward which we are told we are pointed by the *Unheil* as such, that is to say, by the unsafety in which one may also read danger and catastrophe. Ontological catastrophe, I am dangerously tempted to say, meaning by that what is said by the phrase "as such" that qualifies Heidegger's noun *Unheil.* And in the light of this phrase one discovers that, in comparison with the chain as put together in the Letter, the one in the essay only seems to be missing a link. The question one wants to ask now is whether as described in both places the chain contains a link too many. Before I attempt to answer that question I should say something about what I called ontological catastrophe and would have called essential catastrophe were not that adjective to invite a misinterpretation that would bring with it an even greater risk of offense.

THE MANUFACTURE OF CORPSES

At the risk, after Auschwitz, of the highest possible blasphemy, something about ontological catastrophe and its relation to ontic catastrophe needs to be said despite Levinas's utterly understandable refusal to comment upon Heidegger's statement: "Agriculture is now a mechanized food industry. As for the essence, it is the same thing as the manufacture of corpses in the gas chambers and the death camps, the same thing as the blockades and the reduction of countries to famine, the same thing as the manufacture of hydrogen bombs."[6] The same thing, Heidegger might have added, as the housing shortage that prompts him to scandalize many of the readers of his essay "Building Dwelling Thinking" by saying that as soon as the homeless bethink themselves of their homelessness, it is no longer distress.[7] Are we distressed in reading this statement because we take it to say that what we experience as suffering ceases to be experienced as suffering the moment we give thought to it? But this is not what Heidegger is saying. Just as the homelessness referred to in this sentence is to be distinguished from not having a house, so too the suffering of pain, *Schmerz*, as passion opposed to activity, is to be distinguished from a sense of pain that is not so opposed. In the last section of "Overcoming Metaphysics" he does not turn his back on what he there calls "the immense suffering which pervades the earth."[8] He says that suffering thus experienced as passive suffering is experienced as the will to will precisely because it is opposed to action experienced as the will to will. They belong together in the same realm of being. It is our being in this realm of the will to will that stands in the way of our seeing (*Wiss-en,* vision) that our highest distress is our not being distressed by our failing to see (*wissen*) in what the essencing or presencing (*wesen*) of truth consists.[9] Now if the highest distress of suffering here referred to is not the opposite of action, it is not opposed to action. That is to say, it is not inconsistent with taking measures to remove the cause of suffering in the sense of hunger, thirst, or corporeal and mental pain. But the deep ground of the cause of such suffering is the absence of suffering of which Heidegger says, in words we associate more often with the thinking of Levinas, that it is more passive than the passivity opposed to activity. Only when we see through to this common root of that opposition is there a chance of rescue from the profound indifference that leads to and allows to be committed acts of cruelty such as those that Heidegger in fact did little or nothing directly to prevent.

My writing of the immediately preceding paragraphs was interrupted by the viewing of a series of television documentaries about the manufacture of corpses in the gas chambers and the death camps and about the ghettoes of Warsaw and Lodz. During one of these programs, before a cart laden with human corpses like a butcher's wagon loaded with the bodies of animals on their way to the market, a witness speaks of "the wholesale business" and of how one becomes indifferent to death. Another witness exclaims, "Why is the world so silent? Does Israel have no God?" And with this I return to the question whose answering I postponed.

DIVINITY

Does thinking of the truth of being require thinking of the essence of "divinity among the Greeks, the Jewish prophets, in the preaching of Jesus," not to mention other places left unmentioned in Heidegger's short list, but mentioned much more since the manufacture of corpses on the morning of a certain Eleventh of September?[10] The sequence cited earlier from the "Letter on 'Humanism' " is a series of hypotheticals of which the last consequence is the thinking of the truth of being and the first antecedent is the thinking and saying of what can be properly named "God." One cannot do the latter unless one does the former. But does one have to think and say what can be properly named "god"? Why can't one, as Kant says of the sequence "If God exists then he exists necessarily," simply remove the antecedent, deny it? The Kantian analogy here puts us on the way to at least the beginning of an answer to this question. Both atheism and theism are consistent with what Heidegger is wanting to say. Like those questions about the existence of houses, hydrogen bombs, and gas chambers, the question about the existence of God or gods is indeed one about actual or possible existents. It is an ontic question. The atrocious misery, fear, and horror about which those other questions ask is real, but precisely in being real, *wirklich,* they call to be seen as symptoms of a disposition to regard human and other beings as commodities ready to be manhandled in the service of the will to will. The question about the existence of God is a blasphemy unless it is raised out of a sense of what divinity means, whether or not any being is divine. The question as to what the word "God" should name, if it should name anything, is not properly posed unless it rises from that sense, any more than we understand what understanding, *verstehen,* is unless we understand that all understanding is *bestimmt,* that it owes its direction to a motivating mood or passion. (Indeed, Heidegger's analysis in *Being and Time* of understanding [*Verstehen*] and the mood or humor in which Da-sein finds itself [*Bestimmung-Befindlichkeit*] as supplementary of each other explains why the opposition of passion and action is superseded by a higher doing that grows from the common root that is imagination that generates time.)

Apparently, therefore, Heidegger's chain of being need not have the question of God as a link except insofar as that question is raised by the philosophical, theological, mythological, and poetic texts of the various epochs of the history of being Heidegger interprets or destructs. Except in those cases then, could his chain not discard the question of divinity? Would not that be unessential to essential thinking? There seems to be no reason why the truth of being cannot prevail without the splendor of divinity, not to mention the glory, the *kavod*, of God. If wisdom is seeing or vision, the prophetic seeing of a seer or visionary or at least the non-optical seeing on which optical seeing depends, then perhaps one could achieve that wisdom, perhaps one could see to see, without seeing through, in the sense of thanks to, divinity or God. One could see right through divinity, look right through God without seeing him, her, or it and yet not be blind; one could see wisely even though, like Tiresias, Oedipus, Homer, or Milton, one were ocularly blind. Through the other thinking one could see the essential otherwise than through God, otherwise than by his or her or its grace.

But what about the next link of the liaison that the "Letter on 'Humanism'" constructs? What about the holy? We have already stumbled on a reason for saying that thinking of the unconcealing of being may be inseparable from an experience of the holy. For we noted the concatenation made in the essay "What Are Poets For?" of the *Unheil* and the *Heil* with the *Heilig*. The unsafe or dangerous as the unsafe or dangerous, *Unheil als Unheil*, puts us on the track of the *Heil*, of the *sain et sauf*, the safe and sound or salvation. And the *Heil* evokes the holy, *erwinkt rufend das Heilige*. If this *rufend erwinken* is compelling, then, since the way to salvation is the thinking of the truth of being, it seems to follow that the way to the thinking of the truth of being passes through holiness. But this *rufend winken* may have to be interpreted less compellingly, as no more than a hint, a *Wink*. And it may be that this hinting is meant to be read not from left to right, from *Unheil* and *Heil* to *Heilig*, but in the opposite direction. Read as meaning that the *Heilig* hints in the direction of the *Heil* and *Unheil*, that is to say, read as meaning that the holy indicates safety and unsafety, Heidegger's sentences in "What Are Poets For?" turn out to have the same order of unfolding as is followed by the sentences cited from the "Letter on 'Humanism.'"

This order is reflected in what Heidegger writes about the relation of the thinker to the poet in the postscript added in 1943 to "What Is Metaphysics?" We are told there that the thinker says being, the poet names the holy, and that perhaps *Dichten* and *Danken*, thanking, arise in different ways from an originary *Denken* of which they are themselves not capable but of which both are in need. I shall not pursue in this chapter the question of this relationship.[11] I mention it only as a confirmation of my reading of the direction of the implication, indication, or flow of the moments in the two sequences of sentences with which we have been concerned. But I must now mention and remention other sentences of Heidegger's with which this reading is at odds.

Again without pursuing the matter in any detail,[12] the play of the Fourfold (*Geviert*) or Fouring (*Vierung*) of sky, earth, mortals, and immortals is an *inter*play. Describing in turn what he means by each of these, Heidegger adds that when we are speaking of each of them we are already thinking of the simple oneness of the four. Thus of the divinities, the *Göttlichen*, he says, using a word on whose strengths and weaknesses we have already re-marked, they "are the beckoning (*winkenden*) messengers of (the) deity (Godhead, *Gottheit*). Out of their hidden sway appears (the) God in his essencing (*Wesen*) which removes him from all comparison with beings that are present."[13] If in this fourfold *Spiegel-Spiel* of the simple onefold no mem-ber, so at least not the last of the immortal gods, is dispensable, it is not surprising that Heidegger should say in the interview in *Der Spiegel* "Nur noch ein Gott kann uns retten." Yet the dispensability of God does seem to be implied in the two sequences of sentences in the Letter and in the essay "What Are Poets For?" According to both of these pieces God is a possible but not a necessary starting point on the way to the thinking of being in which our salvation is said to consist. There is no suggestion there that if we take another starting point, say human or non-human beings other than divine ones, the way can lead to salvation only if the way leads through God.

It is tempting to infer then that after the period from 1936 to 1946, the dates of the Letter and "What Are Poets For?" Heidegger's thinking under-goes a revision so far-reaching that whereas in those writings God or a god is only an optional point of departure of the path to salvation, by 1950, the date of the essay "The Thing," in which the ecology of the Fourfold is sketched out, the path to salvation must go via God or a god, as emphasized by the statement in *Der Spiegel*.

A reconciliation of these passages might seem to be offered through recognition that the word *Gottheit*, "Godhead," that occurs in the passage from "The Thing" can mean either a divinity or the divine nature. That the latter is intended seems to be implied by the fact that the divinities have been referred to at the beginning of the sentence as beckoning messengers of something, but presumably not of themselves. We might say that Heideg-ger is less interested in drawing our attention to whatever gods there may be than to the divinity or godhood to which they point. It might be suggested that the Fourfold is to be understood as an intertwining, a *symplokē*, of categories or Ideas in something like a Kantian sense. However, to treat the Fourfold as an organon of categories would be to return to the notion of a world as a world-picture, a spectacle, a totality of objects or objective facts owing its structure to, as it were and as one says in introductory courses on Kant, spectacles worn by the mind. It is precisely as an alternative to this modern conception of the world that the ecology of the Fourfold is pro-posed. For similar reasons the analogy with Kantian Ideas of Reason breaks down, for although they apply to the world at one remove, and are regula-tive rather than constitutive principles, the teleological orderedness toward which they beckon is still something that is imposed by the subject, demanded by what the American television announcer calls "viewers like you and me." The best analogy is the one by which Kant says his Ideas of Reason are inspired. The most promising way of overcoming the appearance of conflict or revision in Heidegger's texts is to take as a clue the belonging together, *koinōnia,* of Platonic forms. But in doing so we must not jump to the conclusion that, in Heidegger's thinking of the Fourfold, divinity would be one of these. *Eidos* or *idea* is nothing other than being itself according to Heidegger's interpretation of Plato. And, on that interpretation, divinity is an aspect of *eidos,* an aspect of aspect, of ad-spection.

We must inspect more closely this "ad-" in the light of what Heidegger writes in his *Parmenides.* From these lectures and from certain other texts of Heidegger, for example the *Beiträge,* one learns that despite the apparently one-way linear inference set out in those sequences in the Letter and the essay "What Are Poets For?," apparently in contrast to the mirror-play stressed in the Fourfold, the implication starting as it were from below with God is already a starting from above. In one of the *Parmenides* lectures a reference is made to "This 'address' or 'claim' of the divine which is grounded in being itself," "Dieser im Sein selbst gründende 'An(-)spruch' des Gotthaften."[14] But since through Parmenides' sayings *chrē to legein te noein t'eon emmenai* and *to gar auto noein te kai einai* Heidegger too says that being needs the thinking and speaking of human beings and that these belong together, it is no more than we should expect when in this lecture dedicated to Parmenides we are told that this address or claim or call of the divine — that is to say, of that which does not die notwithstanding the death of God — although and because it is grounded in being, calls to be taken up by the being, the mortal human being, the being who has the word, "das Wort hat," and the being whom the word has, "das Wort hat."[15] Now it is true that Heidegger is here speaking specifically of the Greeks, but how is that restriction to be understood? A few paragraphs earlier he has said that the Saying (*Sage*) of the Gods in "myth," Godsaying, Gospel, is of the essence of the Greekly experienced man, and only him, *der griechisch erfahrene Mensch, aber auch nur er.*[16] Although after the coming to pass of the age of the world picture we do not experience Greekly, it is not impossible for us to enter into an anticipatory relationship (*in einen ahnenden Bezug*)[17] with the Greek experience of the presencing of truth as *alētheia* and therewith of what the Greeks called *to daimonion,* the haunting, *das Un-geheure.* If we cannot experience this we can rethink it. And it is this that Heidegger assists his readers to do by distinguishing seeing from the functioning of eyes. "We do not see because we have eyes, but we have eyes because we can 'see.'"[18]

Incidentally, Heidegger's explanation of this last statement may not be inapplicable to the words "I could not see to see —," the last words of Emily Dickinson's poem "I heard a Fly buzz — when I died —." The question whether the Fly could die is one that has been pursued elsewhere.[19] Seeing (or "seeing"), as contrasted with using one's eyes, is something of which only mortals are capable. And seeing is possible only if looking, *blicken,* is possible in a sense best elucidated by asking what looking is for the Greeks. In asking this a distinction must be made between what Heidegger says that looking is for the Greeks and Heidegger's own restrictions upon the kinds of being that can look in the sense he elucidates by asking what looking is for the Greeks.

In Greek to look is *theaō.* We apply the word "looking," understood by us as looking at, to what spectators do at a theater. But for the Greeks *theaō* has the sense of being looked at. One gives oneself to be looked at: *daiō,* which can be both giving as well as the shining of eyes. My looking is self-exposure; *exposition,* Levinas would say. It is as though in my seeing I say, "See me." Thought *Greekly,* my seeing says what is said by the *Hebrew* word(s) *hineni*! But although in the first place it is in respect of another human being's looking at me that Heidegger construes Greek seeing, he writes, "The Greeks experience looking first and authentically as the way the human being with the other being, but the human being *in its essencing,* itself emerges and presences," "Die Griechen erfahren das Blicken zuerst und eigentlich als die Weise, wie der Mensch mit dem anderen Seienden selbst, aber als Mensch in sein Wesen aufgeht und anwest."[20] And on the next page he writes: "The one who looks appears in the look and 'outlook' or 'aspect' of the familiar, of beings," "Der Blickende erscheint im Anblick und 'Aussehen' des Geheuren, des Seienden." There seems to be nothing in what Heidegger says here that entails that the other being has to be a human being. The same holds for his comment on the Greek *idea* in the *Beiträge* that "The being is a being in its continuing presence, *idea,* the seen in its seenness (*alētheia*)."[21] In its seenness or in its having a face, a *Gesicht,* one is encouraged to say when one reads in the *Sophist* lectures that other beings of whatever kind are not just encountered but encounter us, they are *begegnende,*[22] and when one reads in the *Parmenides* lectures: "The 'faces' (*Die 'Gesichter'*) that things make, their 'outlook' or 'aspect' (*'Aussehen'*), are called *eidos* or *idea,*"[23] and "Encircled by the horizon of 'faces' (*Im 'Gesichts'-kreis*) of this originary look the human being is 'only' the looked at."[24] Having explained that this "only" is nothing less than man's being, as being looked at, his being in relation with being, he goes on to say that man's looking or seeing is his insight into truth as unconcealing. But at the root of this *a-lētheia* is the *lēthē* of the concealed. The concealed is nothing other than being itself, which, through the human being, shines in beings. Being, as the strange that haunts the familiar, gives itself (*daiō*) as the *to daion-daimōn.* Hence looking or seeing, *to theaōn,* is *to theion.* So it is not incorrect to say that in this Greek way of seeing we see through God. Or, to repeat, through a goddess, since for Parmenides *alētheia* is a *thea.*

Daiō. Es gibt divinity. God gives. But God also needs. Given the belonging together of divinity and being, and given that being needs man, then divinity calls on man. Its looking at man is a looking to man, a calling, a *rufend anblicken*. Admittedly, the Germanic word "Got" and its Sanskrit source mean the one who is called and for whom libations are poured, whereas, Heidegger tells us, the Greek words *theos-theaōn* and *daimōn-daiōn* do not carry this sense of being called. The Greek gods nevertheless call to be called. To be called by man, like the man who calls to be called Ishmael-Shem, whose name means "called by God." The Greek god calls to be named, as though being that likes to hide itself can just as well hide behind a name as the Hebrew God can hide itself by calling not to be named. "The word as naming of being, *muthos*, names being in its originary inseeing and shining appearance (*Hereinblicken und Scheinen*) — names *to theion*, that is, the gods."[25] *Theos* needs *muthos; eidos*, being, needs *logos*, the word. *Sein heisst Nennen*. God and being are the same. They belong together and to saying.

So to the gerundial grammar of being, *Sein*, a gerundivity belongs. It will be recalled that in the sequence examined in "What Are Poets For?" we were told that the holy binds (*bindet*) the divine. Now beyond the being of the Platonic *idea* is *to agathon*. This is not the place to do more than raise the question what it might mean to say that the *agathon* of Plato is in the trace of the *dikē* of Anaximander. In so doing we cannot call the latter justice without raising the question of an *adikia* that is before the question, a justice and an injustice of an out of joint time before the justice and injustice whose criterion is the law of the land, for example the law of the state of Denmark, or the law of the intelligible kingdom of ends. Nor can we leap from noticing these hints of an ethico-legal dimension of being to drawing an analogy with the Kabbalistic themes in the teaching of Rabbi Hayyim of Volozhin, referred to by Levinas, according to which God contracts himself in order to make room for an obligation humans have to cooperate with him and each other in the sustaining of the world: a primordial contraction (*tsimtsum*) that is the condition of contract. If that teaching is understood onto-theologically it cannot be understood to say something of the god through, thanks to whom, we see. Its god will be the god we see through, the God that Nietzsche rumbled. On the other hand, if the Kabbalistic god is a god of faith, it is, by the admission Heidegger makes to the students at Zurich, of no intrinsic relevance to the originary thinking of the being of divinity and the divinity of being toward which he seeks guiding threads from the Greeks.[26] And Levinas would say that this god thus understood as the god of confessional faith, or understood metaphysically in Heidegger's usual sense of the word, belongs to a universe of discourse other than that of the metaphysical in his own special sense of that word, the metaphysical in the sense of the ethical beyond being. This does not mean that no God can be seen through the other human being of Levinas's humanistic ethics of the other human being, even if through the face of the other man, woman, or child looking at me I see no more than the divinity's back. (And was even its back to be seen when the children were being burned half a century or so ago?)

DIVINATION

If we see through, rumble, the God of onto-theology and see through, see thanks to, the God of originary Greek thinking or the thinking of the other God who alone can save us, do we see in both of these senses through a God who haunts some of the pages written by Derrida?

In *Of Spirit* Derrida imagines certain theologians saying of what Heidegger says about being, that that is exactly what they themselves are trying to say about God.[27] God and being are the same. And that is exactly what Levinas is trying to call into question by invoking what is older than any question and any answer, namely my answerability before the other human being and before God who are neither the same as being nor the same as me, as the I who is what Levinas often means by the same. And it is by speculating on Derrida's speculations on Levinas, Heidegger, and others that I shall end this chapter by beginning again with the question as to what Derrida might say there remains of divinity after not only the death of the God of traditional metaphysics, but when the traces of justice and the good in Heidegger's rethinking of the Greek beginning of the thinking of being are followed to their source. What in short does Derrida say at length of the Source? What, if anything, have we got left of the Gothic or Greek *Got,* what other *Gott,* if any, is our only source of salvation according to him?

We have been told by both Heidegger and Levinas that God does not make a spectacle of itself, and that divinity is not to be categorized like a pair of either removable or irremovable spectacles. Following Derrida's reflections on Benjamin, Marx, and others, we may speculate that God is a specter. Except, *sauf,* this "is" must be construed otherwise than the being-there of *Da-sein* or *Fortsein,* and otherwise than being's *es gibt.* Ontology, onto-theology, and the thinking of being are pre-vented by hauntology or spectrography. Refracted at the edge of the psyche — and in French a *psychē* is a kind of mirror — the light we see through loses the simplicity it appears to have at its source. Reflected at the mirror's center, the very idea of source disappears in its image, re-tained, it could be said,[28] like an *eidōlon* without *idea,* but also unlike an *eidōlon,* for the spectral *revenant* looks at and speaks to the person to whom it comes back, and is only seen through, without being an object that is seen. It is therefore not an epiphenomenon, and cannot become an object of idolatry. The source of both skepticism and skepticism about skepticism, the spectral is a representation that causes what it represents to disappear.[29] The source is always a resource, the original is always already a copy, therefore it is not a copy, and *a fortiori* not necessarily a fake. God was always a second-comer and ever more shall be so. The paradox of the first mover is that it was always at a remove. Its originality demands this. The paradox of the source is the paradox of iterability. In order to be original, the original must represent, repeat itself, re-seek itself, for it is repetition itself, *semper se re-petens,* hoist by its own petard, always already destroyed so always already undeconstructible. He who seeks God has found him? He who has found him still seeks him even after he has been declared dead, so that, not having been nothing, God is still in a strange way available even if, because he seems not to have answered our prayers, he has been punished by being dispatched to a limbo and so can still meet the need for a scapegoat or a suffering servant, preserving the meaning of what we do when we curse and commit blasphemy, albeit a blasphemy against being.

According to a Kabbalistic tradition the creative imperative word "Let there be light" is a word that is written. God is the archetype of the writer. And the letters of the Torah are the enscripted blueprint of the world from before creation, which therefore is re-creation, reinscription.[30]

The law of the law is the law of iteration. So that because the second coming is first, though with a firstness to which secondness is not opposed, then if God comes back he will again show only his back. Visitation will be revisitation. His *visiter* will be a vis-*iter.* He and we shall be repeatedly *unterwegs.* It is as though in order to be the living God, one can never look back to a time when the being whom Meister Eckhart calls *Gott erst Gott* appeared for the first time. As though, if man is made in the image of God, God must be made at the same time in the image of man. Which might mean that God, like the other man and myself, is from all time immortal: immortally mortal. And that the Father, like the father of the Prince who pondered the difference between being and non-being, must, in order to be capable of living, be capable also of death. Hamlet's father then, like God, was destined not to show his face. His eyes were destined to remain unseen behind his helmet and his voice to be rumbled from the subterranean depths. *Rufend erwinkend,* the specter comes demanding of us justice in a world that is out of joint: *akusala,* as the earth-touching Buddha would say. Undeconstructible justice, Derrida says.[31] For the justice in question is justice before the question and before the alternative, where this is a before of time out of joint before the time out of joint of the *Augenblick* of decision that Kierkegaard says tears time in two and is mad, as Derrida reminds us.[32] Undeconstructible justice is before the right and the wrong decided by law. Yet undeconstructible justice is the condition of deconstruction *in* deconstruction and decision, and in process in their *procès verbal,* exercised at the tribunal, haunting the bar like the unexorcizable ghost of Portia. (Here is another reason for saying that the whole of philosophy might be regarded as a commentary on Shakespeare.)[33] Undeconstructible justice would be the residue of madness that exceeds calculation according to law. Both before and in laws, outside and inside legitimation, an uncomfortable itch under the skin of the legitimation theory of discourse ethics and prefixing an irreducible deontology of dissensus to its teleology of consensus, the specter contaminates *l'esprit des lois.* Dispiriting, the specter both laughs at the *je(u) d'esprit* and weeps over grief. Tragicomic, it is mirth at the graveside of poor

Yorrick and of every other singular soul. Singular justice is the justice of the signaturality that allows natural law and custom law to care for and watch over each and every so-called case that the law represents only because each and every so-called case represents the law's universality. Although the justice of legality is blind, and although my following of a rule is blind,[34] so also is a certain kind of love. Erotic love is blind not only in not having regard for persons other than the loved one, such regard being synonymous with the blindness of justice; it also turns a blind eye to some of the very particulars to which the rule of justice bids us be blind. Henri de Montherlant says somewhere that we hate on account of, but love *malgré*.

However, maybe we should agree with Andrew Marvell, who, speaking of blind Milton, says, in words cited by Derrida and anticipated by Heidegger's Greeks, man thinks his eyes. So that more terrible than eyes that cannot see may be eyes that cannot shed tears of joy or of grief.[35] The *Augenblick* of applying a law, of what Kant calls determinant judgment, is a moment at which, despite its manifold eyes, the Fly, if also it can think and can die, flies blind across some part of the space of the room that is not covered by the law. That is the moment when *le mot juste* may be found only by seeking another law, by what Kant calls reflective judgment. The justice of reflective equilibrium is the judgment of the double mirror of the imagination, which is practical in the sense that it is the faculty of interpretation not as contrasted with change as it is by Marx, but in interpreting the world also changes it. Productive, as Kant and Marx would say, performatory as Derrida and Lyotard say after John Austin, the philo-sophy *en effet* of the imagination is reflected in judgments that are both determining and determined, *bestimmend* and *bestimmt*. Its judgments seek understanding in both the intellectual and moral senses of that word. Made not only out of the love of wisdom, but also out of the wisdom of love — where, remember, wisdom is vis-dom, seeing, if only the seeing of the blind seer — the duple judgments of the operative imagination, the operatively historical imagination (*wirkungsgeschichtliche Einbildungskraft*), construing reflection with determination, seek to give voice, *Stimme,* that changes every so-called case into the bearer of a proper name, a signifying signatory calling for justice that is no longer opposed to love. So what may be called Derrida's nominalism is not opposed to realism of the idea or the *idea*. And it is a nominalism that sees in the affirmativity of constative theory — in *theaō,* that is to say in seeing — a moment, an *Augenblick*, of performativity. As for the unspectacular specter, if in seeing through him or her we are seeing through God, it is a God that parodies what used to be named God, *to theion,* or that is not named by the Tetragamme. *Rufend erwinkend,* this God whose love is not set above its justice just on the sabbath, but whose justice is supplied by love and whose love is supplied by justice on every day and night of the week, may be winking behind its visor. This see-through ghost of a ghost, specter of spirit, may be having a joke at our expense, a joke we may or may not see. Or it may not. I have elsewhere noted the role played by the word "maybe," *peut-être,* in Levinas's exposition of the enigma of the trace,[36] his response to what in Heidegger's references to the enigma (*Rätsel*) of origins is marked by the word *Wink.* The same word *peut-être,* sometimes italicized, punctuates strategically again and again the paragraphs in *Force de loi*[37] and *Spectres de Marx*[38] in which Derrida writes of the undeconstructible justice. Maybe it marks there the watershed between the blinding tears of laughter and blinding tears of grief, or the *Augenblick* in which they blend. Where one cannot see, *voir,* one must believe, *croire.* Or not. Certain atheologians would say that what Derrida says about the spectral is exactly what they are trying to say when they say they have seen through God. You can choose to say *adieu,* or choose to say *au-revoir.* With Pascal you can calculate the risk of hellfire versus the chances of salvation, then either opt for the one or the other or choose Purgatory's excluded third. But before choice and beyond calculation there is a faith so immensely unfirm that only the emptiness of the word "God" can contain it. Jabès: "God was, or was *no more than* the only word for grief sufficiently vast, sufficiently empty that all griefs may be contained within it."[39] Hovering between being or nothingness and beings, the non-constative "maybe" of the precovenantal fiat of this God who will not let me go spans the difference between the time of the child who survived the burning of other children, the time when God itself seemed to have been reduced to ash, husk, or kellipathic shard, and the time when, as depicted in one of those fiftieth-anniversary films the watching of which on television interrupted my writing of the paragraphs I am about to interrupt again, the woman into whom that surviving child grew returned after the war to the block at Auschwitz where her own mother died, and it seemed to her that, yes, Israel still has a God. This yes and the no out of which it grew across time has the Yes of undeconstructible justice and Desire as its quasi-condition, like the way in which the ways of being of beings have being as such as their ground or abyss. Also, however, unlike. For since that justice is a responsibility to the singular, what conditions the moment of decision must be also conditioned by it. What conditions the moment of decision is the incalculable risk or the guess. If a divinity haunts deconstruction, it is that of a God who divines. Its *Déité* is of a deity that plays dice. God keeps us guessing. Divinity allows room for divination. But the words "divinity" and "deity" repeat the ambiguity of "Godhead." And as applied to any spectral *Ça* or *Id* or It that haunts the action-passion of deconstruction's quasi-middle-voiced *se déconstruit,* the words "divinity," "deity," and "godhead" do not name a being before whom one can kneel, offer libations of salt water, or dance, any more than one can do that before any *Es* that may haunt the *gibt* of *Sein.* But, whatever may be said of onto-theology and the thinking of being, given that undeconstructible justice is a responsibility to the singular, then its spectrality is unexorcizable, as I have said that it is, only if it does not turn its back on but rather faces and welcomes both the girl's denial of God and the grown woman's refound faith, the one running into the other like the stem and the branches of the tree of Jesse, of the initial *Y grec* of the word "Yes," and of the unpronounceable Yod of God.

In-zwei-, in-drei-, in-vier-, in-n-bildend, the exemplary s(c)hematism could be heresy, *hairesis,* that is to say bi-, tri-, quadri-, n-section, were it not also *In-eins-bildung, Einbildungskraft,* across time and times. It could be idolatry, were the *Bilden* not also a *Blicken,* the look that speaks louder than words. However, idolatry is not limited to vision, the sense we think was primary for the Greek; it can extend to "Hebrew" hearing, and the other senses too. And it hardly needs saying that idolatry can extend very much further, for instance to Islam and beyond. Islam, which can mean safe, is not safe.

The strange manner of the specter's never being quite at home, unendingly and ateleologically on the way either to visibility or to invisibility, must leave open the optical option between *seeing* through God and seeing *through* God. Whether the deity in question be the god of the poets or the God of this or that revelation, *rufend erwinkend,* the voice of conscience in the eye of wisdom, *Gewissen* in *Wissen,* and the call of justice and love to each other, seeing through (*dia-*) deity — divine dioptrics — is a saying through it too, whether across the footlights or at the brink of the grave: a *dialectique, adikialectique,* a *daiōlectique,* a *deuilectique,* a *dieulectique, à-dieulectique, adieulectique.*

SALVATION AS SALUTATION

Dialectic or "dialectic" without reconciliation. If there is hope of rescue, it does not nullify despair. *Denn nichts als nur Verzweiflung kann uns retten.*[40] Nor is reconciliation promised in the following final, summary, and perspectival remark, by way of *envoi,* on the dialectic or "dialectic" among the authorial or Authorial trinity or quaternity with whom this chapter has been concerned.

If one asserts that being is more holy, more *heilig,* than the God of ontotheology or that it is not more holy than the God of revelation, then, since being and these Gods are being compared in respect of holiness, they cannot be as set apart as the author of the "Letter on 'Humanism' " would have its reader believe. They communicate through the justice of the preformatory, performatory, and deformatory signaturality that prepares the way to and from jus-naturality and legislated right. This — rescue, *Rettung, salut,* or salvation as salutation — is a point of difference from Heidegger and from his thinking of the ontological difference on which Derrida and Levinas agree, however we construe the latter's teaching on the relation of the alterity of the human being to the alterity of God. A point of difference between Derrida and Levinas, it seems to me, is that Derrida does not limit ultimate alterity to these. This is a respect in which undeconstructible justice and alterity in the Derridian gospel range more extensively than they do according to Levinas. Their scope extends at least as widely as and maybe more widely than Heidegger's thinking of being and beings when in "What Are Poets For?" he asks, "Wie könnte je dem Gott ein gottgemässer Aufenthalt sein, wenn nicht zuvor ein Glanz von Gottheit in allem, was ist, zu scheinen begänne?" "How could there ever be for the god a place of sojourn fit for a god if the brillig glance of godhead did not first shine in every thing that is?"[41]

9

REGARDING REGARDING

PAINT, THEREIN LIES SALVATION

Gaston Bachelard's words "tout ce que je regarde me regarde" point toward and beyond the ocularly phenomenological context to which he seems to have wanted to limit their import.[1] His words may be translated provisionally as "everything I regard regards me." It is especially with regard to the eye that he would appear to wish his words to be understood. For elsewhere in the book in which he writes them their import is expressed in the phrase "tout ce qui brille voit," "everything that shines sees." His piece is an eyepiece. My concern in the present and concluding chapter is with what is beside, aside, or askance from the eye. These final chapters are concerned not only with the part played by the eye, with regard as look or gaze. They are concerned not only with vision, but also with pro-vision. They are concerned with regard as concern.

Is not this double "regard" doubly concerned both in painting, the plastic art of the eye, and in the rigorous philosophical art of what shows itself, phenomenology? Is it not uncircumspect to say that the work of art and the phenomenologically reduced field are made for each other, reciprocally illustrative and mutually metaphorical, in the sense that just as the work of art suspends responsibility and is, as Levinas and others have said, a shadow of reality, so too the phenomenological reduction cuts all empirical and ethical ties? It could be said that in the case of the work of art, as in the case of a system of pure mathematics, there seems already to have been initiated the parenthesizing of ethical and empirical questions required by the phenomenological reduction.[2] But this *requirement,* if not an obligation imposed by a special empirical or ethical system, is nevertheless and all the more a most exacting responsibility: the responsibility to depict and describe the *Sache selbst.* Now if this responsibility to depict and describe the *Sache selbst* is the responsibility to describe *being,* it cannot be met without meeting the responsibility of depicting and describing *beings.*[3] If the phenomenology of perception aims to discover laws, these are no less pro-visional than the laws of an empirical science. If its findings are the outcome of a serious concern to tell the truth regarding the *Sache selbst,* concerning being and the advening of its to-be, this concern is still lacking in seriousness unless it is a concern to tell the truth regarding beings. The truth in phenomenology is inseparable from this seriousness. Yet for the very same reason the phenomenology of perception lacks this seriousness and cannot take itself seriously unless it refrains from taking itself so seriously that it is unwilling to let itself run the risk of being led astray on the loose leash held by the artist who takes a line for a walk, unwilling to let itself take the chance of *Le voyage du dessin.*[4] The painter's regard for truth in painting, his regard for what he regards and for what regards him, his aesthetic conscientiousness, is lacking in seriousness unless it is sufficiently relaxed to indulge the enjoyment of play so free that it can tolerate even the changing of the rules of the game *ambulando,* in progress,[5] *in viaggio.*[6] The same must be said of phenomenological conscientiousness if regard for being as such demands regard for beings as depicted by the practitioners of the art of the eye. If the responsibility of phenomenology is to let being and beings be, that responsibility must extend to the letting and the *laisse* of its leading questions. It must extend as far as to allow the restraint of its *Koppelleine* to be coupled with pro-ductive release, like those extendable sprung dogleads from Germany that combine discipline with *Spielraum,* mixing a modicum of control with a margin of error. *If* there is a necessary condition of art, this pro-ductivity could perhaps be proposed as one, hence as a condition of the artfulness of science, including the so-called rigorous science of phenomenology. The finesse that is the rigor of that artful science, like the fineness of fine art, is never quite in earnest unless there is in it an earnest, a foreshadowing, of something to come that is unforeseen. This incompleteness, which is the condition even and especially of the finest and most finished art, explains why, to repeat Merleau-Ponty's remark, the phenomenological reduction is never complete,[7] why essentialist phenomenology is finished, supposing it ever began, why, as Heidegger says of metaphysics, without our straining to overcome it, it can be left to itself.[8]

This incompleteness also explains why truth in painting, hence truth in phenomenology, which feeds on it and is attached to it by an umbilical cord, is not only not correspondence, even when painting is at its most representational. This incompleteness explains further why truth as unconcealing and as unconcealing of concealing is at the same time truth as unspecific troth. Veracity, Levinas would say. Derrida would say loyalty before the law, *loyauté devant* and *avant la loi:* fidelity or pre-onto-theological *foi.*

Could we say both that beyond and within the *alethic* truth of to-be lies, logically as well as anagrammatically, the *ethical* truth of to-say, and that the doubly coming into and going out of itself of being — *Ereignis* and *Enteignis* — come to pass and come to *la passe,* to pass being, to *passer par tout,* to transgress totality, in the ethical truth of to-paint? If the truth in what is said, in *le dit,* goes back to a truth of the to-say, of *le dire,* then does not truth in a painting, depicted truth, truth of *le peint,* go back to the truth of the to-paint, the truth of *le peindre*? Is even the condition expressed in the protasis of this sentence true? Why cannot what is said or entertained be true and yet the saying be frivolous, deceitful, or false? Because frivolity and intent to deceive presuppose that one takes seriously the semantics and logic of address. I cannot withhold my word from another unless I can give my word to another, and I can give my word to another only if I have received it from another as a gift. But how is the word "another" here to be glossed? Should we say that it stands for a plurality? Should we say that it stands for a singular? Must it not stand for the singular plurality signified by the word "*autrui,*" a word that, like the word "*passe-partout,*" by reason of grammatical law, cannot be written in the plural, yet can be comprehended in the plural, can *passer par tout,* and passes especially by me (as does *Elohim,* which is plural by reason of another grammatical law, but is so theographically singular that it can in no way be comprehended)? Whether or not this plurality is already invoked in the logic of vocative saying, if the logic and rhetoric of vocative saying are inseparable from a semantics of the said, then the word "another" must embrace the indefinite plurality of the words "one" or "*das Man.*" On this at least there would be agreement among Levinas, Heidegger, and Wittgenstein.

But what of the other question left in suspense? Does truth in what is painted go back to a truth of to-paint? With this question, the apodotic question, we go back to the one we have just supposedly left behind, the question posed by the protasis, for it can be answered only when we have decided whether truth in what is painted or truth in to-paint goes back to the truth of what is said or the truth of to-say. This does not mean that this latter question, the protatic question, may not also revert to the apodotic question. This would seem to be the case if the picture theory of linguistic meaning is valid, a possibility or eventuality that Derrida appears to be aiming not to close off when in the foreword to *The Truth in Painting,* after referring to the French language, he guardedly adds more than once, "if there is one that is one and if it is not a painting."[9]

The picture theory of meaning, at least as outlined in the *Tractatus Logico-Philosophicus,* would seem to entail a picture theory of truth. Such a theory of truth would be what Derrida refers to in his foreword as a theory of truth as representation or adequation. Truth as unconcealing, that is to say truth as unconcealed in "The Origin of the Work of Art" — what I have referred to as alethic truth and what Derrida refers to as truth as presentation — would require a different theory of the picture from Wittgenstein's if such truth were to be capable of being accounted for by a picture theory of truth. Where truth as pictorial representation is grounded in calling things by their names, truth as pictorial presentation would be grounded in invocation, in calling up things by naming them "as though for the first time"; it would be grounded in grounding, or in the *Abgrund,* the abyss. It is doubtful whether there could be a theory of such truth that did not conceal that truth precisely because it was a theory, a *theōria,* a descriptive or explanatory account of a look. It would throw us into the *abîme* to which Derrida alludes, the perpetual oscillation between the presentation of representation and the representation of presentation, the *Abgrund* of the doubly genitive unconcealing of truth.

But this degeneration and regeneration of truth could be regarded as Levinas regards the repeated rebirth of skepticism from the ashes of its self-refutation.[10] Perhaps it is evidence or testification of a still other and higher or deeper truth, the truth of altitude and alterity for which Levinas and Derrida use the words "veracity," "truthfulness," "fidelity," and "sincerity." When alethic truth is spelled out, when, as Levinas would say, the spell of the truth of phainaesthetic presentation or presencing (*Anwesen*) is broken, that is, when we hark back beyond the truth of the saying of the *Sagen* in which according to Heidegger *Dichten* and *Denken* belong together, will we hear the ethical truth that exceeds phenomenological and ontological presentation, the Good that according to Levinas "cannot enter into a present nor be put into a representation"?[11] More particularly, and most improbably, will this ethical truth be audible in the truth in painting, where the aesthetic is most sensibly present? Are ethics and aesthetics one? And are they one not for the reason that, whatever they may *show,* they *say* the same thing, namely nothing, because they are at the limit of language and meaning and truth? Are ethics and aesthetics one rather for the reason that they are both the truth of truth and the reason of reason, saying respect for the difference without which respect for the moral law would be disloyalty to whoever or whatever — him, her, or it — stands before its tribunal?

The reason of reason is sensibility, ethical responsiveness; therefore responsibility; therefore, where painting is concerned, our being concerned, affected, and moved by painting or moved to painting what Cézanne calls its "*motifs,*" that is to say, what moves him. This sensibility is aesthetico-ethical regard. Without this sensibility the moral law lacks moral sense. I have been maintaining in this book and have maintained elsewhere that it makes sense to allow that the moral sense is affected — moved, touched — by non-human beings no less than by human beings and that even inorganic things give rise to as direct, underivative ethical responsibility as do other human beings.[12] Because I am, so to speak, in the place in the sun that could be occupied by someone or something else, someone or something commands my responsibility provided, first, it or he or she is other than me and, second, it or he or she is in need.

Otherness than me is marked by the asymmetry of the Levinasian ethics of the face to face — though this asymmetry is also to be found in the Christian ethics of the neighbor, at least as I interpret it. I also argue, on the basis of an evocation of world ecology suggested by Heidegger's fourfold regioning of mortals, immortals, earth, and sky, that every being is in need, the need to be let be. This need may be the need to be left alone. It may be the need not to be left alone, not to be left alone to die, to perish, or to suffer destruction. It will often be, most obviously in the case of beings that cannot speak for themselves, the need to have someone speak on their behalf, to be their agent, like a parent or guardian, to act for them, to perform a speech-act for them — or a painting-act.

"I owe you the truth in painting and I will tell it to you," Cézanne writes on October 23, 1905 to Emile Bernard. But he owes the truth also to whatever thing in nature he takes as his motif. He owes it not only as a return for the color sensations his motif enables him to enjoy. He owes the truth also, as he says in one of the last letters he wrote to his son, because he becomes more clear-sighted before nature, *devant la nature. Devant,* he owes the truth for the lesson nature teaches, for its *enseignement.* He owes it above all on account of the ensignment with which the tree and the rock, no less than the subjects of his human portraits, summon his regard and through him the regard of the recipient of his letter and of those who regard his painting. To the recipient of the letter to whom he says *en écriture* that he owes him the truth *en peinture* Cézanne says in an earlier letter (dated July 25 1904), "Do not be an art critic, but paint, therein lies salvation." He could be meaning the salvation of the world. For the painter is a preserver of the truth of his motif as much as the person whom Heidegger calls the preserver (*die Bewahrende*) is a preserver of the truth of the painting he or she beholds. Salvation here may be no more than acknowledgment, a salutation like saying "*Salut,*" a recognition of the truth that, as Wallace Stevens all but says, death is the mother of loveliness, and that, as Levinas writes, vulnerability is the dominant sense of sensibility, prior to sensibility in the sense of cognitive sensation, somewhat as someone might write, under the irresistible French title "*Conscience conscience,*" that moral conscience is prior to cognitive consciousness, that cogitative self-consciousness is younger than the againbite of inwit, looking back to, regarding, the *re* of re-morse.[13] Where I am affected by the loveliness of a thing I am moved by its transience. I am therefore called to respond. So I am called to respond by the painter who draws my attention to the thing's loveliness if only by singling it out by enclosing it in a frame, for the found object and the ready-made are limiting cases of the artist's motif. Talk of moral responsibility is apt where the transience in question is the transience of, for example, the fragile tree depicted in Cézanne's São Paulo painting *The Great Pine*, perhaps the only tree that will survive in Brazil. If the transience in question is my transience, my mortality before, say, the seemingly eternal Montagne Sainte-Victoire, talk of moral responsibility may be misplaced. Where being toward *my* disappearance is said to mark the circumference of the circle of my concern, we can expect it to be said too, as it is said by Heidegger, that ethics is not yet quite on the scene. In any case, since vulnerability is the signification of aesthetic sensibility, the enjoyment of loveliness, the enjoyment of, say, the beauty of a pair (or unpair) of old boots, will have to be such as makes sense of a notion of enjoyment that is enjoyment not only of pleasure, but also of pain—which latter, anyway, is not a symmetrical opposite of pleasure. This notion of enjoyment is the one with which Levinas works. Yet he says that aesthetic enjoyment is irresponsible. Art according to him is interlude. Ethics comes on the scene and the work of art awakens to reality only when the artist faces his critics. I am saying that this is too narrow a notion of ethics and of the experience of art. It disregards a vast range of things that call for an ethical response. Cézanne is nearer the truth when he tells Bernard to give up criticism and to paint. That is the truth in painting he owes it to him to say. But we owe it to Levinas to say that he, Levinas, has a deeper conception of criticism than does Cézanne, a conception according to which criticism is decisive for what it is to owe, for criticism as Levinas defines it is ultimately the demand for a justification, and we never cease owing that.[14]

THE TEARS OF THINGS

Let us try to take seriously the remark Merleau-Ponty cites from Marchand citing Klee, that it can look as though one is being looked at and addressed by things—for instance, his instance, trees—that have no eyes to see or mouths to speak.[15] In the present discussion I have left the literal looking to the painter, leaving what may be referred to provisionally as metaphorical regard to the often sightless things the painter represents or presents. But I spoke of a mutual metaphoricity. In so speaking I was thinking of Derrida's essay on the so-called white or blank mythology of Anatole France's *The Garden of Epicurus*.[16] I was also thinking of the essay published in the following year where Levinas too treats of France's book and where he adverts to Karl Löwith's citation of Bruno Snell, who, as paraphrased by Levinas,

> points out that when in the *Iliad* the resistance to an attack by an enemy phalanx is compared to the resistance of a rock to the waves that assault it, it is not necessarily a matter of extending human behavior to the rock, through anthropomorphism, but of interpreting human resistance petromorphically. Resistance is neither a human privilege, nor a rock's, just as radiance does not characterize a day of the month of May more authentically than the face of a woman.[17]

Levinas adds, though it is questionable whether this thought is expressed by Snell, even if it is by Heidegger, "The meaning precedes the data and illuminates them." Yet for the author of *Otherwise Than Being or Beyond Essence* the ultimate meaning of data resides in their being things to be given to the other. Not indeed in their being present at hand, nor in their being ready to hand, and certainly not in their being handsome, but in their being handsels, presents, things I can give to the other. Data are in the first place *donanda*. How does this thought, when conjoined with the thought that the thing is that which I am called to give to a being with a face, relate to the thought that radiance does not characterize a day of the month of May more authentically than the face of a woman? Does not this last thought suggest that I am called to give back things to themselves? And does this thought not suggest that what in a "literal" sense lacks eyes with which to see or lips with which to speak should nonetheless be granted a face? Can one say not only "tout ce qui voit brille" but also "tout ce qui brille voit," "Everything that is brillig sees"? Does glory, which for Levinas is the privilege of human or divine beings, spread over the face of all things?

To return for a second time to another phrase, what would a "mutual metaphor" be? Would it be metaphor's death, a dead metaphor, a metaphor that has been put under the ground? Or would it be a metaphor that never got off the ground? And what would literality be? Would that be a dead letter too? Are the letters l-i-t-e-r-a-l, framed by quotation marks as in the previous paragraph, another way of spelling "metaphor"? Again, what would a perfect chiasmus look like? Perhaps it would be a mirror-imaging, like that which goes on between the sign χ on page 189 of *La vérité en peinture* and the reverse of this sign on its cover, where, instead of the *pas au-delà*, the step forward to the right of that properly inscribed sign, we have a sinister *Schritt zurück*, an "anagrammatical inversion." Look at the jackets of that book and its English translation, and, for instance, at page 190 of *La vérité en peinture* and page 153 of *The Truth in Painting*. Compare the footless sign within the frame (not even a pair of feet here, let alone a pair of shoes) with the sign (is it a letter or is it a drawing?) outside at the top, which, it seems, combines the Greek right-foot-forward version and its left-foot-backward inversion, as though it were doing the splits, like lines being taken for a walk but taken apart, deconstructed, through being drawn excruciatingly in different directions at once. *Regardez le regard.* The differences between these signs may be signs that a chiasmus of regard could and could not be a mirror image of itself, that it could and could never be perfect, that it is essentially perfectly imperfect, that, never a perfect fit, it is made up of incongruous counterparts, and, maybe, that if literal visual regarding and metaphorical ethical regarding take in each other's washing, we shall never be in a position to judge which washes whiter than white. But this may be because, if we are in a position to compare, we have moved too quickly ahead or not moved far enough back. In the words Derrida writes in *Droit de regards*—and Levinas would agree—*jamais un troisième regard ne surprendra le face-à-face de deux autres.*[18] That these words about the excluded third are left in French in my text here is a sign (in French, in English, in Esperanto, *en peinture?*) of the hopelessness of trying to say respectfully in English or French the truth that is said respectively in French or English. Or in drawing or painting. It is a sign of the redrawn-withdrawn "metaphoricity" of the literal, a sign of *Le retrait de la métaphore,*[19] a sign in particular of the postponement *sine die* of the day when we shall have got straight, unbeveled, *débiseauté,*[20] unbedeviled (*biseauter* is to bevel, but in card games it is to mark or to nick),[21] complete *entendement,* that is to say understanding-hearing, regarding whether "regard" and "*regard*" see eye to eye, a sign of the deferment of the *Augenblick* when we see how regard as looking intently or gazing at something or someone stands vis-à-vis regard as looking upon something or someone with understanding.

In asking how these words look when viewed across the Rhine, the English Channel, or the Atlantic, we expect that the different values the etymologically related words have in German, French, and English may have something to do with the way English, whatever we or Derrida might say about French, is not one language, but at least two, a Latin one that is almost French, and a Germanic one. This may indeed be relevant, but not directly, for "regard" and "look" are both of Germanic origin, as is the French "*regard.*" What Heidegger calls the guarders of the work of art are those who regard it. They regard and guard not only the painting as product but the painting as working or pro-ducing. Painters are careful seers, themselves guardians of truth, wardens of the *wahr,* who enable those who see or read their works to have regard for what is painted in both the presentative and the representative senses of this "what"—an ambiguity that is perhaps only partially presented and represented in Magritte's paintings entitled *La condition humaine,* where there is an ambiguity between what is seen through a window and what is seen on a canvas, a canvas painted on the canvas on which the painter paints. The painter, like the poet, brings out the painter and the poet in us, teaching us that, as Hölderlin might have said, *malerisch, wohnet der Mensch auf dieser Erde,* "painterly dwells humankind on this earth," teaching us, after Poussin had taught Cézanne to redo nature after him, to, as best as we can, redo nature after Cézanne. This work is love's work. The beautiful, *to kalon,* is the lovely, *to erasmiōtaton,* but not in a narrowly erotic sense. To see something as lovely, as the artist must see his motif, is to regard it with regard, with a seeing, a *Schaun,* as Rilke writes in *Requiem for a Friend,* that is *besitzlos,* unpossessive. It is to see it as calling to be loved agapeistically, that is to say ethically. *To kalon* and *to agathon* are one. Loving something unpossessively is loving it for itself, being affectionately its devoted servant, venerating it, revering it without reserve, *a-lēthes,* reguarding it *re vera,* being true to it, being its truly and its sincerely — or, rather, yours truly and yours sincerely, since we can only respond in the mode of address. To bring out the loveliness in something in painting is to bring out the painter in the beholder, to bring out in ourselves its and our truth. The sovereignty of the good is at the same time the sovereignty of the beautiful and the true.

Maybe the painter's eye, and the human eye insofar as it lets itself see painterly and poietically, that is to say, lets itself paint truth in seeing, is the eye less of a seer than of a "seer," less an organ of vision than of a visionary, of a prophet, painting on behalf of things unseen. Maybe second sight is first. A volume of Paul Klee's reflections on painting is entitled *Das bilderische Denken.* That the English translation of this volume is entitled *The Thinking Eye* could teach us something relevant to the Heideggerian chiasmus of poietic thinking, *dichterisches Denken* and thinking poietics, *denkerisches Dichten.* This is not a question that will be pursued here.[22] Nor shall we pursue here that other related Heideggerian line of thinking, the trace of *Danken* in *malerisches Denken.* It must suffice here merely to evoke in passing the trace of thoughtfulness in thinking and in painting that gratitude implies, the considerateness in consideration that links regard to the economy of reward in which thanks is the least or most one can give in return. Thoughtfulness, keeping in mind, holding in memory, may imply not being able not to weep, for example — in case the truth that might be revealed in painting is not only that I am my brother's keeper, but that fraternity is Franciscan — to weep for the departed trees of Brazil and Indonesia. The painter's eye may be less the seeing eye than the eye that sheds *lacrimas rerum.* In *Mémoires d'aveugle* Derrida cites one prophet, Marvell, saying with regard to and for another, blind Milton, that first of all man *thinks* his eyes. Eyes are thoughtful as they may be tearful, full or on the brink of tears. Even the eyes of someone who is blind. How much more terrible than blindness would be the blindness of eyes that could not cry. Eyes that could keep nothing in the mind's eye, in memory; eyes that could not mourn or shed tears of joy. The painter's eyes, and ours thanks to the painter, before they are seeing eyes, before they are eyes that regard in the sense of look or look back, regardant, as the Anglo-French language of heraldry says, are eyes that regard in the sense of re-guard, eyes that keep in memory even the immemorial past. Derrida quotes some verses from a poem of Marvell. I recite its last verse here, a not quite last chiasmus in which "each the other's difference bears," followed by the dialogue with which Derrida ends his essay, but invites us to go on:

> Thus let your streams o'erflow your springs,
> Till eyes and tears be the same things:
> And each the other's difference bears;
> These weeping eyes, those seeing tears.

> — Tears that see . . . Do you believe that?
> — I don't know, one can but believe. (. . .)

> — *Des larmes qui voient . . . Vous croyez?*
> — *Je ne sais pas. Il faut croire. (. . .)*

In the space where Derrida provides us with these *points de suspension*, like dazzling tears exposed to a painter's view, between the parentheses of the *epochē* that reduces and raises aesthetic regard to ethical regard, suspending *l'art de l'œil* from *l'à part de l'œil*, let us ask a question and suspend an answer one more time:

> — Everything that shines sees . . . *Tout ce qui brille voit.*
> *Tout ce que je regarde me regarde . . .* Do you believe that?
> — I don't know, one can but believe. (. . .)

One can but believe because seeing is believing. But one cannot see this, that seeing is believing, except on and in the same condition, the *condition humaine*. There is no seeing at all without blind faith.[23] Without truth as troth, betrothal, skepticism itself has no scope, skepticism, for example, whether this betrothal is fourfold, *vierfältig Vertrauung*, as Heidegger would say. Without regard in the sense listed second in the *Oxford English Dictionary*, namely regard as respect or concern, there is no regard in the sense it lists first, namely regard as gaze or steady look. This explains perhaps why it says "steady or *significant* look." This supplement of significance — or *signifiance*, as Levinas would say, and signi-fiance, as Heidegger might write — is significant in two regards. It provides some lexicographical backing for my earlier avowed feeling that the English word "regard" is hard put to shake off the sense of concern. And it makes a chiasmic concession to the French dictionary (Littré at least) where the ordering of senses recognizes explicitly that *regard* in its moral — as Derrida would say, abocular — sense must come first, *devant*. Must have come first. *Aura-t-il obligé?* Am I beholden? Am I beholden by everything I behold? *Il faut croire. (. . .)*

But we are beholden to observe that the text's final words

> *Des larmes qui voient . . . Vous croyez?*
> — *Je ne sais pas. Il faut croire. (. . .)*

are plurally inconclusive. Among the many questions they open are these: if the last three words affirm anything, do they affirm that one should believe that tears see, or do they affirm that, whether one believes or does not believe this, there is room here only for belief or faith as opposed to knowledge? Then "*Je ne sais pas,*" which could be one response to this question as well as to "*Vous croyez?*" might at the same time be the expression of skepticism that always returns, Levinas suggests, because of the enigma that a trace can always be disregarded by being regarded as a sign or a symptom. The plight of prehistorically plighted troth is the risk it inevitably runs of being misrepresented as representable and cognitive truth or falsity. The latter, like alethic presentation or presencing and absencing, calls for the former. But where something is called for there is something that is or could be missing, in default, like the letter *l* that has fallen from the third person singular of *falloir* and *faillir,* and like the trust of which the default is avowed to be a possibility by the declaration *il faut croire.*

ASLANT OF LIGHT

In Chapter 5 we learned that the poet-thinker Martin Heidegger never views the landscape: *Ich betrachte die Landschaft gar nie.* We have learned now that from his never viewing the landscape it by no means follows that the landscape does not regard him in the sense of regard explained in the present chapter. For in this chapter regard as viewing and considering has been distinguished from regard as being respectful and considerate in response to a being looked at or to what could be as well described as a being called and a being addressed. Here the language of hearing is as natural as the language of sight and light. The two senses cross, as they do in the Latin word *os,* which can mean either face or mouth. And if hearing is aslant of light in the sight of regard, touch too is tangential to both sight and hearing here. Toward the end of Chapter 8 it was remarked that idolatry is not limited to vision, the sense we think was primary for the Greeks, but that it can extend to "Hebrew" hearing, and to other senses too.

Ethical regard lends itself to being construed as a non-idolatrous hearing, looking, and touching. Other senses may be appealed to also. For example, if taste can be idolatrous, it can also be non-idolatrous. And there is no doubt a good way and a bad way of scenting ritually burned incense. In other words, it is the sensing shared by all these particular senses that gives sense to the notion of ethical regard. From this it follows that if in spelling out what this regard entails we turn from invoking sight to underlining hearing, this (to mix our metaphors still more) is in order to keep in touch with the resonances elicited by such locutions as "the voice of conscience." This voice is heard as though from within us, as though our hearing of it were our hearing ourselves speak. But this voice of seeming self-affection is broken by the voice that seems also to come from over and above us when conscience speaks. A source of the voice that seems to come from above may be deemed to be a god or a law or pure reason. But justesse and honor regarding the singular things of our world demand that they too be recognized and acknowledged to be its source. This is a recognition that is not a cognition and an acknowledgment that is not a knowledge. It is an affect that saves the distance between the affector and the affected, a distance such as is necessary if we are to be able to see anything, for example the starry skies above, rather than only the "stars" and flashes and shadows produced by something so close that it exerts pressure upon our eyes.

However, just as "the voice of conscience" is a turn of speech, so too is "being called" by the thing. The thing is abvocally clamant. To say that it makes a claim is to say no more nor less than that we have a responsibility toward it. With this reservation, therefore, it may be said that the thing addresses us. In saying this I may be or at least may appear to be disagreeing with Jean-François Lyotard when he writes that "matter would be something which is not addressed, what does not address itself to the mind (what in no way enters into a pragmatics of communicational and ideological destination)."[24] However, what Lyotard calls matter is also what he calls the Thing, *la Chose*. Now an upper-case initial can introduce a proper name. But if the Thing is matter, it is not the proper or even improper name of a singular thing. Its status is, paradoxically, more like that of Reason, except that Reason does address the mind, does "call on the mind" and is called for by it. The Thing or matter "sists 'before' questioning and answer, 'outside' them. It is presence as unpresentable to the mind, always withdrawn from its grasp. It does not offer itself to dialogue and dialectic."[25] All this holds for the lower-case thing. It does not com-municate, least of all with the mind or the understanding. Did we not say that acknowledgment of it is not knowledge and that recognition of it is not cognition? The singular thing affects, touches our feelings, hurts them, moves us to a response and an answerability that is indeed "before" questioning and answer, an asymmetry unre-collectively "older than" their symmetry. Let us look again at this singularity by looking again to the landscape.

10

SEEING THROUGH SEEING THROUGH

LANDSCAPE AND INSCAPE

What force does the *schaft* of the *Landschaft* acquire in the light of what has been written by the thinker-poet Gerard Manley Hopkins?

Calling Hopkins a poet does not exclude the possibility that he is also a scientist, at least insofar as poetry, *poieō, schaffen,* is at the beginning of science — *Wissenschaft* — not only for the so-called pre-Socratic scientist-poets Heraclitus, Anaximander, Anaxagoras, Empedocles, and so on, but for modern scientific methodology too, as was demonstrated in our chapter (Chapter 3) on the methodologies of the so-called rationalist Descartes and the so-called empiricist Bacon. The question how the natural sciences might be related to creatively aesthetic practice and how both are related to an ecologically sensitive ethics can be approached by asking how the relationship between certain tenets of Aristotelianism and Thomism, on the one hand, and of Scotism, on the other, was crucial in Hopkins's life and work.

It is important to remind ourselves that one of the tenets of the Aristotelianism and Thomism that Hopkins's Jesuit education impressed upon him is that there is nothing in the intellect that was not first in the senses. The kind of hylomorphism advocated by Aristotle, however, does not allow that there can be a science of the singular. The genus informs the species and the species informs matter, but there is no science, no knowledge, of the singular or individual *this*. Duns Scotus, a follower of Saint Francis of Assisi, upheld the subtle doctrine that there is an essence of the singular thing that is its thisness, its *haecceitas*. On February 20, 1875 Hopkins wrote to Robert Bridges from Saint Beuno's College in North Wales that he had been reading Duns Scotus and that he cared for him "more even than Aristotle and more *pace tua* than a dozen Hegels."[1] But well before this date, and before he had begun reading Scotus seriously three years earlier, Hopkins had experienced what he called the inscape of things. This scape, this *Schaft*, in a thing is the thing's uniqueness, selfhood, or ipseity. Hopkins also found this thisness in species. It would therefore be in the inscape of the species that science would come face to face with the poetry and prose in which Hopkins endeavored to inscape his motif, that is, to express its inscape. Face to face, because the inscape of the maximally specific, of the *infimae specii*, is the place where the scientists Polanyi and McClintock and the poet Hopkins discover what they all three call a personal knowledge of things, a *Wissenschaft*, where the Aristotelian universal, conceptualized in the Critical philosophy of Kant, is not merely instantiated by a particular, but is singularized, and the It regains the respect accorded to it by, among others, Martin Buber, if not by Emmanuel Levinas, or by the latter only derivatively from its relationship to another human being.

In his self-styled "Greek" thinking, Levinas repeatedly maintains that there is no way to God except through the other human being. Buber seems to make the possibility of an I-Thou relationship with something we would usually refer to as an It depend upon the relationship of the It to God. Unsurprisingly, this latter dependence, *mutatis mutandis*, is often affirmed by Hopkins. Levinas's humanism does not posit any such onto-theological dependence. Nor does it rule out such a dependence. But it eschews the language of onto-theological relations. Its language is the language of the ethical relation from which Levinas holds they derive their sense. So the most he can say is that the word "God" derives what sense it has from the humanism of the other human being. On several occasions he goes as far as to allow that the work of art may present a face, and therefore may have an ethical force. But he appears never to allow that works of nature themselves exert any ethical force upon humans. The forces of nature call for no ethical response. He leaves it to scientists such as Einstein to speak of "cosmic religiosity." Whether with Cicero we take *religio* to derive from *religare* and to imply nothing more than the idea of a ligature, or with Lucretius take it to derive from *religere,* meaning to re-collect, gather, or, perhaps, read together,[2] for Levinas cosmic religiosity would amount to either pantheistic idolatry, the worst polytheism of all, or, as represented by one reading of the *Deus sive Natura* of the *Ethics* of Spinoza (which is not the reading of these words adopted in the present book), neutral monism's last dying gasp.

The breath of fresh air, the *ruah,* that survivors of the death of a certain god will welcome in Levinas's "Greek" writings is his suspension of onto-theology. Rational theology had already been suspended by Kant. Redefining the categorical imperative, Levinas redefines rationality. His idea of the ethical that overflows any idea is a super-rationality, the rationality of rationality. Yet it is a rationality of affect, affect that singularizes. The ethical is the excessively rational in the excessively affective or aesthetic. That is a formula that would fit the rational intuition of the exemplar in the philosophy of Schelling. But there it would appertain to totality. Could the oxymoronic forces of that totality be experienced at the level of the inscaped This that *saves* the singular from the fate of absorption into the genus that sense-certainty suffers in the *Phenomenology of Spirit?*

When Hopkins speaks of "instress" he sometimes means an affect. To affect is sometimes what is meant by *strictiare,* the popular Latin verb (based on *strictus,* the past participle of *stringere*) from which it is said that English gets "to stress." Hopkins often uses the word "feeling" in conjunction with "instress." For example: "Looking all around but most in looking far up the valley I felt an instress and charm of Wales." But he writes not only of feeling instress. He writes also of "the instress of feeling." So this "of" marks a genitive that is both subjective and objective, the phenomenological product of possession and being possessed. When Hopkins speaks of feeling in this context he does not mean a vague romantic emotion, but a sense of value denoting nearness to or remoteness from God. Is the "or" here exclusive or non-exclusive? Is it equivalent to *vel* or to *aut?* Is the feeling of nearness simultaneous with the feeling of remoteness? And is the feeling of the remoteness of God the feeling one might have at the thought that God is dead? Or does that thought exclude even such a feeling as that of the remoteness of God? Is that thought an exception to the Heideggerian rule that all understanding has an affective modification (*Stimmung*)? If it is not an exception to that rule, what is the mood that is felt along with the thought that God is dead? According to Heidegger it could still be a feeling of the holy, to wit the holiness of being. But because finally according to Heidegger there is no being without beings, even the thought of the death of one of those beings, to wit God understood as a being, might be accompanied, as a spin-off from the holiness of being, by a feeling of the holiness of beings, the things whose instress we feel. That Hopkins too may be saying something like this is confirmed by some of his comments on Parmenides. He took Parmenides to be treating of being and not only of beings, what is, when he used the expression *to eon.* Hopkins writes: "His great text, which he repeats with religious conviction, is that Being is and Not-being is not — which perhaps one can say, a little over-defining his meaning, means that all things are upheld by instress and are meaningless without it."[3] He goes on to say, "There would be no bridge, no stem of stress between us and things to bear us out and carry the mind over: without stress we might not and could not say / Blood is red / but only / This blood is red / or / The last blood I saw was red / nor even that, for in later language not only universals would not be true but the copula would break down even in particular judgements." That is to say, in view of the fact that *stringere* also means to bind, Hopkins's quaint use of the words "stress" and "instress," whether as verbs or nouns or verbal nouns, is aimed at recovering the forgotten resources of the lexemes of ontology, at "instressing," he would say, the religious and recollective forces of the Yes of affirmation and predication in which the binding of a property to its bearer signified by the copula is bound to the binding of the signator to the things of which he or she speaks: to what Hopkins would call our quaintance with them.

If Hopkins's feeling of instress and instress of feeling is the feeling of value, it will be a feeling of positive value if it is the feeling of the nearness of God. Will it be a feeling of negative value if it is the feeling of the remoteness of God, or will it still be a feeling of positive value in the latter case too? Many of his statements about instress and inscape are made in his "Comments on the *Spiritual Exercises* of St. Ignatius Loyola." And if at least in 1868 Aristotle is "the end-all and be-all of philosophy," it is an Aristotle filtered by St. Thomas.[4] Our question is whether enough would survive the erasure of his religious faith from Hopkins's notions of instress and inscape for these and the connected Scotist notions to serve as the nerve of an ethics broad enough to allow existents of the natural world to make an underivative claim on human responsibility alongside responsibility toward other human beings. Not irrelevant to this question is the fact that eleven years after his letter declaring that Aristotle is the alpha and omega of philosophy and seven years after beginning his intensive study of Scotus — "He . . . who of all men most sways my spirits to peace," as the poem "Duns Scotus's Oxford" says of that philosopher — it is to Plato that Hopkins awards the title of "the greatest of Greek philosophers."[5] Admittedly, that title is conferred in a sermon that leaves open the possibility that among his grounds for rating Plato so highly is Hopkins's belief that the Crucifixion of Christ is foreshadowed by the persecution of the just man described at *Republic* 361e. But what chance is there that one of the prolegomena for any future ecological ethics might be found in what Hopkins would qualify as a "heathen" interpretation of the Platonic Idea of the Good? Relevant to this question is W. H. Gardner's statement that instress is akin to what, following Plato, Shelley — the author of the tract on "The Necessity of Atheism" — called " 'the One Spirit's plastic stress,' which sweeps through the 'dull dense world' of matter and imposes on it the predestined forms and reflections of the Prime Good."[6] If instress is affect, affect is effectivity. So it is *energeia* or *actus*. The feeling or affect I experience is a response to the effectuation of the power of the singular thing, the *dunamis* of its inscape, the potency it possesses to move me, the force of its unique nature, the *Potenz* of its haecceity, of its secret self. The world is full of inscape, but this is "buried away," "unwitnessed," waiting to be "called out everywhere again" by anyone with eyes to see. An entry in the Notebooks records: "I saw the inscape though freshly, as if my eye were still growing."[7] There is in this reference to the education of the eye a hint of Hopkins's idea that in realizing the inscape of the thing, I realize my own inscape in the gnosiological and ontological sense of "realize." In inscaping the thing I am inscaped by it. The education of the eye is the *Bildung* of the I. My perception, my *vernehmen,* of the inscape is contingent—with a contingency that Hopkins would translate as grace—upon my being *benommen* by the ungenerality of the thing. How can *Benommenheit* contribute to the selving of myself? Is not *Benommenheit* being transported from myself? It is indeed this, but it is a transporting away of the self preoccupied with itself. Only in being occupied with the self of the other is my self selved. Only then is my self salved and savored:

> God's most deep decree
> Bitter would have me taste: my taste was me;
> Bones built in me, flesh filled, blood brimmed the curse.
> Selfyeast of spirit a dull dough sours. I see
> The lost are like this, and their scourge to be
> As I am mine, their sweating selves; but worse.[8]

Only when that gustatorily savored self, mine and yours, is decentered from itself is it soteriologically sav-our-ed. From this it follows that the saving of my self is not something that can be the object of my concern without that concern being frustrated. There is an absolute contingency here, a contingency "either," Hopkins says, "of grace, which is 'supernature,' to nature or of more grace to grace already given."[9]

Grace is affect, and affect is the double genitivity of feeling of instress and instress of feeling. Although Hopkins finds Hegel disagreeable, he, like Kierkegaard, would not disagree with the assertion in the *Philosophy of Mind* (§400) that feeling is a mode of individuality. Hopkins, unlike Kierkegaard, would agree with Hegel's assertion that "It is . . . silly to consider intellect as superfluous or even harmful to feeling, heart, and will; the truth and, what is the same thing, the actual rationality of the heart and will can only be at home in the universality of the intellect, and not in the singleness of feeling as feeling."[10] What Hopkins would disagree with is the interpretation Hegel would put upon this universality of intellect. For although instress is indeed affect as feeling and is not independent of intellect, the intellect from which it is inseparable is not that which grasps a generality. It is the intellect that is seized by the individuality of a thing. The "logic" here is analogous to that of the uniqueness of the face of the other and how it picks out *me* in Levinas's doctrine of superrationality, where that superrationality is nonetheless traumatizing and thaumatizing affect, and where Levinas is reinterpreting the saying considered above in Chapter 4 that philosophy begins in *thaumazein*.

The disagreement with Hegel is a disagreement with Hegel's ancestor Aristotle, now regarded by Hopkins more as end-all than be-all or begin-all. Hopkins writes in "Comments on the *Spiritual Exercises* of St. Ignatius Loyola": "And as a mere possibility, passive power, is not power proper and has no activity it cannot of itself come to stress, cannot instress itself."[11] Only *energeia* can come to stress, and *energeia* or actuality only of the singular, knowledge of which Aristotle and Thomas deny, but Hopkins joyfully affirms.

Joyfully. Yet in instress there is more than a hint of distress, *dusdaimonia*. How could happiness and well-being, *eudaimonia*, be the end of human beings who are conscious of the part they play in bringing about the end of things? "The ashtree growing in the corner of the garden was felled. It was lopped first: I heard the sound looking out and seeing it maimed there came at that moment a great pang and I wished to die and not to see the inscapes of the world destroyed any more."[12]

Destruction and harming in any way are the frustration of a thing's good, whatever that good may be. Minimally, a thing's good is its persistence in being, even if the time of its existence be as limited as that of a wave that destroys itself on the shore. What a thing's good may be, other than its continuing in being, is that thing's inscape, the singularity that it is not only, as Rilke says, the task and duty (*Aufgabe*) of the poet to learn, for to protect whatever one can from harm is on everyone's agenda. The instress that responds to the perception of inscape is the response to a need.

Anyone who insists that only a sentient creature can be subject to a need may be willing to speak here at most only of a quasi-need, and consequently at most of a quasi-ethicality. The idea of deep ecological ethicality may be ahead of the concepts and rules with which many people feel comfortable. An ethics embracing nature may seem to them not a little perverse, if not a contradiction in terms. A first step is made toward seeing that it is not when the simple truth dawns that as well as the natural world being the environment of the human world, the human world is the environment of the natural. It is not enough to recognize that in inhabiting its own corporeality among other human beings inhabiting theirs the human being already inhabits the natural world. Recognition of that would be enough to give us ground for gratitude for the support our natural needs as human beings receive from our non-human natural surroundings, but it would not be enough to take us the further step, to acknowledging that we have at the very least a responsibility independent of human needs not to do anything that contributes to the ending of the existence of any natural thing. For a thing's that it is, its *hoti estin* or its *quod*, whatever may be its what, its *ti estin* or its *quid*, is already a good reason for its maker, if it has one, to say "behold, it is good." If it has a maker or if it does not, human beings will nevertheless find themselves in circumstances of lightning, tempest, plague, pestilence, or famine that will be a good reason for them to say "behold, it is bad." That both of these declarations may be made simultaneously is perhaps the truth behind Lovelock's hypothesis that nature can look after itself. It reminds us that as well as the natural world being the environment of the human world, the human world is the environment of nature.

In "On Truth and Lying in an Extramoral Sense" Nietzsche writes:

> In some remote corner of the universe, poured out and glittering in innumerable solar systems, there once was a star on which some clever animals invented knowing. That was the haughtiest and most mendacious minute of "world history" — yet only a minute. After nature had drawn a few breaths the star grew cold, and the clever animals had to die.
>
> One might invent such a fable and still not have illustrated sufficiently how wretched, how shadowy and fleeting, how aimless and arbitrary, the human intellect appears in nature. There have been eternities when it did not exist; and when it is done for again, nothing will have happened. For this intellect has no further mission that would lead beyond human life. It is human, rather, and only its owner and producer gives it such importance, as if the world pivoted around it. But if we could communicate with the midge, we should discover that it floats through the air with the same self-importance, and feels within itself the centre of this world.[13]

The truth behind this is perhaps the truth behind the Gaia Hypothesis. In neither case is its sense extra-moral, I believe.

COSMIC CLEANSING

Schelling, preceded and followed by others, is wonder-struck by the thought that there is something rather than nothing. He is struck by the "that it is" as such, and so by the quoddity not only of everything, but by the quoddity of every thing. It was in the destined-to-be-disappointed hope of hearing more said about this "that it is" that in 1841 Kierkegaard traveled to Berlin to attend the lectures of Schelling. He might have done better to travel to England, where Coleridge too was bearing witness to this itness. From Coleridge he might also have learned, as Eckhart might have learned from Duns Scotus when their paths crossed in Cologne, that an authentic relation with the Thou of God may not mean an acosmic and ananthropic disappearing of every other Thou.[14] As regards the ananthropy, this is a lesson taught also by Levinas and indeed entailed by his teaching that the anthropic Thou of alter-humanism is the only way to the Thou and the He-She-or-It of God. But this is the way of the world, he maintains, only insofar as the anthropic has the cosmic as its condition. Otherwise, Levinas teaches, we can do away with the way of the world. Except insofar as it is from the world that the needs of the other human being arise and from the world that they are met, the world can be disappeared, as cleanly cleansed as in the soteriology of Eckhart, who tells us that we must be quit of all creatures and things if we are to reach the reality of the Godhead in which lieth our salvation. The sermon from which words have been cited above is based on the text of Matthew 5:3: "Blessed are the poor in spirit, for theirs is the kingdom of heaven." The poor in spirit are those whose spirit makes room for the spirit of God. And "God" is here spelled with a capital G, so that when spelled with a lower-case initial it refers to an idea invented by the human being. One of the editors of Eckhart's works comments that the distinction between the upper- and lower-case spellings

> reflects the reading of Plato's *Timaeus*, where the divine name is spelled both ways. . . . The *Timaeus* tells about the "created gods," who were responsible for the soul. There is, however, the other distinction in Eckhart, perhaps more important: God is beyond thinking; god is what I think he is.[15]

To speak in the manner of Descartes and Levinas, God and the Good beyond being overflow every idea. To speak in the manner of Luther and Kierkegaard, the *deus absconditus* who is hidden in his revelation, where strength appears as weakness and wisdom as folly, hides the *Deus absconditus* who is hidden behind his revelation.[16] So Eckhart would have us turn our attention from ourselves. God is not in my environment. I am in his. But this *Kehre* away from oneself toward God goes along with what Eckhart terms a disinterest or disinterestedness in what is neither human spirit nor God's.

> God cannot give his properties away and so he can do nothing for the disinterested mind except to give himself to it and it is then caught up in eternity, where transitory things no longer affect it. Then the man has no experiences of the physical order and is said to be dead to the world, since he has no appetite for any earthly thing. This is what St. Paul meant by saying: "I live; yet not I, but Christ liveth in me."[17]

Let these words stand for the thousands of others that could be cited instead from the Christian tradition beginning with Paul, and from a Judaic tradition before that and an Islamic tradition since, testifying to a refusal or reluctance to allow that it is possible to have a disinterested (*abgeschieden*) love for earthly things that is not appetitive. One of the reasons Eckhart gives for ranking love of God below disinterest is as follows:

> love compels me to suffer for God's sake, whereas disinterest makes me sensitive only to God. This ranks far above suffering for God or in God; for, when he suffers, man pays some attention to the creature from which his suffering comes, but being disinterested, he is quite detached from the creature.[18]

The creature from whom the disinterested man is quite detached is not God, since God is not a creature. It must be the creature that would be the object of man's love, either something in the world other than himself, or himself, or both. But why might not man's love of things of this world be disinterested? Why might it not be agapeic? There is a deficiency in suffering on account of the suffering of another human or non-human being or on account of a thing's destruction only if, like Eckhart, we rank being sensitive to things of this world below being sensitive to nothing but God. But it is precisely the latter sensitivity that is "phenomenologically suspended" in the experiment being conducted throughout the present book. Such suspension does not mean that the experiment cannot allow for imagining how the world might look from the point of view of a divinity, provided the limits to such an imaginative exercise be acknowledged, as they usually are by the theologian and by the phenomenologist alike when they consider it necessary to issue a reminder that that imagining is being exercised from the point of view of the human experimenter.

Having cited paragraphs from Eckhart, one could cite ones from certain of the Greek and Latin Fathers, for instance St. Bonaventure, in which the possibility of an agapeic love of earthly things is allowed, but only insofar as these things are regarded as glorious creatures of god, modes of his self-revelation (and therefore, Luther and Kierkegaard would say, irrelevant to and possibly in contradiction with the God of faith). One could cite volumes in the same vein from certain contemporary theologians, for instance Urs von Balthasar. But, again, they would be beside the point of the volume now approaching its end.

At critical moments in his life Hopkins finds himself between, on the one hand, those who allow this second possibility, namely the possibility of an agapeic love of earthly things based on the belief that these things are creatures of god, and, on the other hand, those who allow a third possibility, namely the possibility that earthly things are to be loved non-concupiscently, agapeically, in and for themselves, not on account of their making up the environment of the human being or the environment of their Maker. These are moments between the nearness of God and remoteness from him, where Hopkins is drawn on the one hand to say with Gavin Maxwell, "Whatever joy she gave to you, give back to Nature" and on the other hand to say, in the words of his poem *The Golden Echo*, "Give beauty back . . . back to God, beauty's self and beauty's giver." Without prejudice to those who have ears to hear the second of these injunctions and to accept only the second of these three ways of seeing things, the aim of the present book has been to make space for a third way, a space in which the earth and the transitory things therein can be honored by those who, while not being, in Eckhart's phrase, dead to the world, are either dead to God or find that for them God is dead, in a sense of that fashionable phrase in which the G-word stands for the God to whom in his sermon on the text "Blessed are the poor" Eckhart prayed that God would quit him of god.

THEOLOGICAL VANDALISM

Certain questions touching on vandalism arise relative to the logical, epistemological, and theological teachings of the Dominican Eckhart, the Franciscan Scotus, and the Jesuit Hopkins.

According to Eckhart the poor are blessed because they are poor in world, *weltarm,* insofar as by the world we mean the world of whose climates Hopkins writes in his journal for May 7, 1868: "Warm; misty morning; then turquoise sky. Home, after having decided to be a priest and religious but still doubtful betw. St. Benedict and St. Ignatius . . . ," then, four days later: "Dull; afternoon fine. Slaughter of the innocents." That last phrase apparently refers to his burning of his poems, an act of vandalism for which Hopkins may be to some extent exonerated by the pressure imposed by his superiors and the pressure of a conscience that also led him to discontinue his learning of Welsh for fear that his motive for beginning to study that language and its literature was not a desire to acquire a medium through which to convert the Episcopalian, Nonconformist, and pagan population of Wales. So our questions may be rephrased. Is theological vandalism the only alternative to an ecological ethics based on the idea that nature bears witness to the glory of God? Can that witness be suspended in a reading of the teaching of Duns Scotus in a manner that will open the way either to a secular ecological ethics or, better, to one that neither entails nor excludes the theological dimension?

Why do I say better? Because to exclude God ab initio from the provisional ecological schema by opting for the faith of atheism would be no less dogmatic than to assume that an ecological ethics must have a theological base. However, it is difficult to see how the theological component of Scotist realism can be suspended without suspending the logical and epistemological components that seem to offer hope for an ecologically ecumenical ethics. The Subtle Doctor seems to offer hope for this through his argument that we have knowledge by acquaintance of the singularity of every thing, so that it would begin to make some sense to think of things as fitting topics of ethical, "ethical," religious, or "religious" regard. On closer inspection this hope is disappointed. Where does Scotus let us down?

Leibniz maintains that there is no sense in the hypothesis of two leaves of which one and the same full description holds. The description identifies the thing, so there is only one leaf of which such a description holds. Where there is indiscernibility, there is identity. Behind Leibniz's defense of the principle of the identity of indiscernibles lies the theological premise that without this principle there would be no assurance that God had created the best of all possible worlds. For without the principle there would be no reason for creating this leaf in preference to its identical twin, and a world in which there was repetition of two identicals would be less good than one in which there was the greater variety made possible by the avoidance of repetition. But why not ground the identity of things on singularity referred to deictically yet not described by common names connoting universals? That is the ambition of Occam's nominalism, which, guided by the principle of maximum economy, maintains that universals are otiose. If that principle is not a theological principle but, as Wittgenstein maintains, a logical principle, would not nominalism provide exactly what we are looking for, namely a theologically neutral theory based upon the singularity of things? The objection to this theory, the objection made against it by Scotus, is that there can be no knowledge of a manifold of separate singulars unconnected by real universals. So Scotus is a friend of universals.

On the other hand, Scotus maintains that there can still be no knowledge if we have no way of knowing that universals and laws are instantiated in singulars. For that to be possible it must be possible for human beings to have knowledge of singulars. It is to safeguard this possibility that he posits singular essences. These haecceities are related to universal natures in every individual thing somewhat as the differentiating properties of a thing are related to its nature, except that whereas the latter combination yields generic or specific difference, the combination of the haecceity with the nature yields the thing's numerical difference from other things and, more than its oneness, which other things also possess, it yields the uniqueness of what Heidegger calls, in quotation marks, the "*Hinblick,*" that is to say, the "view" or "*coup d'œil*" that two leaves on the same tree have of the sky.

It is worth noting in passing that although Heidegger expresses this point thus in his dissertation of 1915 on a treatise mistakenly attributed to Scotus, Thomas of Erfurt, to whom that treatise is now attributed, was a follower of Scotus and his doctrine of the univocality of being. It is not difficult to conceive the debate this must have stirred up in the mind of the young Heidegger, for whom, since 1907, as he later wrote, "Brentano's dissertation 'On the Manifold Meaning of Being since Aristotle' had been the chief help and guide of my first awkward attempts to penetrate into philosophy."[19] Heidegger's Habilitation thesis is dedicated to Heinrich Rickert, who wrote many pages on the topic of historical individuality that merit closer inspection than they have received. Also meriting closer inspection is the relation the Scotist notion of the uniqueness of things bears to the uniqueness attributed to God. But here the attempt is being made to hold theology in suspense.

Any hope of furthering this endeavor by appealing to Scotus is dampened the moment we learn that his appeal to singular essences preserves the possibility of human knowledge only if certain theological assumptions are made. Scientific knowledge of singular essences is not possible in our state of sin, he tells us. It is possible only in the world to come. That paradise garden is placed by Platonists like Wordsworth and Henry Vaughan in the bygone world of our "Angel-infancy" or earlier, the world of the *infans,* before one has the word — or before the first word fades away.

Not all hope may be lost, not if the verbal *Machenschaft* of Hopkins may help us to direct our regard not upon some world to come or gone by, but upon the vulnerable face of the world here and now, and to regard that face with something like the same respect that we feel when, at our best, we regard the face of another human being. The task set us by all three of these English and Welsh wordsmiths, all three of them in their different ways and degrees adherents of theistic transcendentalism, is to find a way of preventing the image of God represented in the face of the other human being from being not only the begin-all but also the be-all of the world that was our kindergarten, that will become our graveyard, and that is here and now our *oikos,* our ecology, our home.

Our home. The adjective is stressed because it is to instress of the human beings with whom we inhabit the world that Hopkins accords special importance in comparison with instress of the non-human things of this world:

> my selfbeing, my consciousness and feeling of myself, that taste of myself, of *I* and *me* above and in all things [. . .] is more distinctive than the taste of ale or alum, more distinctive than the smell of walnutleaf or camphor, and is incommunicable by any means to another man (as when I was a child I used to ask myself: What must it be to be someone else?). Nothing else in nature comes near this unspeakable stress of pitch, distinctiveness, and selving, this selfbeing of my own. Nothing explains it or resembles it, except so far as this, that other men to themselves have the same feeling.[20]

In our attempt to suspend theology we pass over Hopkins's argument that because human nature is "more highly pitched, selved, and distinctive than anything in the world," it can have been "developed, evolved, condensed" only by a power of "finer or higher pitch and determination than itself and certainly than any that elsewhere we see." But let us not pass over the sentences cited earlier in this chapter in which the instress of human beings is said to be deepened by the instress of non-human beings. Human selves are the more deeply selved the more instress of nature grows in truth. So if of the foci of the present book the supernatural has been eclipsed by the natural, that is because the book is motivated by a sense of grief shared with Hopkins that more and more of the inscapes of the natural world are being destroyed. That is why the book is written not *coram Deo* nor only *coram hominibus,* but principally *coram rebus,* facing things: things natural — but it is high time we took note that Hopkins mourns also the defacing, disregard, loss, or overlooking of the inscapes of human artifacts.

> Stepped into a barn of ours, a great shadowy barn, where the hay had been stacked on either side, and looking at the great rudely arched timber-frames — principles and tie-beams, which make them look like bold big A's with the cross-bar high up — I thought how sadly beauty of inscape was

unknown and buried away from simple people and yet how near at hand it was if they had eyes to see it and it could be called out everywhere again.[21]

How sadly, too, beauty of inscape was burned when a holocaust was made of some of the artifacts in which Hopkins would have given his readers eyes to see. It is however of the natural world that he writes in the previous year in a note that anticipates the remark made by Bachelard and the remark made by Klee as recollected by André Marchand and referred to in our last chapter, that sometimes when you stand facing a forest, the trees seem to be looking at and speaking to you.[22] Hopkins observes:

> What you look hard at seems to look hard at you, hence the true and the false instress of nature. One day early in March when long streamers were rising from Kemble End one large flake loopshaped, not a streamer but belonging to the string, moving too slowly to be seen, seemed to cap and fill the zenith with a white shire of cloud. I looked long up at it till the tall height and the beauty of the scaping — regularly curled knots springing if I remember from fine stems, like foliation in wood or stone — had strongly grown on me. It changed beautiful changes, growing more into ribs and one stretch of running into branching like coral. Unless you refresh the mind from time to time you cannot always remember or believe how deep the inscape in things is.[23]

You grow as the scaping of things grows on you. Hopkins's closer and closer observations feed his poetry, as those made by John Muir and referred to in our first chapter feed his descriptive prose. But they could equally well be the basis of science. The way in which these observations are gathered is no different from the method of Descartes and Bacon examined in Chapter 3. Muir and Hopkins share with Descartes and Bacon the *technē* of education that is prior to the technology of application.

HOW THINGS LOOK

If we want a technical name for this technique, as good as any is the German term *Anschauung*. Not *Anschauung,* however, as this term is usually used by Kant of passive sensibility or "intuition" as opposed to active conceptual understanding. Nor *Anschauung* as specifically seeing or as perception generally. *Anschauung* rather as looking, and in both of the senses of looking mentioned in the first sentence of those just reproduced from Hopkins's *Note-Books:* being looked at by the thing at which you look. *Weltanschauung* then, not as purely passive registration of the data of sense nor as purely active imposition of a preconception, but as the quiet work of imagination where first impressions are adjusted, made just, in responsive looking and listening to what looks to us. A detachment from oneself in order not to use or enjoy, but to honor and be en-joyed by the thing that regards us, this practice of ambiguous looking with which both art and science begin is also the beginning of ethics and religion in a fundamental sense of these terms. It is an experiment of imagination *coram re* and a spiritual exercise in something like Loyola's meaning of that term, though also something unlike. Loyola's *Spiritual Exercises* opens with the proclamation that "Man was created to praise, reverence, and serve God our Lord, and thereby to save his soul. And the other things on the face of the earth were created for man's sake, and to help him in the following out of the end for which he was created."[24] The exercise carried out in our book suspends the proposition that "the other things on the face of the earth were created for man's sake." It makes bold to entertain the thought that the face of the earth has a sake of its own. In a letter from Oxford to Robert Bridges dated May 26, 1879 Hopkins writes as follows about the words "sake" and *Sache*, both words we found it necessary to write about as early as our opening chapter:

> *Sake* is a word I find it convenient to use: I did not know when I did so first that it is common in German, in the form of *sach* [*sic*]. It is the sake of "for the sake of," *forsake, namesake, keepsake.* I mean by it the being a thing has outside itself, as a voice by its echo, a face by its reflection, a body by its shadow, a man by his name, fame, or memory, *and also* that in the thing by virtue of which especially it has this being abroad, and that is something distinctive, marked, specifically or individually speaking, as for a voice and echo clearness; for a reflected image light, brightness; for a shadow-casting body bulk; for a man genius, great achievements, amiability, and so on. In this case it is, as the sonnet says, distinctive quality in genius.[25]

The sonnet referred to is the one in praise of Henry Purcell in a prefatory note to which Hopkins says that "whereas other musicians have given utterance to the moods of man's mind, he has, beyond that, uttered in notes the very make and species of man as created both in him and in all men generally." Moods or modes or modalities are the accidental states, whereas it is the "rehearsal of own, of abrupt self" that Hopkins rehears in Purcell's music. It takes a phenomenologist to recognize a phenomenologist. So the *Sachen selbst* that Hopkins hears and sees through hearing — "I'll have an eye to the sakes of him" — are not re-presentations in the way of echoes, reflections, or shadows. That is to say, they are not what Plato calls *eidōla* or what Bacon calls idols of the theatre. Nor, on the other hand, are these sakes the quintessential being or substantial presences of which echoes and reflections are re-presentations. They are qualities, *Eigenschaften*, selfscapes, the distinctive qualities of persons and things of which Hopkins seeks to mark the distinctness by coining or recoining the Anglo-Saxon words "inscape" and "instress," much as, for the sake of enabling us to see and hear as though for the first time, Heidegger forsakes the Latinisms of metaphysics and metaphysical theology for their less adulterated German namesakes.

The experimental method or way followed by Hopkins is akin also to a meditational technique of Buddhism, with the difference that, unlike these "Oriental" practices, the saving of the self through the losing of the self to which we are introduced by what Hopkins writes about inscape and instress is at the same time a salutation and an honoring of things earthly. Like those techniques, inscaping would enable us to escape subjectivity, but the objectivity it would thereby enable us to reach is the objectivity of a science of the earth, the geology or geography Nietzsche would have called *gaia scienza*.

It may be asked at this late stage why this geotechnology is invoked, given that we have earthed the responsibility we owe to a thing in the thing's sheer existence. It may be asked how, if a thing's minimal need not to be destroyed is implied by its existence, there can be any room left for the responsiveness of stethoscopy or other subtle *Doktorschaft* such as Hopkins displays. There is still room for this because only thanks to such attentiveness, listening, looking, and tact can one learn what harms and what protects this thing or that and what is to be given priority over what. For example, should a pigeon wounded by a sparrow-hawk (or windhover!) be left in pain for the bird of prey to return to it? Should it be finished off and given decent burial, thereby putting another pigeon at risk from the still-hungry hawk? Should the visibly distressed pigeon be hidden from or shown to the very young children approaching the scene?[26] What treatment of the non-human being is called for may be as difficult to learn as what our treatment of our fellow human beings should be. As our being looked at by a person is what leads us to take pains to make our observations of the person looking at us as carefully as we can, so is it also with the looking of the thing. As I am looked at and touched by it, con-tacted by it, tested and *getastet* by its taste, my observational regard is disarmed to the point that any desire to reach out to palpate and manipulate the thing is suspended. This is a suspension by its judgment of me of any judgment I might make of it. But its judgment of me is its demand that I respond to it with justice and justesse. This means at the very least that when it comes to my making a judgment of it I seek the most just word. And it must come to that if I am to keep faith with it and with myself as artist or as scientist and as human being. The moment of my being addressed by the thing is a moment of practical religion in which I am secretly bound to expose myself and the prejudices I inevitably bring with me to being proved wrong. The moment in question is the moment of the challenge posed to the posing of any question, the moment of the good faith of truthfulness demanded by truth. That the word "religion" is here the *mot juste* is confirmed by one further statement of the phenomenon witnessed to by Marchand, Klee, Bachelard, and Hopkins:

> What one looks like contains in it an active element of looking at something, but also includes the passive element of being looked at. This is true in the strict sense of the encounter between one person and another, face to face, but is also applicable to the relationship to everything which is

looked at as present. This aspect of looking is also true of things when man looks at them. Man not only looks at them, but sees himself as looked at by them. This is because he recognizes that he is in a certain sense dependent upon them, though in such a way that the way in which things look at him is inseparable from the way he looks at things.

These sentences were written neither by a painter nor by a poet nor by a scientist. They come from the pen of a theologian in a volume on the theology of Luther.[27] They are offered as an interpretation of Luther's statement *Facies rerum est omnia in omnibus*, "the (look of the) face of things is all in all." And they bring us to our final questions.

Is not all this talk about being looked at and looked to by things inanimate or animate derivative from the polytheisms or pantheisms whose gods dwell in and keep an eye on us from out of interstices in the things of what we are accustomed to call the natural world? Alternatively, does not such talk originate in the idea of the great monotheisms with their idea of a God whose gaze never leaves us? Given the theological context of the remarks about being looked at just cited, the pertinence of these questions cannot be denied. But are they pertinent to phenomenology? Given the phenomenological context of the remarks made in the first section of the first chapter of this book about the openness to historical variation in the concept of phenomenology itself, we cannot say whether these questions are bound to remain aslant of any future phenomenological ecology and therefore to exceed this book's bounds. We cannot know whether that openness to historical variation is open enough for the meaning of phenomenology to stretch so far that this openness to variation becomes closed. That is to say, "phenomenology" might be one of those Abelian words admitting contradictory senses to which reference was made at the beginning of this book. Phenomenology—and this may be one of its limitations—does not have eyes to see whether the experience of being looked at by things of the earth upon which we rely relies on the God upon which some say we rely ultimately. It does not have eyes to see whether we see how things look by seeing through God in the sense of thanks to God, by seeing through God in the sense of rumbling God, or by seeing through God in the sense of seeing through the transparency of God's revisiting ghost. Phenomenology as familiarly envisaged today does not have eyes to see whether we, in our place in the sun, see how things look only through the slant of the sun's rays. Does geophenomenology?

> *Tout ce que je regarde me regarde* . . . Do you believe that?
> —I don't know, one can but believe. (. . .)

NOTES

1. PROLEGOMENA TO ANY FUTURE PHENOMENOLOGICAL ECOLOGY

1. Martin Heidegger, *Being and Time,* trans. John Macquarrie and Edward Robinson (Oxford: Blackwell, 1962), trans. Joan Stambaugh (Albany: SUNY, 1996), p. 35.

2. Edmund Husserl, *Ideas Pertaining to a Pure Phenomenology and to a Phenomenological Philosophy, First Book: General Introduction to a Pure Phenomenology,* trans. Fred Kersten (The Hague: Nijhoff, 1982), §§24, 141.

3. Robert Musil, *The Man without Qualities,* trans. Sophie Wilkins and Burton Pike (New York: Knopf, 1995). I thank Percy Jack for drawing my attention to this passage. For comments on what is said by the other writers named in the text at this point, see John Llewelyn, *Derrida on the Threshold of Sense* (London: Macmillan, 1986), chs. 5 and 6.

4. For a discussion of some of the complications to which this connection has given rise see John Llewelyn, "Meanings Reserved, Re-served, and Reduced," *Southern Journal of Philosophy* 32, Supplement (1993): 27–54.

5. Heidegger, *Being and Time,* p. 15 and §15.

6. Ibid., p. 175.

7. Maurice Merleau-Ponty, *Phenomenology of Perception,* trans. Colin Smith (London: Routledge and Kegan Paul, 1962), p. viii.

8. Heidegger, *Being and Time,* p. 35.

9. Ludwig Wittgenstein, *Philosophical Investigations,* trans. G. E. M. Anscombe (Oxford: Blackwell, 1953), para. 24.

10. Aristotle, *Nichomachean Ethics,* 1094b, 11–12.

11. William J. Richardson, *Heidegger: Through Phenomenology to Thought* (The Hague: Nijhoff, 1967).

12. Martin Heidegger, *Vorträge und Aufsätze,* vol. 2 (Pfullingen: Neske, 1954), p. 55, *Poetry, Language, Thought,* trans. Albert Hofstadter (New York: Harper and Row, 1975), p. 182.

13. Heidegger, *Vorträge und Aufsätze,* vol. 2, pp. 178–80, *Poetry, Language, Thought,* pp. 50–52.

14. John Muir, *My First Summer in the Sierra* (Edinburgh: Canongate, 1988), p. 14.

15. Martin Heidegger, *Unterwegs zur Sprache* (Pfullingen: Neske, 1959), p. 198, *On the Way to Language,* trans. Peter D. Hertz (New York: Harper and Row), p. 92.

16. The expression "*question-savoir*" is Merleau-Ponty's. See *Le visible et l'invisible*

(Paris: Gallimard, 1964), p. 171, *The Visible and the Invisible,* trans. Alphonso Lingis (Evanston, Ill.: Northwestern University Press, 1968), p. 129.

17. Edmund Husserl, *Cartesianische Meditationen* (The Hague: Nijhoff, 1950), p. 183, *Cartesian Meditations,* trans. Dorian Cairns (The Hague: Nijhoff, 1960), p. 157.

18. Heidegger, *Being and Time,* p. 54.

19. John Rawls, *A Theory of Justice* (Oxford: Oxford University Press, 1972), p. 223. See John Llewelyn, *The Middle Voice of Ecological Conscience: A Chiasmic Reading of Responsibility in the Neighbourhood of Levinas, Heidegger and Others* (London: Macmillan, New York: St Martin's Press, 1991), pp. 35 and 192. I can underline how important for my argument is the coherence of the notion that human beings may be advocates for non-human beings if I reproduce here the following helpful comment by an anonymous editorial reviewer of this chapter, a chapter in a book that is itself a case of such advocacy: "Rawls claims that his ethic is not one based essentially on self-interest, but rather is a Kantian ethic based on rational choice. It just so happens that the most rational universalization in this instance is one that maximizes self-interest. Yes, this is hogwash, but it is his position. This is why, for instance, a tree can't enter the Original Position. It supposedly has no rationality that would be left behind the Veil of Ignorance." On my argument the most rational universalization for the human advocate in the Original Position would be more universal than the universalization contemplated by Rawls and Kant.

20. John Muir, *A Thousand Mile Walk to the Gulf* (Boston: Houghton Mifflin, 1916), p. 58.

21. Heidegger, *Vorträge und Aufsätze,* vol. 2, p. 53, *Poetry, Language, Thought,* p. 181.

22. Husserl, *Ideas,* §§4, 70, 140.

23. John Muir, "Thoughts on the Birthday of Robert Burns," cited by Graham White in his introduction to John Muir, *The Wilderness Journeys* (Edinburgh: Canongate, 1996), p. xviii.

24. See John Llewelyn, *The HypoCritical Imagination: Between Kant and Levinas* (London: Routledge, 2000).

25. Emmanuel Levinas, *Autrement qu'être ou au-delà de l'essence,* 2nd ed. (The Hague: Nijhoff, 1978), p. 172, *Otherwise Than Being or Beyond Essence,* trans. Alphonso Lingis (The Hague: Nijhoff, 1981), p. 135.

26. G. W. F. Hegel, *Phenomenologie des Geistes* (Frankfurt am Main: Suhrkamp, 1970), p. 92.

2. GAIA SCIENZA

1. Martin Heidegger, "Nur ein Gott kann uns retten," *Der Spiegel* 23 (1976): 195–217, trans. William J. Richardson, in Thomas Sheehan, ed., *Heidegger the Man and the Thinker* (Chicago: Precedent Publishing, 1961), pp. 45–57.

2. James Lovelock, *Gaia: A New Look at Life on Earth* (Oxford: Oxford University Press, 1991), *The Ages of Gaia: A Biography of our Living Earth* (Oxford: Oxford University Press, 1991).

3. The thought that can be read on the plaque above a passageway leading off Edinburgh's Royal Mile announcing "World's End Close."

4. Lovelock, *Gaia,* p. 152.

5. Ibid., p. 9.

6. Llewelyn, *The Middle Voice of Ecological Conscience;* Lawrence E. Johnson, *A Morally Deep World: An Essay on Moral Significance and Environmental Ethics* (Cambridge: Cambridge University Press, 1991).

7. Peter Carruthers, *The Animals Issue: Moral Theory in Practice* (Cambridge: Cambridge University Press, 1992).

8. Ibid., p. 160.

9. Ibid., p. 137.

10. John Rawls, *A Theory of Justice* (Oxford: Oxford University Press, 1972).

11. Carruthers, *The Animals Issue*, pp. 99–100.

12. Thomas Scanlon, "Contractualism and Utilitarianism," in Amartya Sen and Bernard Williams, eds., *Utilitarianism and Beyond* (Cambridge: Cambridge University Press, 1982), pp. 103–24.

13. Carruthers, *The Animals Issue*, p. 66.

14. Ibid., p. 57.

15. Thomas Nagel, "What Is It Like to Be a Bat?" in *Mortal Questions* (Cambridge: Cambridge University Press, 1979), pp. 165–80.

16. See John Llewelyn, "Am I Obsessed by Bobby?" in Robert Bernasconi and Simon Critchley, eds., *Re-reading Levinas* (Bloomington: Indiana University Press, 1991), pp. 234–45; and *The Middle Voice of Ecological Conscience*, ch. 3.

17. Frans de Waal, *Chimpanzee Politics* (London: Unwin, 1982), p. 207, cited by Rosemary Rodd, *Biology, Ethics, and Animals* (Oxford: Clarendon Press, 1990), p. 241.

18. Carruthers, *The Animals Issue*, p. 196.

19. Ibid., p. 99.

20. Peter Singer, *Practical Ethics* (Cambridge: Cambridge University Press, 1979); Peter Singer, "Killing Humans and Killing Animals," *Inquiry* 22 (1979): 145–56.

21. J. J. C. Smart, "An Outline of a System of Utilitarian Ethics," in J. J. C. Smart and Bernard Williams, *Utilitarianism For and Against* (Cambridge: Cambridge University Press, 1973).

22. R. G. Frey, *Interests and Rights: The Case against Animals* (Oxford: Clarendon Press, 1980).

23. Peter Singer and Paul Cavalieri, eds., *The Great Ape Project* (London: Fourth Estate, 1993). See also note 30, below.

24. So I can with consistency subscribe to the Jane Goodall Society, a society dedicated specifically to the welfare of chimpanzees.

25. Immanuel Kant, *The Metaphysical Principles of Virtue* (part 2 of *The Metaphysics of Morals*), trans. James Ellington (New York: Bobbs-Merrill, p. 105). See Llewelyn, *The Middle Voice of Ecological Conscience*, ch. 3.

26. Johnson, *A Morally Deep World*, p. 94.

27. Michel Serres, *Le contrat naturel* (Paris: Bourin, 1990).

28. Johnson, *A Morally Deep World*, p. 106.

29. Martin Heidegger, *Grundbegriffe der Metaphysik: Welt — Endlichkeit — Einsamkeit*, Gesamtausgabe [hereafter G] 29/30 (Frankfurt: Klostermann, 1983), *The Fundamental Concepts of Metaphysics: World, Finitude, Solitude*, trans. William McNeill and Nicholas Walker (Bloomington: Indiana University Press, 1992).

30. Dorion Sagan and Lynn Margulis, "The Gaian Perspective of Ecology," *Ecologist* 13 (1983): 161–64.

31. Johnson, *A Morally Deep World*, p. 288.

32. David Farrell Krell, *Daimon Life: Heidegger and Life-Philosophy* (Bloomington: Indiana University Press, 1992). For a discussion of this see John Llewelyn, "The De(p)rivation of Life," *Research in Phenomenology* 24 (1994): 236–45.

3. OCCIDENTAL ORIENTATION

1. Francis Bacon, *Novum Organum*, Aphorisms Concerning the Interpretation of Nature and the Kingdom of Man, Book 1, nos. 1, 3, *The Philosophical Works of Francis Bacon*, reprinted from the texts and translations, with the notes and prefaces of

Robert Leslie Ellis and James Spedding, ed. John M. Robertson (London: Routledge, 1905), p. 259.

2. *The Philosophical Works of Descartes*, trans. Elizabeth S. Haldane and G. R. T. Ross, vols. 1 and 2 (New York: Dover, 1931).

3. Ibid., vol. 1, p. 33.

4. Ibid., p. 16.

5. Ibid.

6. His arguments for simplicity of nature are not always convincing. It is plausible to assert that equality is simpler than inequality and that the latter is more complex, and this is a good reason for saying, as Descartes does, that one must make comparisons between equals before one can know whether when A is unequal to B and B is unequal to C, A is unequal to C. But he also says that if we are to know an effect we must first know the cause, whereas the converse does not hold. His reasoning here seems not to turn on the correlativity of the concepts of cause and effect. His argument seems to be that from a given event one cannot predict its effects, whereas from a given event one can retrodict its cause. This assumes that there is no indefinite plurality of causes.

7. Jean-Luc Marion, *Sur la théologie blanche de Descartes: analogie, des vérités éternelles, et fondement* (Paris: Presses Universitaires de France, 1981), pp. 162–63.

8. *The Philosophical Works of Descartes*, vol. 1, p. 92.

9. *De Interpretatione*, 2, 3, *Poetics* 20; W. D. Ross, *Aristotle: A Complete Exposition of His Work and Thought* (New York: Meridian, 1959), pp. 27 and 294, note 13.

10. Werner Jaeger, *Aristotle: Fundamentals of the History of His Development*, trans. Richard Robinson (London: Oxford University Press, 1948), p. 375.

11. Bacon, "Preface to the Great Instauration," *Philosophical Works*, p. 247

12. Max Horkheimer and Theodor W. Adorno, *Dialectic of Enlightenment*, trans. John Cumming (New York: Continuum, 1944), p. 4.

13. Bacon, *De Sapientia Veterum*, *Philosophical Works*, p. 830.

14. John Black, *The Dominion of Man: The Search for Ecological Responsibility* (Edinburgh: Edinburgh University Press, 1970), pp. 40–41.

15. Francis Bacon, *Valerius Terminus*, *Philosophical Works*, pp. 194–95.

16. Bacon, *Novum Organum*, "The Great Instauration," *Philosophical Works*, p. 251.

17. Bacon, *De Augmentis Scientiarum*, *Philosophical Works*, p. 484.

18. Genevieve Lloyd, *The Man of Reason: "Male" and "Female" in Western Philosophy* (London: Methuen 1984), p. 14.

19. Bacon, *Novum Organum*, Aphorisms, Book 1, no. 95, *Philosophical Works*, p. 288.

20. Peter Urbach, *Francis Bacon's Philosophy of Science: An Account and Reappraisal* (La Salle: Open Court, 1987), pp. 59ff.

21. Bacon, *Of the Advancement of Learning*, *Philosophical Works*, pp. 92–93. Compare "Knowledge . . . is power," in *Works*, vol. 7, ed. James Spedding, R. L. Ellis, and D. D. Heath (London: 1857–74, New York: Garrett Press, 1968), p. 253.

22. Bacon, *Novum Organum*, Aphorisms, Book 1, nos. 19, 20, 104, *Philosophical Works*, pp. 261, 290; Urbach, *Francis Bacon's Philosophy of Science*, p. 35.

23. Bacon, *Novum Organum*, Aphorisms, Book 1, no. 82, *Philosophical Works*, p. 281.

24. Bacon, "In Praise of Human Knowledge" (*Miscellaneous Tracts upon Human Knowledge*), in *The Works of Francis Bacon*, vol. 1, ed. Basil Montagu (London: n.p., 1825), pp. 254ff.

25. Bacon, *Historia Ventorum*, cited in Benjamin Farrington, *Francis Bacon: Philosopher of Industrial Science* (London: Macmillan, 1973), pp. 149–50. See also *Valerius Terminus*, *Philosophical Works*, p. 189, and *Novum Organum*, Aphorisms, Book 1, no. 67, *Philosophical Works*, p. 274.

26. Bacon, *Temporis Partus Masculus*, cited in Urbach, *Francis Bacon's Philosophy of Science*, p. 85.

27. Bacon, *Novum Organum,* Aphorisms, Book 1, no. 129, *Philosophical Works,* p. 300.

28. Bacon, *Novum Organum,* Aphorisms, Book 1, no. 117, 3, *Philosophical Works,* pp. 295, 259.

29. For such an attempt see Urbach, *Francis Bacon's Philosophy of Science,* pp. 71–72.

30. Bacon, *Of the Advancement of Learning,* in *Philosophical Works,* p. 45.

31. Ibid., p. 125.

32. *Redargutio Philosophorum, The Refutation of Philosophies,* cited in Urbach, *Francis Bacon's Philosophy of Science,* p. 96.

33. Ludwig Wittgenstein, *Tractatus Logico-Philosophicus,* trans. D. F. Pears and B. F. McGuinness (London: Routledge and Kegan Paul, 1961), 6.43.

34. Ibid., 6.52.

35. Evelyn Fox Keller, *A Feeling for the Organism: The Life and Work of Barbara McClintock* (San Francisco: Freeman, 1983), pp. 198, 200.

36. Ibid., p. 201, citing E. Broda, "Boltzman, Einstein, Natural Law and Evolution," *Comparative Biochemical Physiology* 67B (1980): 376.

37. Robert Nye, cited in Llewelyn, *The Middle Voice of Ecological Conscience,* p. 207.

38. Keller, *A Feeling for the Organism,* p. 201, citing Banesh Hoffmann and Helen Dukes, *Albert Einstein, Creator and Rebel* (New York: New American Library, 1973), p. 222.

39. Ibid., p. 204, citing Niels Bohr, *Atomic Physics and Human Knowledge* (New York: Wiley, 1958), p. 33.

40. Ibid., p. 204, citing Robert J. Oppenheimer, *Science and the Common Understanding* (New York: Simon and Schuster, 1954), pp. 8–9.

41. Ibid., p. 207.

4. ON THE SAYING THAT PHILOSOPHY BEGINS IN WONDER

1. Martin Heidegger, *Sein und Zeit* (Tübingen: Niemeyer, 1967), *Being and Time,* p. 370.

2. Ibid., p. 12.

3. G. W. F. Hegel, *The Philosophy of History,* trans. J. Sibree (New York: Dover, 1956), p. 234.

4. Sigmund Freud, *Standard Edition of the Complete Psychological Works,* vol. 11 (London: Hogarth Press and the Institute for Psycho-analysis, 1957), pp. 154ff.

5. See Jacques Derrida, "Plato's Pharmacy," in *Dissemination,* trans. Barbara Johnson (Chicago: University of Chicago Press; London: Athlone Press, 1981), *La Dissémination* (Paris: Seuil, 1972).

6. Martin Heidegger, *What Is Philosophy?* trans. E. Kluback and Jean T. Wilde (London: Vision, 1958), p. 79.

7. Emmanuel Levinas, *Existence and Existents,* trans. Alphonso Lingis (The Hague: Nijhoff, 1978), p. 95, *De l'existence à l'existant* (Paris: Vrin, 1981), p. 163.

8. G. W. F. Hegel, *Lectures on the History of Philosophy,* vol. 1, trans. E. S. Haldane (London: Kegan Paul, Trench, Trübner, 1892), pp. 151–52.

9. Hegel, *Philosophy of History,* p. 234.

10. Hegel, *Lectures on the History of Philosophy,* p. 99.

11. Martin Heidegger, *Existence and Being,* trans. R. F. C. Hull and A. Crick (London: Vision, 1949), p. 386, *Pathmarks,* ed. William McNeill (Cambridge: Cambridge University Press, 1998), p. 234, *Wegmarken* (Frankfurt am Main: Klostermann, 1976), p. 307.

12. Martin Heidegger, *Grundfragen der Philosophie* (Frankfurt am Main: Klostermann, 1984), p. 190.

13. See especially Robert Bernasconi, *The Question of Language in Heidegger's History of Being* (Atlantic Highlands, N.J.: Humanities Press; London: Macmillan, 1984).

14. For a discerning treatment of the question of whether scientific explanation reduces the scope for wonder, as well as of other topics related to the ones raised in the present essay, see R. W. Hepburn, "Wonder," *Aristotelian Society Supplementary Volume* 54 (1980): 1–23, reproduced in *"Wonder" and Other Essays: Eight Studies in Aesthetics and Neighbouring Fields* (Edinburgh: Edinburgh University Press, 1984), pp. 131–54. See also Richard Dawkins, *Unweaving the Rainbow: Science, Delusion and the Appetite for Wonder* (London: Allan Lane, Penguin Press, 1998).

15. Heidegger, *Grundfragen der Philosophie*, p. 174.

16. Heidegger, *Existence and Being*, p. 392, *Pathmarks*, p. 237, *Wegmarken*, p. 312.

17. Heidegger, *Introduction to Metaphysics*, trans. R. Manheim (New York: Doubleday, 1961), p. 129, *Einführung in die Metaphysik* (Tubingen: Niemeyer, 1953), p. 117.

18. Hegel, *Philosophy of History*, p. 235.

19. Heidegger, *Existence and Being*, p. 392, *Pathmarks*, p. 238, *Wegmarken*, p. 312.

20. Heidegger, *Introduction to Metaphysics*, p. 132, *Einführung in die Metaphysik*, p. 120.

21. Heidegger, *Introduction to Metaphysics*, p. 133, *Einführung in die Metaphysik*, p. 121.

22. Freud, *Standard Edition*, vol. 17 (1955), pp. 218ff. See also Llewelyn, *Derrida on the Threshold of Sense*, pp. 94ff.

23. *The Philosophical Works of Descartes*, vol. 1, p. 358.

24. Martin Heidegger, *The Essence of Reasons*, trans. T. Malick (Evanston, Ill.: Northwestern University Press, 1969), p. 113, *Pathmarks*, p. 129, *Wegmarken*, p. 168.

25. Heidegger, *Grundfragen der Philosophie*, p. 170.

26. Martin Heidegger, *Erläuterungen zu Hölderlins Dichtung* (Frankfurt am Main: Klosterman 1981), p. 76.

27. Heidegger, *Grundfragen der Philosophie*, p. 2, *Existence and Being*, p. 380, *Pathmarks*, p. 96, *Wegmarken*, p. 122.

28. Maurice Merleau-Ponty, *The Visible and the Invisible*, p. 129, *Le visible et l'invisible*, p. 171.

29. Hegel, *Lectures on the History of Philosophy*, p. 254.

30. Alexander of Aphrodisias, *In Aristotelis Metaphysica Commentaria*, ed. M. Hayduck (Berlin: Reimer, 1891), pp. 15–16.

31. Heidegger, *Grundfragen der Philosophie*, p. 170.

32. Heidegger, *What Is Philosophy?*, p. 80.

33. Heidegger, *Grundfragen der Philosophie*, p. 2.

34. Martin Heidegger, *Basic Writings*, ed. D. F. Krell (New York: Harper and Row, 1977; London: Routledge and Kegan Paul, 1978), p. 379, Martin Heidegger, *Zur Sache des Denkens* (Tübingen: Niemeyer, 1969), p. 67.

35. Martin Heidegger, *Early Greek Thinking*, trans. D. F. Krell and F. A. Capuzzi (New York: Harper and Row, 1975), p. 108, Martin Heidegger, *Vorträge und Aufsätze*, vol. 2, p. 60.

36. Heidegger, *Basic Writings*, p. 386, *Zur Sache des Denkens*, p. 74.

37. Heidegger, *Basic Writings*, p. 390, *Zur Sache des Denkens*, p. 78.

38. Heidegger, *Basic Writings*, p. 242, *Pathmarks*, p. 276, *Wegmarken*, p. 364.

39. Heidegger, *Early Greek Thinking*, p. 121, *Vorträge und Aufsätze*, pp. 279–80.

5. BELONGINGS

1. Martin Heidegger, "Das Ding," in *Vorträge und Aufsätze*, vol. 2, p. 52, *Poetry, Language, Thought*, p. 179, where Albert Hofstadter's translation has: "The mirror-

ing that binds into freedom is the play that betroths each of the four to each through the enfolding clasp of their mutual appropriation."

2. Jacques Derrida, *La vérité en peinture* (Paris: Flammarion, 1978), p. 404, *The Truth in Painting*, trans. Geoff Bennington and Ian McLeod (Chicago: University of Chicago Press, 1987), p. 354.

3. Martin Heidegger, *Unterwegs zur Sprache*, p. 198, *On the Way to Language*, p. 92.

4. André Gide, *Les nourritures terrestres* (Paris: Gallimard, 1947). Emancipate yourself from this book, the author bids his readers in it *avant-propos* and its *envoi*, for if he had done so in the book itself, the request could not have been met.

5. Martin Heidegger, *Die Selbstbehauptung der deutschen Universität* (Frankfurt am Main: Klostermann, 1983), p. 18. However, in November 1933, Heidegger tells his students that "The Führer himself and he alone is German reality and its law, today and henceforth."

6. Martin Heidegger, *Identität und Differenz* (Pfullingen: Neske, 1957), *Identity and Difference*, trans. Joan Stambaugh (New York: Harper and Row, 1969).

7. Friedrich Hölderlin, *Poems and Fragments*, trans. Michael Hamburger (Cambridge: Cambridge University Press, 1980), p. 462.

8. Derrida, *La vérité en peinture*, p. 292, *The Truth in Painting*, p. 257.

9. This description can be read at Martin Heidegger, *Holzwege* (Frankfurt am Main: Klostermann, 1972), pp. 22–23, *Poetry, Language, Thought*, pp. 33–34, *Chemins qui ne mènent nulle part*, trans. W. Brockmeier and F. Fédier (Paris: Gallimard, 1962), pp. 34–35.

10. This description can be read at Derrida, *La vérité en peinture*, pp. 334–35, *The Truth in Painting*, pp. 292–23.

11. Derrida, *La vérité en peinture*, p. 335, *The Truth in Painting*, p. 293–94.

12. Derrida, *La vérité en peinture*, p. 336, *The Truth in Painting*, p. 294.

13. Derrida, *La vérité en peinture*, p. 334, *The Truth in Painting*, p. 292.

14. Friedrich Hölderlin, *Die Wanderung*, *Poems and Fragments*, p. 392.

15. Derrida, *La vérité en peinture*, p. 336, *The Truth in Painting*, p. 294.

16. Derrida, *La vérité en peinture*, p. 299, *The Truth in Painting*, p. 262.

17. Derrida, *La vérité en peinture*, p. 330, *The Truth in Painting*, p. 288.

18. Derrida, *La vérité en peinture*, p. 311, *The Truth in Painting*, p. 272.

19. Derrida, *La vérité en peinture*, p. 315, *The Truth in Painting*, p. 276.

20. Harold G. Alderman, "The Work of Art and Other Things," in *Martin Heidegger: In Europe and America*, ed. Edward G. Ballard and Charles E. Scott (The Hague: Nijhoff, 1973), p. 168.

21. Derrida, *La vérité en peinture*, p. 311, *The Truth in Painting*, p. 272.

22. Derrida, *La vérité en peinture*, p. 420, *The Truth in Painting*, pp. 367–68.

23. Martin Heidegger, "Schöpferische Landschaft: Warum bleiben wir in der Provinz?" in *Denkerfahrungen* (Frankfurt am Main: Klostermann, 1983), p. 11, "Creative Landscape: Why Do We Stay in the Province?" trans. Thomas Sheehan, in *The Weimar Republic Sourcebook*, ed. Anton Kaes, Martin Jay, and Edward Dimendberg (Berkeley: University of California Press, 1994), p. 427.

24. Derrida, *La vérité en peinture*, p. 355, *The Truth in Painting*, p. 311.

25. Meyer Schapiro, "The Still Life as a Personal Object—A Note on Heidegger and van Gogh," in *The Reach of Mind: Essays in Honour of Kurt Goldstein*, ed. Marianne L. Simmel (New York: Springer, 1968), p. 207. The full title of the MS numbered D 17 in the Husserl Archive is "Umsturz der kopernikanischen Lehre in der gewöhnlichen weltanschaulichen Interpretation. Die Urarche Erde bewegt sich nicht. Grundlegende Untersuchungen zum phänomenologischen Ursprung der Körperlichkeit, der Räumlichkeit der Natur im ersten naturwissenschaftlichen Sinne. Alles notwendige Anfangsuntersuchungen." Merleau-Ponty's references to the short title are not quite correct. The piece is reproduced in *Essays in Memory of Edmund Husserl,*

ed. Marvin Farber (Cambridge, Mass.: Harvard University Press, 1940), pp. 305–25. There is an English translation by Fred Kersten in *Husserl: Shorter Works,* ed. Peter McCormick and Frederick A. Elliston (Notre Dame: University of Notre Dame Press, 1981), pp. 222–33. There is a French translation by Didier Franck in *Philosophie* 1 (January 1984): 5–21. D 18 is a sequel published under the title "Notizen zur Raumkonstitution" with an editorial introduction by Alfred Schuetz in *Philosophy and Phenomenological Research* 1 (September 1940 and June 1941): 21–37 and 216–26. Both of Husserl's pieces are dated May 1934. The first version of "Der Ursprung des Kunstwerkes" was a lecture delivered in November 1935. I am grateful to Phil Buckley and the staff of the Husserl Archive at Louvain for assistance in establishing some of these facts.

26. Derrida, *La vérité en peinture,* p. 405, *The Truth in Painting,* pp. 354–55.

27. Heidegger, *Being and Time,* p. 370.

28. Heidegger, G39, p. 142.

29. Heidegger, *Holzwege,* p. 16, *Poetry, Language, Thought,* p. 26.

30. My references to what Heidegger says on p. 70 of *Being and Time* gave rise to the following exchange when an early version of the present chapter was read at the Reading Heidegger colloquium organized by David Farrell Krell at the University of Essex in 1986:

> *D. Krell:* Toward the end of *Being and Time* Heidegger talks about the peculiar power of certain aspects of our environment to shape time. He talks about the passage of the sun through the sky, the housing of the sun, as it were; it is almost a discussion of the zodiac. Would that be one of the places in *Being and Time* where you would want to see something like the power of the earth, and would it not be somehow stronger in *Being and Time* than it is in "The Origin of the Work of Art"?
>
> *J. Llewelyn:* It might be. I would need to refresh my memory. . . . My first reaction is to say that it sounds rather as though that would come under the heading of nature as wherewithal, as being used to mark time, as a clock, as an instrument, which Heidegger also refers to earlier on when he talks about what the South wind is to the farmer. But you may well be right to say that there is something hinted at there that would be germane to what he says on page 70 of *Being and Time.* However, if it involves measuring time, it is an instrument, and so it seems to me that it is not that power of the earth which Heidegger later invokes.
>
> *D. Krell:* Yes, but isn't it the instrument of instruments, to use an Aristotelian phrase; isn't it somehow beyond *Zeughaftigkeit?* The passage of the sun across the sky, or the coming of the South wind, is not an artifact, it is not *Zeug.* . . .
>
> *J. Llewelyn:* That is true. But I was very careful to say that *Zeug* may need human intervention, not that it has to have human intervention, because we have to accommodate what he says in the fairly unambiguous passages early in the book, about what the wind is to the farmer, and the rain, and the rest of it. This may well be a problem for Heidegger. But it does seem that there one is regarding nature as equipment. One's so regarding it is, you might say, performing an operation on it; and it is very different from an artifact. It is not a human artifact. It is a kind of intermediate stage. Yet I myself don't see what he is talking about on page 70 as the power of nature. But I will go back and look at the later pages: maybe there's more there than I recall.
>
> *D. Wood:* When you talk about the zodiac, you have to note that it is, in a sense the capturing of the sun, not merely the sun moving freely through the heavens. This is obviously something special, because you're dealing directly with the sun and with nature, but . . .
>
> *J. Llewelyn:* . . . but it's *clock* time.
>
> *D. Krell:* No, it is before clock time.
>
> *J. Sallis:* It is the self-interpretation of temporality. . . .
>
> *D. Krell:* The auto-affection of world time. . . .

D. Wood: But it is the beginning of division, the division of the day; that seems to me the sense. It is that intervention, that metrication, the beginning of measurement, the beginning of measuring, that is so important. In a sense the sun is a pre-clock....
D. Krell: Truly, that is the direction Heidegger takes. But what reminds me of the passage on page 70 that John is talking about is the poetics or the rhetoric of the passage, which could take one in quite a different direction.

(Many revolutions of the earth later, John agrees.)

31. Heidegger, *Holzwege*, p. 24, *Poetry, Language, Thought*, p. 35.
32. Derrida, *La vérité en peinture*, p. 353, *The Truth in Painting*, p. 310.
33. Derrida, *La vérité en peinture*, p. 333, *The Truth in Painting*, p. 292.
34. Derrida, *La vérité en peinture*, p. 407, *The Truth in Painting*, p. 356.
35. Derrida, *La vérité en peinture*, p. 335, *The Truth in Painting*, pp. 293–94.
36. Derrida, *La vérité en peinture*, p. 404, *The Truth in Painting*, p. 353.
37. Heidegger, *Denkerfahrungen*, pp. 10–11, *The Weimar Republic Sourcebook*, p. 427.
38. Heidegger, G39, p. 8.
39. Heidegger, *Holzwege*, p. 37, *Poetry, Language, Thought*, p. 48.
40. Heidegger, G39, p. 127.
41. Ibid., pp. 85 and 117.
42. Ibid., p. 88.
43. Heidegger, *Holzwege*, p. 38, *Poetry, Language, Thought*, p. 49.
44. Heidegger, *Holzwege*, p. 38, *Poetry, Language, Thought*, p. 49.
45. Derrida, *La vérité en peinture*, pp. 408–409, *The Truth in Painting*, pp. 357–58.
46. Heidegger, *Holzwege*, p. 37, *Poetry, Language, Thought*, p. 49.
47. Heidegger, *Holzwege*, p. 36, *Poetry, Language, Thought*, p. 47.
48. Heidegger, G45, p. 174.
49. Heidegger, *Holzwege*, p. 41, *Poetry, Language, Thought*, p. 53.
50. Heidegger, *Holzwege*, p. 31, *Poetry, Language, Thought*, p. 42.
51. Heidegger, *Being and Time*, p. 275.
52. Heidegger, *Denkerfahrungen*, p. 38, could be taken to suggest that he would.
53. Heidegger, *Holzwege*, p. 32, *Poetry, Language, Thought*, p. 43.
54. Heidegger, *Holzwege*, p. 24, *Poetry, Language, Thought*, p. 35.
55. Heidegger, *Vorträge und Aufsätze*, vol. 2, p. 51, *Poetry, Language, Thought*, p. 178.
56. Heidegger, G39, p. 111.
57. Ibid., p. 112.
58. Ibid., p. 111.
59. Heidegger, *Holzwege*, p. 32, *Poetry, Language, Thought*, p. 43.
60. Heidegger, *Cézanne*, in "Gedachtes" (1970), *Denkerfahrungen*, p. 163. Roughly:

> Reflective, composed, his face
> earnest with stillness, the old gardener
> Vallier, who attended to inconspicuous things at
> the chemin des Lauves.
>
> In the painter's late work the twofold
> Of what is present and of presence is into a onefold
> turned, "realized" and at the same time overcome,
> altered into an identity with secrecy replete.
>
> Is a path opened up here that to a belonging-
> together of poetry and thinking
> leads?

The lines from *Patmos* cited at the end of this essay may be rendered:

> Dwell near, spent,
> On mountains most separate.

6. A FOOTNOTE IN THE HISTORY OF *PHUSIS*

1. Maurice Merleau-Ponty, *La nature, Notes, Cours du Collège de France* (Paris: Seuil, 1995), pp. 19–20.

2. John Sallis, *Stone* (Bloomington: Indiana University Press, 1994), p. 147. After writing this chapter I realized that it responds to a thought expressed in the final sentence of John Sallis, "Levinas and the Elemental," *Research in Phenomenology* 27 (1998): 152–59. I have also read with great enjoyment papers on the elemental by Alphonso Lingis, among them "The Elemental Imperative," *Research in Phenomenology* 18 (1988): 3–21.

3. Maurice Merleau-Ponty, *Notes de cours* 1959–1961 (Paris: Gallimard, 1996), p. 127.

4. Edmund Husserl, "Grundlegende Untersuchung zum phänomenologischen Ursprung der Räumlichkeit der Natur (Umsturz der kopernischen Lehre)," in *Essays in Memory of Edmund Husserl*, ed. M. Farber (Cambridge, Mass.: Harvard University Press, 1940), p. 324.

5. Heidegger, *Die Grundbegriffe der Metaphysik*, pp. 345–46, *The Fundamental Concepts of Metaphysics*, p. 237. See also Krell, *Daimon Life*, pp. 9–11. I am greatly indebted to that book and its author. I dedicate whatever may be found worthwhile in the present chapter to him and to Cristy.

6. André Lalande, *Vocabulaire technique et critique de la philosophie* (Paris: Presses Universitaires de France, 1951), p. 671.

7. Martin Heidegger, *Einführung in die Metaphysik*, G40, p. 17, *Introduction to Metaphysics*, p. 12.

8. Edmund Husserl, *Zur Phänomenologie der Intersubjektivität*, Husserliana 15, ed. Iso Kern (The Hague: Nijhoff, 1973), p. 178.

9. Jacques Derrida, *De l'esprit: Heidegger et la question* (Paris: Galilée, 1987), *Of Spirit: Heidegger and the Question*, trans. Geoffrey Bennington and Rachel Bowlby (Chicago: University of Chicago Press, 1989).

10. Edmund Husserl, *Ideen zu einer reinen Phänomenologie und phänomenologischen Philosophie*, vol. 2, *Phänomenologische Untersuchungen zur Konstitution*, Husserliana 4, ed. Walter Biemel (The Hague: Nijhoff, 1952), p. 285, *Ideas Pertaining to a Pure Phenomenology and to a Phenomenological Philosophy*, Second Book, *Studies in the Phenomenology of Constitution*, trans. Richard Rojcewicz and André Schuwer (Dordrecht: Kluwer, 1989), p. 298.

11. Edmund Husserl, *Die Krisis der Europäischen Wissenschaften und die transzendentale Phänomenologie: Eine Einleitung in die phänomenologische Philosophie*, Husserliana 6, ed. Walter Biemel (The Hague: Nijhoff, 1954), p. 232, *The Crisis of European Sciences and Transcendental Phenomenology: An Introduction to Phenomenological Philosophy*, trans. David Carr (Evanston, Ill.: Northwestern University Press, 1970), p. 229.

12. See Llewelyn, *The HypoCritical Imagination*. The unword "gl-and" would be a connective in the queer logic of *Glas*. See Jacques Derrida, *Glas*, trans. John P. Learey Jr. and Richard Rand (Lincoln: University of Nebraska Press, 1986).

13. William Wordsworth, "A Slumber Did My Spirit Seal," in *The Poetical Works of Wordsworth*, ed. Thomas Hutchinson (London: Oxford University Press, 1932), p. 187; Martin Heidegger, *Sein und Zeit* (Tübingen: Niemeyer, 1972), G2, *Being and Time*, p. 70.

14. See Theodore R. Schatzki, "Early Heidegger on Being, the Clearing, and Realism," in *Heidegger: A Critical Reader*, ed. Hubert L. Dreyfus and Harrison Hall (Oxford: Blackwell, 1992), p. 93.

15. Martin Heidegger, *Die Grundprobleme der Phänomenologie*, G24, pp. 241, 314–15, *The Basic Problems of Phenomenology*, trans. Albert Hofstader (Bloomington: Indi-

ana University Press, 1982), pp. 170, 220–21. See also Heidegger, *Metaphysische Anfangsgründe der Logik im Ausgang von Leibniz*, G26, pp. 194–95, *The Metaphysical Foundations of Logic*, trans. Michael Heim (Bloomington: Indiana University Press, 1984), p. 153, and *Being and Time*, pp. 212, 226–27.

16. Heidegger, *Die Grundbegriffe der Metaphysik*, p. 319, *The Fundamental Concepts of Metaphysics*, p. 218.

17. Heidegger, *Die Grundbegriffe der Metaphysik*, pp. 290–92, *The Fundamental Concepts of Metaphysics*, pp. 197–98. See also Krell, *Daimon Life*, pp. 116–19.

18. *Being and Time*, p. 75.

19. Ibid., p. 345.

20. Ibid., p. 310.

21. Emmanuel Levinas, *Totalité et infini: essai sur l'extériorité* (The Hague: Nijhoff, 1980), p. 102, *Totality and Infinity: An Essay on Exteriority*, trans. Alphonso Lingis (The Hague: Nijhoff, 1969), p. 129, *Autrement qu'être ou au-delà de l'essence*, p. 60, *Otherwise Than Being or Beyond Essence*, p. 47.

22. Levinas, *Totalité et infini*, p. 108, *Totality and Infinity*, p. 134.

23. See, however, the next chapter of this book and the last chapter, entitled "No Happy Ending," in my *Appositions of Jacques Derrida and Emmanuel Levinas* (Bloomington: Indiana University Press, 2002).

24. For the equation of *bonheur* with *jouissance* see *Totalité et infini*, pp. 84–86, 121, *Totality and Infinity*, pp. 112–13, 147. For the equation of *jouissance* with *joie* see *Totalité et infini*, p. 107, *Totality and Infinity*, p. 134.

25. *Being and Time*, p. 61.

26. Martin Heidegger, *Schellings Abhandlung Über das Wesen der menschlichen Freiheit (1809)*, ed. Hildegard Feick (Tübingen: Niemeyer, 1971), p. 111, *Schelling's Treatise on the Essence of Human Freedom*, trans. Joan Stambaugh (Athens: Ohio University Press), p. 92.

27. Martin Heidegger, *Was heisst Denken?* (Tübingen: Niemeyer, 1971), p. 51, *What Is Called Thinking?*, trans. Fred D. Wieck and J. Glenn Gray (New York: Harper and Row, 1968), p. 16.

28. Heidegger, "Schöpferische Landschaft: warum bleiben wir in der Provinz?" in Martin Heidegger, *Denkerfahrungen 1910–1976* (Frankfurt am Main: Klostermann, 1983), p. 10, "Creative Landscape: Why Do We Stay in the Provinces?," trans. Thomas Sheehan, in *The Weimar Republic Sourcebook*, ed. Anton Kaes, Martin Jay, and Edward Dimenberg (Berkeley: University of California Press, 1994), p. 427. I thank Suzanne Stern-Gillet and Adrian Wilding for assistance with this question.

29. Heidegger, *Was heisst denken?* p. 51, *What Is Called Thinking?* p. 16.

30. Jacques Derrida, *Psyché: Inventions de l'autre* (Paris: Galilée, 1987), pp. 423ff.

31. Jacques Derrida, *Le toucher, Jean-Luc Nancy* (Paris: Galilée, 2000).

32. Martin Heidegger, *Der Satz vom Grund* (Pfullingen: Neske, 1986), pp. 110–14, *The Principle of Reason*, trans. Reginald Lilly (Bloomington: Indiana University Press, 1992), pp. 62–65.

33. Heidegger, *Holzwege*, pp. 22–25, G5, pp. 18–21, *Poetry, Language, Thought*, pp. 33–35.

34. *Being and Time*, p. 70.

35. Levinas, *Autrement qu'être*, p. 190, *Otherwise than Being*, p. 149.

7. TOUCHING EARTH

1. Witness C. S. Lewis, *Surprised by Joy: The Shape of My Early Years* (London: Fount, 1978). I am grateful to David Llewelyn for putting me right about this, as about so many other things.

2. E. D. Saunders, *Mudrā: A Study of Symbolic Gestures in Japanese Buddhist Sculpture* (London: Routledge and Kegan Paul, 1960), p. 124. I am grateful to James Giles for this reference. See also David Michael Levin, "Mudrā as Thinking: Developing Our Wisdom-of-Being in Gesture and Movement," in *Heidegger and Asian Thought,* ed. Graham Parkes (Honolulu: University of Hawaii Press, 1987).

3. Saunders, *Mudrā,* p. 125.

4. Aristotle, *Metaphysics* 1075a 12–19.

5. Friedrich Nietzsche, *On the Genealogy of Morals,* trans. Walter Kaufmann and R. J. Hollingdale (New York: Vintage Books, 1969), first essay, §6, p. 32.

6. Antony Gormley, *Field for the British Isles* (Llandudno: Oriel Mostyn, 1994), p. 62.

7. Antony Gormley, Thomas McEvilley, Gabriel Orozco, and Pierre Théberge, *Field* (Montreal: Montreal Museum of Fine Arts, 1993), pp. 19–21.

8. Gormley, *Field for the British Isles,* p. 62.

9. Gormley et al., *Field,* p. 21.

10. Gormley, *Field for the British Isles,* p. 62.

11. Heidegger, *Pathmarks,* p. 199, *Wegmarken,* p. 330, G9, p. 260.

12. Heidegger, *Pathmarks,* p. 208, *Wegmarken,* p. 342, G9, p. 272.

13. Heidegger, *Basic Writings,* p. 230, *Pathmarks,* p. 276, *Wegmarken,* pp. 182–83, G9, p. 391.

14. Heidegger, *Pathmarks,* p. 206, *Wegmarken,* p. 340, G9, p. 270.

15. Norman Malcolm, *Nothing Is Hidden* (Oxford: Blackwell, 1986).

16. Heidegger, *Pathmarks,* p. 237, *Wegmarken,* p. 107, G9, p. 312.

17. Heidegger, *Pathmarks,* p. 209, *Wegmarken,* p. 344, G9, p. 274.

18. Heidegger, *Pathmarks,* p. 213, *Wegmarken,* p. 349, G9, p. 279.

19. Heidegger, *Poetry, Language, Thought,* p. 62, *Holzwege,* p. 50, G5, p. 50.

20. Heidegger, *Poetry, Language, Thought,* p. 65, *Holzwege,* p. 53, G5, p. 53.

21. Heidegger, *An Introduction to Metaphysics,* p. 129, *Einführung in die Metaphysik,* p. 115, G40, p. 162.

22. Heidegger, *Pathmarks,* p. 210, *Wegmarken,* p. 345, G9, p. 275.

23. Ibid.

24. Heidegger, *Poetry, Language, Thought,* p. 61, *Holzwege,* p. 50, G5, p. 49.

25. Heidegger, *Poetry, Language, Thought,* p. 69, *Holzwege,* p. 57, G5, p. 57.

26. Heidegger, *Poetry, Language, Thought,* p. 62, *Holzwege,* p. 50, G5, p. 50.

27. Heidegger, *Poetry, Language, Thought,* p. 62, *Holzwege,* p. 50, G5, p. 50.

28. Heidegger, *Poetry, Language, Thought,* p. 46, *Holzwege,* p. 35, G5, p. 32.

29. Heidegger, *Poetry, Language, Thought,* p. 75, *Holzwege,* p. 62, G5, p. 63.

30. Heidegger, *An Introduction to Metaphysics,* p. 130, *Einführung in die Metaphysik,* p. 119, G40, p. 164.

31. Heidegger, *Pathmarks,* p. 212, *Wegmarken,* p. 347, G9, p. 277.

32. Heidegger, *Poetry, Language, Thought,* p. 70, *Holzwege,* p. 58, G5, p. 58. See Robert Bernasconi, "Ne sutor ultra crepidum: Erasmus and Dürer at the Hands of Panofsky and Heidegger," in *Heidegger in Question: The Art of Existing* (Atlantic Highlands, N.J.: Humanities Press, 1993).

8. SEEING THROUGH GOD

1. Martin Heidegger, "Brief über den 'Humanismus,'" 1946, *Wegmarken,* G9, p. 171, "Letter on 'Humanism,'" in *Pathmarks,* p. 259, *Basic Writings,* p. 220.

2. Heidegger, "Nietzsche's Wort 'Gott ist tot,'" in *Holzwege* (Frankfurt am Main: Klostermann, 1972), "The Word of Nietzsche: 'God Is Dead,'" in Martin Heidegger, *The Question Concerning Technology and Other Essays,* trans. William Lovitt (New York:

Harper and Row, 1977). Dating from 1943, this essay is based on the lectures on Nietzsche dating from 1936 to 1940.

3. Heidegger, *Wegmarken*, pp. 179–80, *Pathmarks*, p. 265, *Basic Writings*, p. 228.

4. Heidegger, *Wegmarken*, pp. 181–82, *Pathmarks*, p. 267, *Basic Writings*, p. 230.

5. Heidegger, "Wozu Dichter?" in *Holzwege*, p. 294, "What Are Poets For?" in *Poetry, Language, Thought*, p. 141.

6. Cited in Emmanuel Levinas, "As If Consenting to Horror," trans. Paula Wissing, *Critical Inquiry* 15 (Winter 1989): 487, from Wolfgang Schirmacher, *Technik und Gelassenheit: Zeitkritik nach Heidegger* (Freiburg, Munich: Alber, 1983), reporting Heidegger, "Das Ge-stell," *Bremer und Freiburger Vorträger*, G79, p. 27.

7. Heidegger, *Vorträge und Aufsätze*, vol. 2, p. 36, *Poetry, Language, Thought*, p. 160.

8. Heidegger, "Überwindung der Metaphysik," in *Vorträge und Aufsätze*, vol. 1 (Pfullingen: Neske, 1967), pp. 90–91, "Overcoming Metaphysics," in *The End of Philosophy*, trans. Joan Stambaugh (New York: Harper and Row, 1974), p. 110.

9. Heidegger, "Überwindung der Metaphysik," in *Vorträge und Aufsätze*, vol. 1 p. 82, "Overcoming Metaphysics," in *The End of Philosophy*, p. 102. The pattern of Heidegger's statement is reflected in the following "venture" by George Steiner and in the Socratic remark to which he refers: "We can, I think, cite certain things said or unsaid irretrievably, in which Western consciousness, in respect of its literacy and commitment to an 'examined life' (the Socratic ground rule), moves house. This move is first declared in Mallarmé's disjunction of language from external reference and in Rimbaud's deconstruction of the first person singular. These two proceedings, and all that they entail, splinter the foundations of the Hebraic-Hellenic-Cartesian edifice in which the *ratio* and psychology of the Western communicative tradition had lodged. Compared to this fragmentation, even the political revolutions and great wars in modern European history are, I would venture, of the surface." George Steiner, *Real Presences: Is There Anything in What We Say?* (London: Faber and Faber, 1989), pp. 94–95

10. Heidegger, *Nachwort* to "Das Ding," in *Vorträge und Aufsätze*, vol. 2, p. 57, *Poetry, Language, Thought*, p. 184.

11. I have done so in *The Middle Voice of Ecological Conscience*, ch. 5.

12. This matter is pursued in some detail in chapter 6 of the book referred to in note 11.

13. Heidegger, "Das Ding," in *Vorträge und Aufsätze*, vol. 2, p. 51, "The Thing," in *Poetry, Language, Thought*, p. 178.

14. Heidegger, *Parmenides*, G54, p. 169; *Parmenides*, trans. André Schuwer and Richard Rojcewicz (Bloomington: Indiana University Press, 1992), p. 114.

15. Heidegger, *Parmenides*, G54, p. 237, *Parmenides* [trans.], p. 160.

16. Heidegger, *Parmenides*, G54, p. 166, *Parmenides* [trans.], p. 112.

17. Heidegger, *Parmenides*, G54, p. 157, *Parmenides* [trans.], p. 106.

18. Heidegger, *Parmenides*, G54, p. 217, *Parmenides* [trans.], pp. 145–46.

19. Krell, *Daimon Life*; see also John Llewelyn, "The De(p)rivation of Life," *Research in Phenomenology* 24 (1994), *The Middle Voice of Ecological Conscience*, ch. 7, and Will McNeill, *Heidegger: Visions of Animals, Others and the Divine* (Warwick: Centre for Research in Philosophy and Literature, University of Warwick, 1993). Among the texts of Heidegger most relevant to this question are his *Parmenides*, §8, *Die Grundbegriffe der Metaphysik. Welt-Endlichkeit-Einsamkeit*, G29/30, *The Fundamental Concepts of Metaphysics*, and "What Are Poets For?"

20. Heidegger, *Parmenides*, G54, p. 153, *Parmenides* [trans.], p. 103.

21. Heidegger, *Beiträge zur Philosophie (Vom Ereignis)*, G65, p. 209, *Contributions to Philosophy (From Enowning)*, trans. Parvis Emad and Kenneth Maly (Bloomington: Indiana University Press, 1999), p. 146.

22. Heidegger, *Platon: Sophistes*, G19, pp. 204–206.

23. Heidegger, *Parmenides*, G54, p. 154, *Parmenides* [trans.], p. 104.

24. Heidegger, *Parmenides*, G54, p. 160, *Parmenides* [trans.], p. 108.

25. Heidegger, *Parmenides*, G54, p. 165, *Parmenides* [trans.], p. 112.

26. *Aussprache mit Martin Heidegger an 06/XI/1951*, University of Zurich Committee for Guest Lecturers, Zurich, 1952. Part of this is cited in Jean-Luc Marion, *Dieu sans l'être* (Paris: Communio/Fayard, 1982), p. 93. For the French translation by Jean Greisch see Richard Kearney and Joseph Stephen O'Leary, eds., *Heidegger et la question de Dieu* (Paris: Grasset, 1980). A French translation by François Fédier and D. Saatdjian was published in *PoEsie* 13 (1980). For an English translation see John Llewelyn, *Emmanuel Levinas: The Genealogy of Ethics* (London: Routledge, 1995), pp. 221–22.

27. Jacques Derrida, *De l'esprit: Heidegger et la question* (Paris: Galilée, 1987), p. 184, *Of Spirit: Heidegger and the Question*, trans. Geoffrey Bennington and Rachel Bowlby (Chicago: University of Chicago Press, 1989), p. 113.

28. After Rodolphe Gasché, *The Tain of the Mirror* (Cambridge: Mass.: Harvard University Press, 1986).

29. Jacques Derrida, *Force de loi* (Paris: Galilée, 1994), p. 102.

30. Gershom Scholem, *Le nom et les symboles de Dieu dans la mystique juive* (Paris: Cerf, 1983), p. 75.

31. Derrida, *Spectres de Marx: L'État de la dette, le travail du deuil et la nouvelle Internationale* (Paris: Galilée, 1993), p. 56, *Specters of Marx: The State of the Debt, the Work of Mourning, and the New International*, trans. Peggy Kamuf (London: Routledge, 1994) p. 28, *Force de loi*, p. 35.

32. *Force de loi*, p. 58.

33. Emmanuel Levinas, *Le temps et l'autre* (Paris: Fata Morgana, Quadrige, 1983), p. 60, *Time and the Other*, trans. R. A. Cohen (Pittsburgh: Duquesne University Press, 1987), p. 72.

34. Wittgenstein, *Philosophical Investigations*, p. 219.

35. Derrida, *Mémoire d'aveugle: L'autoportrait et autres ruines* (Paris: Réunion des musées nationaux, 1990), p. 36.

36. Llewelyn, *Emmanuel Levinas*, pp. 58, 158, 197. See also John Llewelyn, "sELection," in Alan Milchman and Alan Rosenberg, eds., *Post-Modernism and the Holocaust* (Amsterdam and Atlanta: Rodopi, 1998), reproduced in John Llewelyn, *Appositions of Jacques Derrida and Emmanuel Levinas* (Bloomington: Indiana University Press, 2002), ch. 11.

37. *Force de loi*, p. 60. Derrida's use of "maybe" partners his use of the French *éventuel* as distinguished from *possibilité*. Compare also his employment of *chance* and *mes chances*, and compare and contrast these with the nuances of Heidegger's *vielleicht* as perceptively brought out by Rodolphe Gasché in "Perhaps: A Modality on the Way with Heidegger to Language," *Graduate Faculty Philosophy Journal* 16, no. 2 (1993). In its last sentence he writes: "*Perhaps* is a mark of a response, but as a response to the Other, it remains infinitely suspended from it." It is perhaps also a mark of that thanks, *Danken*, which with *Dichten* remains suspended from that Other *Denken*. All three are incalculably suspended from the sage Saying (*Sagan-Sagen*) of the essay "The Nature of Language," in which Heidegger's reflection upon the essencing (*Wesen*) of speech is no less a reflection upon the proto-grammatical forces of the phrases *Gott sei Dank* and *grâce à Dieu*.

38. *Spectres de Marx*, p. 102, *Specters of Marx*, p. 59.

39. Edmond Jabès, as reported by Elisabeth de Fontaney, introducing the symposium "Le scandale du mal. Catastrophes naturelles et crimes de l'homme," *Les Nouveaux Cahiers* 22 (1986): 5.

40. "For nothing but despair can save us." Hans Dietrich Grabbe, cited by Adorno in conversation with Arnold Gelsen, "Ist die Soziologie eine Wissenschaft vom Menschen?" cited again by Martin Jay, *Adorno* (Cambridge, Mass.: Harvard University

Press, 1984), p. 82. I wonder whether the chiasmus of hope and *Verzweiflung* retains a trace of the *Verweigerung*, the refusal of either flight or arrival of God, referred to in a comment on my reflections for which I owe thanks to Hent de Vries. See Heidegger, *Beiträge, Contributions*, para. 254.

41. Heidegger, *Holzwege*, p. 249, *Poetry, Language, Thought*, p. 92.

9. REGARDING REGARDING

1. Gaston Bachelard, *La poétique de la rêverie* (Paris: Presses Universitaires de France, 1960), p. 159.

2. Llewelyn, *The HypoCritical Imagination*, p. 170.

3. Llewelyn, *The Middle Voice of Ecological Conscience*, ch. 5.

4. Derrida, *La vérité en peinture*, p. 14, *The Truth in Painting*, p. 10.

5. Derrida, *La vérité en peinture*, p. 193, *The Truth in Painting*, p. 169.

6. Derrida, *La vérité en peinture*, p. 197, *The Truth in Painting*, p. 172.

7. Maurice Merleau-Ponty, *La phénoménologie de la perception* (Paris: Gallimard, 1945), p. viii, *The Phenomenology of Perception*, trans. Colin Smith (London: Routledge and Kegan Paul, 1962), p. xiv.

8. Heidegger, *Zur Sache des Denkens*, p. 25, *On Time and Being*, trans. Joan Stambaugh (New York: Harper and Row, 1972), p. 24.

9. Derrida, *La vérité en peinture*, pp. 10–11, *The Truth in Painting*, pp. 6 and 7.

10. Levinas, *Autrement qu'être ou au-delà de l'essence*, pp. 210–18, *Otherwise Than Being or Beyond Essence*, pp. 165–71.

11. Levinas, *Autrement qu'être ou au-delà de l'essence*, p. 19, *Otherwise Than Being or Beyond Essence*, p. 15.

12. See the book referred to in note 3 above.

13. Levinas, *Autrement qu'être ou au-delà de l'essence*, p. 80, *Otherwise Than Being or Beyond Essence*, p. 63.

14. Llewelyn, *The HypoCritical Imagination*, ch. 7.

15. Maurice Merleau-Ponty, *L'œil et l'esprit* (Paris: Gallimard, 1964), p. 31, "Eye and Mind," trans. Carleton Dallery, in *The Primacy of Perception*, ed. James M. Edie (Evanston, Ill.: Northwestern University Press, 1964), p. 167.

16. Jacques Derrida, "La mythologie blanche," in *Marges de la philosophie* (Paris: Minuit, 1972), "White Mythology," in *Margins of Philosophy*, trans. Alan Bass (Chicago: University of Chicago Press, 1982). See also Llewelyn, *Emmanuel Levinas*, ch. 13.

17. Emmanuel Levinas, "La signification et le sens," in *Humanisme de l'autre homme* (Montpellier: Fata Morgana, 1972), p. 23, "Meaning and Sense," in *Collected Philosophical Papers*, trans. Alphonso Lingis (The Hague: Nijhoff, 1987), p. 78; Bruno Snell, *The Discovery of the Mind* (Oxford: Blackwell, 1953), pp. 200–201. Snell's proposal is referred to also by Hannah Arendt, *The Life of the Mind*, vol. 1 (New York: Harcourt Brace Jovanovich, 1971), p. 109.

18. Jacques Derrida, *Droit de regards* (Paris: Minuit, 1985), p. xxviii. One way of translating the sentences would be "the third party's gaze will never surprise the face-to-face of two others."

19. Jacques Derrida, "Le retrait de la métaphore," in *Psyché*.

20. Derrida, *La vérité en peinture*, p. 18, *The Truth in Painting*, p. 13.

21. Diabolized names and disguised descriptions are in play in Jacques Derrida, *Signéponge/Signsponge*, trans. Richard Rand (Ithaca, N.Y.: Cornell University Press, 1984), pp. 118, 119.

22. This question is pursued some distance in the chapter mentioned above in note 3.

23. Derrida, *Mémoires d'aveugle*, p. 36. I thank Michael Naas for a comment that lies behind the last paragraph of this chapter.

24. Jean-François Lyotard, *The Inhuman: Reflections on Time,* trans. Geoffrey Bennington and Rachel Bowlby (Cambridge: Polity Press), p. 142.

25. Ibid.

10. SEEING THROUGH SEEING THROUGH

1. *The Letters of Gerard Manley Hopkins to Robert Bridges,* ed. Claude Colleer Abbott (London: Oxford University Press, 1935), p. 31.

2. W. Warde Fowler, *Roman Essays and Interpretations* (Oxford: Clarendon Press, 1920), pp. 7–15, Jacques Derrida and Gianni Vattimo, *La religion* (Paris: Editions du Seuil, 1996), pp. 43ff.

3. "Parmenides," in *The Note-Books and Papers of Gerard Manley Hopkins,* ed. Humphry House (Oxford: Oxford University Press, 1937), p. 98.

4. Gerard Manley Hopkins, *Poetry and Prose,* ed. W. H. Gardner (Harmondsworth: Penguin Books, 1953), p. 169.

5. Hopkins, *The Note-Books and Papers of Gerard Manley Hopkins,* p. 264.

6. Hopkins, *Poetry and Prose,* p. xxi.

7. Hopkins, *The Note-Books and Papers of Gerard Manley Hopkins,* p. 171.

8. Hopkins, *Poetry and Prose,* p. 62, "I wake and feel the fell of dark, not day," from *Poems (1876–1889).*

9. Hopkins, *The Note-Books and Papers of Gerard Manley Hopkins,* p. 325.

10. G. W. F. Hegel, *Philosophy of Mind,* trans. William Wallace (Oxford: Oxford University Press, 1971), §471, pp. 230–31.

11. "On Principium sive Fundamentum," in "Comments on the *Spiritual Exercises* of St. Ignatius Loyola," in *The Note-Books and Papers of Gerard Manley Hopkins,* p. 310.

12. Hopkins, *Poetry and Prose,* p. 128.

13. Friedrich Nietzsche, *The Portable Nietzsche,* ed. Walter Kaufmann (New York: Viking, 1968), p. 42.

14. Maurice Friedman, *Martin Buber's Life and Work* (London: Search Press, 1982), p. 302.

15. *Meister Eckhart,* trans. Raymond B. Blakney (New York: Harper and Row, 1941), p. 328.

16. Alister E. McGrath, *Luther's Theology of the Cross* (Oxford: Blackwell, 1985), pp. 165ff. Hellmut Bandt, *Luthers Lehre vom verborgenen Gott: Eine Untersuchung zu dem offenbarensgeschichtlichen Ansatz seiner Theologie* (Berlin: Evangelische Verlagsanstalt, 1958).

17. Eckhart, "About Disinterest," in *Meister Eckhart,* p. 84.

18. Ibid., p. 82.

19. Heidegger, "My Way into Phenomenology," in *On Time and Being,* p. 74.

20. Hopkins, *The Note-Books and Papers of Gerard Manley Hopkins,* pp. 309–10.

21. Ibid., entry for July 19, 1872, p. 161.

22. Merleau-Ponty, *L'œil et l'esprit,* p. 31, "Eye and Mind," p. 167.

23. Hopkins, *The Note-Books and Papers of Gerard Manley Hopkins,* entry for March (day not given) 1871, p. 140.

24. Cited by the editor of Hopkins, *Poetry and Prose,* p. 143.

25. *The Letters of Gerard Manley Hopkins to Robert Bridges,* p. 83.

26. Methinks the thing I did was wrong.

27. Gerhard Ebeling, *Luther: An Introduction to His Thought* (London: Collins, 1970), p. 195.

INDEX

JOHN LLEWELYN

first taught philosophy at the University of New England, Australia. He has since been Reader in Philosophy at the University of Edinburgh, Visiting Professor of Philosophy at the University of Memphis, and the Arthur J. Schmitt Distinguished Visiting Professor of Philosophy at Loyola University of Chicago. His publications include *Appositions of Jacques Derrida and Emmanuel Levinas* (also from Indiana University Press); *The HypoCritical Imagination; Emmanuel Levinas: The Genealogy of Ethics; The Middle Voice of Ecological Conscience; Derrida on the Threshold of Sense;* and *Beyond Metaphysics?*